Christendom
A Short History of Christianity
and
Its Impact on Western Civilization

ROLAND H. BAINTON

Christendom

A Short History of Christianity

and

Its Impact on Western Civilization

Vol. I

From the Birth of Christ

to the Reformation

HARPER TORCHBOOKS
Harper & Row, Publishers
New York, Hagerstown, San Francisco, London

To a spiritual contemporary of the Early Fathers,
Hans Freiherr von Campenhausen

CHRISTENDOM: VOLUME I

Copyright © 1964, 1966 by American Heritage Publishing Co. Inc.

The text of this book was first published in *The Horizon History of Christianity* in 1964 by American Heritage Publishing Company and is here reprinted, revised and expanded, by arrangement. The illustrations have been selected for the Torchbook edition by the author.

First HARPER TORCHBOOK edition published 1966 by
Harper & Row Publishers, Incorporated
10 East 53rd Street
New York, N.Y. 10022

Library of Congress catalog card number: 64-19638

81 82   18 17 16

Contents
Volume I

I   Backgrounds of Christianity   1
- Birth of Christ   1
- Judaism   2
- Father Abraham   4
- Moses   6
- Exodus   6
- The Promised Land   7
- David and Solomon   11
- Babylonian Captivity   14
- Alexander the Great   16
- Herod the Great   23
- Messianic Hope   25

II   The Ministry of Christ and the Emergence of the Church   27
- Childhood of Jesus   28
- The Teachings of Jesus   29
- The Disciples   30
- Rejection   31
- Plots   37
- Passion and Death   38
- Resurrection   40
- Early Christians   41
- Apostle Paul   43

III   Christ Against Caesar   51
- The Gods of Rome   52
- The Early Church   55
- Roman Views of Christians   57
- The Christian Way of Life   58
- Persecutions   62
- Gnosticism   64
- Creed and Canon   66
- The Church of Rome   71
- Martyrs   73
- Mysteries   74
- Christian Feasts and Sacraments   76
- Church Fathers   77
- Forgiveness of Sins   80
- Neoplatonism   84
- Celsus   85
- Christian Influences on Roman Society   87

IV The Christian Roman Empire   89
    Persecution of Diocletian   89
    Constantine   91
    Donatists   96
    Arians   97
    Council of Nicaea   99
    Byzantium   100
    Julian the Apostate   102
    The Christian State   103
    Eastern Monasticism   104
    St. Jerome   106
    The Second Rome   107
    Justinian   110
    Byzantine Culture   111
    The Slavic Peoples   116

V The Conversion of the Barbarians   120
    St. Augustine   121
    Barbarian Invasions   131
    Conversions   134
    Western Monasticism   136
    The Papacy and the State   139
    Ireland   143
    Gaul   145
    Mores   147
    The Irish Monks Columbanus and Columba   151
    The British Isles   152
    The Mohammedans   153

VI The Quest for Order   155
    Consolidation of Power   155
    Charlemagne   159
    So-called Dark Ages   162
    Cluny   168
    The Investiture Controversy   172
    The First Crusade   177

VII Medieval Christendom   182
    The Rise of the Universities   183
    Scholasticism   184
    Chivalry   187
    Abelard and Heloise   189
    Cistercians and Bernard of Clairvaux   191
    Gothic   195
    Law and Justice   201
    Innocent III   203

St. Francis and St. Dominic   206
Economy of the Middle Ages   210
Heresies   212
Inquisition   218
Thomas Aquinas   219
Dante Alighieri   221

VIII The Decline of the Papacy   224
The Rise of Nations   225
Avignon   228
Knights Templars   228
Church Revenues   230
The Great Schism   234
John Wycliffe   236
John Huss   238
Council of Basel   241
Renaissance   242
Humanism   243
The Renaissance Popes and Princes   247
Renaissance Art   250
The Mystics   253

Selected Bibliography   255

Index   266

Illustrations

The illustrations pertaining to each chapter will be found in groups following pages 26, 50, 88, 118, 154, 180, 222, and 254.

Acknowledgments

I wish to tender my thanks to the libraries of Yale University for the extension of every courtesy: the Sterling Library, the Divinity Library, and the Beinecke Library. I am particularly indebted to the university photographer, Frederic Ludwig, whose glossy prints are often improvements upon the originals.

I

Backgrounds of Christianity

Birth of Christ

"In those days a decree went out from Caesar Augustus that all the world should be enrolled. This was the first enrollment, when Quirinius was governor of Syria. And all went to be enrolled, each to his own city. And Joseph also went up from Galilee, from the city of Nazareth, to Judea, to the city of David, which is called Bethlehem, because he was of the house and lineage of David, to be enrolled with Mary, his betrothed, who was with child. And while they were there, the time came for her to be delivered. And she gave birth to her first-born son and wrapped him in swaddling clothes, and laid him in a manger, because there was no place for them in the inn.

"And in that region there were shepherds out in the field, keeping watch over their flock by night. And an angel of the Lord appeared to them, and the glory of the Lord shone around them, and they were filled with fear. And the angel said to them, 'Be not afraid; for behold, I bring you good news of a great joy which will come to all the people; for to you is born this day in the city of David a Saviour, who is Christ the Lord.' "[1]

In these words the historian Luke records that event which in the Western world divides all history. Our chronology is reckoned up to and as of the birth of Christ. All the years prior to his coming are tallied in descending order, those thereafter in ascend-

---

[1] Luke 2:1–11.

ing order. How incredible it would have appeared to the ancient Sumerians and Assyrians, the Babylonians and Persians, the Greeks and Romans, had they been told that the days of their years would come to be reckoned in terms of an event to occur in a village too insignificant to be mentioned on their monuments or in their annals! How amazing it would have been to Augustus to be informed that he would be famed less as the founder of the Roman Empire than as that emperor under whose rule this child was born! And as for Quirinius, what surprise it would have caused him had he foreseen that he, of all the governors of Syria, should be remembered best, and solely because of his connection with that event.

Augustus and Quirinius would have been not only amazed but shocked had they been told that the child who would make them memorable was a Jew, for the Jews alone would do no homage to the emperor as divine. Jesus was a Jew who went up to Jerusalem for the great religious feasts of his people and who regularly attended the synagogue on the Sabbath. He declared that he had not come to destroy but to fulfill the Jewish Law. If we would understand Jesus, we must understand the religion in which he was reared, and if we would understand Christianity, we must begin with Judaism.

Judaism

The Jews began as an agglomeration of small tribes who later attained political independence, but did so only in the interludes between the fall and rise of great empires. They have bequeathed no monuments testifying to magnificence. They built no pyramids like the Egyptians, no ziggurats like the Sumerians. There are no tombs of the Hebrew kings with chaplets of finely wrought gold and chariots studded with jewels, no palaces and fortresses like those of Crete and Mycenae. Palestinian archaeology has unearthed no statues of David and Solomon but only water pots like the one from which Rebecca watered the camels of Abraham's servants or the sickle like that with which Boaz reaped while Ruth gleaned.

But the ancient Hebrews, contemptible in the eyes of their contemporaries, created something more enduring than palaces and pyramids. They created a literature, traditionally classified as law, prophecy, and writings, comprising twenty-eight books which in the century before Christ were canonized as Holy Scripture. (*Canon* is derived from the Greek word for a measuring stick; the writings canonized were those that measured up.) Some of the works thus gathered deal with the events of the writers' own times; others record traditions that were transmitted orally for quite possibly a thousand years, often with amazing accuracy.

This body of scriptures, called by Christians the Old Testament, in unique. Even in its earliest portions it sets forth a philosophy of history such as the peoples of the Levant never envisioned and the Greeks approximated only later. History was for the Hebrews the plan of God, focused on his chosen people, whose very weakness served all the more to manifest his power. Through all their vicissitudes he was leading them. In all their disasters he was chastening them. In all their sufferings he was using them that they might be a light to the Gentiles who someday would come to the House of the Lord and receive the Law from Mount Zion. History to the Hebrews was a drama investing the future with a mighty hope.

Judaism is a religion of history and as such it may be contrasted with religions of nature and religions of contemplation. Religions of nature see God in the surrounding universe; for example, in the orderly course of the heavenly bodies, or more frequently in the recurring cycle of the withering and resurgence of vegetation. This cycle is interpreted as the dying and rising of a god in whose experience the devotee may share through various ritual acts and may thus also become divine and immortal. For such a religion, the past is not important, for the cycle of the seasons is the same one year as the next.

Religions of contemplation, at the other extreme, regard the physical world as an impediment to the spirit, which, abstracted from the things of sense, must rise by contemplation to union with the divine. The sense of time itself is to be transcended, so that here again history is of no import.

But religions of history, like Judaism, discover God "in his mighty acts among the children of men." Such a religion is a compound of memory and hope. It looks backward to what God has already done. The feasts of Judaism are chiefly commemorative: Passover recalls the deliverance of the Jews from bondage in Egypt; Purim, Esther's triumph over Haman, who sought to destroy the Jews in the days of King Ahasuerus; and Hanukkah, the purification of the Temple after its desecration by Antiochus Epiphanes. And this religion looks forward with faith; remembrance is a reminder that God will not forsake his own. The faith of Judaism was anchored in the belief that God was bound to his people by a covenant, at times renewed and enlarged.

Father Abraham

The first covenant was with Abraham, the traditional progenitor of the Hebrews. The Bible relates that he migrated to Palestine from Ur of the Chaldees (in the land between the Tigris and Euphrates rivers, later known as Babylonia) sometime between 2000 and 1700 B.C. That the Hebrews had close cultural relations with this region is likely: the accounts of the creation, the flood, and other traditional stories in the Old Testament are clearly related to Babylonian myths; the Ten Commandments are reminiscent of the Code of Hammurabi; the Tower of Babel recalls the ziggurat at Ur.

But, how marvelously did the Hebrews transform these ancient materials! In their version of the creation we find no union of sky god and earth goddess, no mere analogy with procreation. God, the unutterable majesty, spoke from out of the shroud of mystery and said, "Let there be light,"[2] and before ever there was a sun or a moon there was light. Out of sheer nothing, by the fiat of divine will, all that is began to be. In the Hebrew version the flood was occasioned by the vileness of man. But, from out of the mass of the wicked, God chose one righteous man and all his house, that by these few the divine purpose for the ages might be fulfilled. And if one compares the Ten Commandments with the Code of Hammurabi, one passes from the conditional—"If a man steal . . . then . . ."—to the imperative—"Thou shalt not steal."

The God of Abraham—he was called El, and his name survives in such compounds as Beth-El and Isra-El—commanded Abraham to leave his father's house and to journey to a country which should be shown him. The Bible relates that he and his descendants journeyed to the land of Canaan, to be known as Palestine. They were probably semi-nomads, migrating annually with their flocks for pasturage and were not settled on farms or in the cities of Canaan. God made a covenant with this Abraham, by promising that he and his descendants would possess the land of Canaan and that they should be blessed with prosperity and progeny, numerous like the stars of heaven or the sands of the sea. Abraham begat Isaac, and Isaac Jacob, and Jacob in turn twelve sons from whom stemmed the twelve tribes of Israel. The name Israel, meaning "he that strives with God," was given to Jacob after he had wrestled all night with an angel and had received a blessing.[3] In later history that name came to be applied to the ten northern tribes, while the name Judah (whence the word Jew) was applied to those in the south of Palestine. But, after the Ten Tribes were deported in the eighth century B.C., and lost to history, the name Israel was extended, and now Israelite, Hebrew, and Jew are virtually synonymous.

In the age of the patriarchs, all Palestine was under the suzerainty of Egypt, and when a famine afflicted the land, as it peri-

[2] Gen. 1:3.
[3] Gen. 32:28.

odically did, the inhabitants sought the verdant valley of the Nile —not only the Hebrews, but their neighbors as well. The Hebrews interpreted their own migration as a part of God's plan, for he had brought to pass the sale of Joseph by his brethren as a slave into Egypt, as well as Joseph's subsequent elevation there to the office of Pharaoh's viceroy in charge of the supplies of grain at the very time of the famine. Thus he was in a position to save his father's house.

Moses

The fugitives from drought stayed on in Egypt until there came a Pharaoh, possibly Ramesses II (1304–1237 B.C.), who impressed the Hebrews into servitude so rigorous that their leader, Moses, came before Pharaoh with the demand, "Let my people go." Not until God had smitten Egypt with ten plagues did Pharaoh consent. In the last plague, the death of the first-born in the homes of the Egyptians, God spared—"passed over"—the children of the Hebrews. The commemoration of this event, called Passover, remains probably one of the oldest religious festivals celebrated today.

Exodus

Then, when Pharaoh gave in, Moses led his people into the wilderness. How many they were cannot be determined. The biblical account cannot be corroborated from Egyptian annals, which do not refer to the Sojourn or the Exodus, but the number could not have been large, since not all the Hebrews came down into Egypt and not all those in Egypt went back to Palestine. Perhaps the band did not exceed a thousand.

But for these, whether few or many, the religion of Israel took on a new quality when Moses conducted them to the foot of

Mount Sinai and there, from out of the cloud brooding over the brow of the mountain, the God of Abraham, Isaac, and Jacob disclosed himself with a new name. Henceforth he is called Jehovah, or in a more exact vocalization, Yahweh. And he made there with Israel a new covenant: not simply a promise of prosperity and progeny, but a covenant of commitment that they should observe the Law, including the Ten Commandments,[4] given to Israel by the hand of Moses. Yahweh said: "You have seen what I did to the Egyptians and how I bore you on eagles' wings. . . . Now therefore, if you will obey my voice and keep my covenant, you shall be my own possession among all peoples . . . and you shall be to me a kingdom of priests and a holy nation."[5] This concept of the covenant related the Hebrews to their God in a manner that was unique in history. He had chosen them, not by reason of their merit, but through his sheer grace, to be the instruments of his purpose.

The Promised Land

After the Exodus from Egypt, the Bible tells of the wandering in the desert wilderness, and then, after these forty years of trial and discipline, of the conquest of Canaan—the "promised land" of Abraham's covenant—under Joshua in the late thirteenth or early twelfth century B.C. This is portrayed in the Books of Joshua and Judges as swift, gory, and drastic. The walls of Jericho collapsed miraculously at the blowing of the trumpet. When the cities of the Canaanites were stormed, the inhabitants were put to the sword by the victorious Israelite warriors.

At some points the biblical account is not accurate. The Canaanites were obviously not exterminated since, as told elsewhere in the Bible, they remained an irritant to Israel for centuries. Indeed, whether this was in fact a military conquest or

---
[4] Exod. 20:1–17; Deut. 5:6–21.
[5] Exod. 19:5–6.

rather a process of gradual settlement of the land by the Israelites cannot be fully determined. Jericho had been destroyed before Joshua's time, and he may have had only to occupy the ruins of the city. Also, it has been argued that the Israelites were not sufficiently advanced in the arts of warfare to capture the Canaanite cities, defended as they were by chariots drawn by horses, of which the Israelites had none. Even much later, in David's day, when horses were captured from the Philistines, they were not used for military purposes.[6]

In any event, the Hebrews did settle in Palestine. From the standpoint of subsequent Christian history, that event of itself is more important than the manner in which it came to pass, although the manner in which it is described in the Book of Joshua is of great significance in that the conquest is there described as a war of aggression, deemed just and even holy simply because commanded by God. The enemy who resisted his will was accursed and was therefore to be annihilated with unflagging zeal, with no humanitarian scruples, and with less reliance on military efficiency than on God's miraculous assistance. God was believed to be present on the field of battle in a chest called the Ark of the Covenant. This view of war was to be revived with direct appeal to the Old Testament in the Christian crusades about two millenniums later.

At the outset, the Hebrews certainly did not have Palestine to themselves. The Canaanities remained, and there were other invading peoples with whom the Hebrews had to contend: Moabites, Edomites, and Ammonites, who established kingdoms east of the Jordan and in some cases lasted into the Christian era. Into northern Syria came the Aramaeans, and to the south, bordering on Arabia, were the Midianites, who confounded the Hebrews as much with their camels as the Canaanites did with their horses and chariots. Probably only after centuries of slow penetration did

[6] Martin Noth, *The History of Israel* (New York, 1960), p. 82, against W. F. Albright, who in numerous articles defends the essential historicity of the biblical account.

the tribes of Israel assume their ascendancy over this land and its many peoples.

In the Old Testament, the Canaanites are often called the Amorites, a people also of many tribes: the Hivites, the Girgashites, the Jebusites (who held the walled town of Jerusalem), and so on. From the Canaanites the Hebrews learned much, both of the arts of agriculture and of city dwelling. In this period, the Hebrews adapted their Aramaic speech to a dialect of the Canaanites, thereby producing the classical Hebrew tongue, in which the larger portion of the Old Testament is written. They later returned to Aramaic and some of the Old Testament is in this language, which was to be the language of Jesus. The Hebrews also took over from the Phoenicians—a group of Canaanites along the north coast of Palestine—their most brilliant invention, the alphabet, which also passed to the Greeks, to the Romans, and to the rest of the Western world.

But, one aspect of Canaanite culture the Hebrews would not assimilate, namely, religion. For the Canaanites were practicing the fertility cults of a god called Baal, appearing in many local forms, and a goddess Astarte, whose rites included child sacrifice and sacred prostitution. The story in the Old Testament of how God arrested Abraham's hand when he was about to sacrifice his son Isaac may indicate that the Hebrews either had never practiced child sacrifice or came to reject it. And, to associate sexual practices with religion was to them utterly abhorrent. The gravest danger to Israel was not that her sons would apostatize, as some did, but rather that they might transform Yahweh into a Baal. Lest this should happen, the Baalim (the plural of Baal) were to be exterminated from the land.

If the Hebrews had rivals for the conquest of Canaan to the north, east, and south, a more formidable rivalry threatened from the west, where the Philistines, a people perhaps of Illyrian origin, invaded the coastal plain toward the end of the thirteenth century B.C. It was they who gave their name to the land: *Palestine* is a modification of *Philistia*. They were pushing farther inland and gaining control over the land of the Hebrews. This assault could not be met by a loose confederation of tribes who came together only when the spirit of Yahweh inspired some leader to summon them to conflict. Such a procedure was altogether too casual. Therefore, the seer Samuel agreed to anoint Saul, an inspired captain, as king. But Samuel himself had grave misgivings over this course and warned the people that the monarchy would impose on them exacting burdens.

Even more serious was the foreboding that the rule of a king would compete with the rule of God. Israel up to this point was a theocracy. The very word *theocracy* was later coined by the Jewish historian Josephus (A.D. 37–95?) to describe this people ruled by God,[7] whose will was made known to them by seers and prophets. In matters of war, God's will was executed by inspired bands of warriors, like the band of Gideon, which was deliberately reduced in size to prove that God, not human prowess, had given the victory. In place of this system would come standing armies, taxes, and, worst of all in the eyes of the purists, foreign alliances, principally because they entailed religious alliances. Those who made military covenants were expected to recognize each others' gods. The resolve on the part of Israel that Yahweh should not be made to fraternize with alien gods was to be for them a source of both inner division and outward isolation. The unswerving loyalty of the Jews to their God has been both their tragedy and their glory.

The anointing of Saul by Samuel toward the close of the second millennium B.C. is very important for later political theory in Western Europe. This anointing meant the institution of a sacral rather than secular kingship; however, it involved a point of ambiguity. Was royal authority conferred directly by God or through the mediation of a priest or prophet as his earthly representative? By anointing Saul, did Samuel confer upon him kingship, or did he merely ratify what God had already done by sending upon him his

[7] Steward Perowne, *The Later Herods* (New York, 1958), p. 33.

spirit? These two theories of kingship gave rise to much controversy in the Christian Middle Ages.

David and Solomon

Saul did not vanquish the Philistines; that was the work of David, who had been the leader of a mercenary band serving under the Philistines. They were willing that he should become the king of Judah, believing that the tribes would thus be divided. But, instead, David went on to become king of all the tribes of Israel (1005–970 B.C.), and he succeeded in decisively breaking the power of the Philistines. His kingdom reached to the north into Galilee. In the south, he took Jerusalem from the Jebusites and made this city the religious center for all the Hebrew tribes. The choice was very wise, because a shrine located in the existing territory of any single Hebrew tribe would have been unacceptable to the others. David brought the Ark of the Covenant to Jerusalem. Yahweh was thus localized in space, but not embodied, materialized, or depicted in any earthly form.

David was succeeded by Solomon (970–930 B.C.), whose name in Hebrew contains the root *shalom*, meaning peace—an appropriate appellation, since Solomon eschewed war and did not seek to extend his boundaries, but rather to glorify his holdings with such costly structures as the great Temple at Jerusalem. But as war was waged, so peace was conserved by alliances, and these alliances meant foreign marriages, which in turn involved setting up shrines of other gods than Yahweh. Solomon married a daughter of Pharaoh and also a daughter of the king of Tyre, and many other princesses. For the gods of his numerous foreign wives this builder of the Temple of Yahweh constructed shrines on the Mount of Olives. More sumptuous than any other structure, however, was Solomon's own palace, which took thirteen years to build. The two builders of magnificent temples at Jerusalem were essentially secular spirits. The first was Solomon and the second Herod the Great. Little wonder that to Solomon should have been ascribed the least religious books in the Jewish Scriptures: Proverbs, Ecclesiastes, and the Song of Songs, as well at the Book of Wisdom in the Apocrypha!

Such sumptuous building required money which had to be raised by taxation. Under Solomon the people groaned beneath their burden; when he died, their grievances became outspoken. Solomon's son Rehoboam was accepted as his successor in Judah, which had come to believe that the monarchy was divinely vested in the dynasty of David. But the Ten Tribes of Israel still had much of the ideology of the old confederation. They applied the principle of the covenant to the kingship, thus subjecting it to conditions, and demanded that Rehoboam lighten the financial burden and relieve them of the forced labor under which they had been suffering. He replied that, whereas his father had beaten them with rods, he would beat them with scorpions. In consequence they called Jeroboam to be their king, and thereby the northern and southern kingdoms were divided.

In the early centuries of the first millennium B.C., the rising power was Assyria, in Mesopotamia, a nation of ruthless, warlike people who threatened their neighbors on all sides. The menace to the Hebrews became acute when Tiglath-pileser III came to the throne in 745 B.C. The northern kingdom of Israel united with Damascus to resist the Assyrian hordes. When King Ahaz of Judah refused to join the coalition, he was besieged by the other two, and when he appealed to the Assyrians for help, they overran Israel. Then, in 721 B.C., when Israel rebelled, the Assyrians under the great Sargon deported the ruling aristocracy of the Ten Tribes and replaced them with people from Mesopotamia. The peasants of Israel remained, and the mingling of these peoples produced those later known as Samaritans. In time the Mesopotamian immigrants accepted Yahweh as their god. Judah was allowed to continue as a vassal state, after paying ransom that stripped the very gold from the Temple doors. But this meant that an altar to the god of the Assyrians had to be erected near the altar of Yahweh in Jerusalem. King Hezekiah destroyed the pagan shrine, but when Sennacherib, the Assyrian, "swept down like a wolf on the fold," the altar removed by Hezekiah had to be restored.

In the seventh century B.C. a new power, Babylonia, arose to threaten Assyria, whereupon Egypt, although long the enemy of Assyria, rallied to her help in order to preserve the balance of power. With this division among his towering neighbors, King Josiah of Judah seized the chance to shake off Assyrian dominance. He swept Jerusalem clean of idolatrous abominations and issued the biblical Book of Deuteronomy, the "Book of the Law" that had recently been discovered in the Temple. As Pharaoh Necho proceeded across Palestine to help Assyria, Josiah stood in his way. A historic battle was fought at Megiddo in 609 B.C., and Josiah, the reforming king, was "carried . . . dead in a chariot . . . to Jerusalem."[8]

But Necho failed to restore the balance; he was himself crushed by Nebuchadnezzar, king of the Babylonians. Then came Judah's turn. Jerusalem fell before the Babylonians in 587 B.C. King Zedekiah, the last king of Judah, was spared having his eyes put out only long enough to see his sons slain.[9] The Judean aristocracy was carried off to its long captivity in Babylon, the Temple of Solomon was razed, and the Ark of the Covenant forever disappeared. The monarchy in the united kingdoms had lasted two and a half centuries; Judah as a vassal state had had a king of the House of David for another one and a half centuries. For the next four centuries there was to be no native king at all.

---

[8] II Kings 23:30.
[9] II Kings 25:7.

Babylonian Captivity

The captive Jews sat by the waters of Babylon and wept. Why had Yahweh abandoned his people; as the psalmist sang, "My God, my God, why hast thou forsaken me?"[10] When the Assyrian had just begun his oppressions, the prophet Isaiah answered this lament by asserting that the calamity was a chastisement for Israel's sins and that the Assyrian was the rod of God's anger. To propose that God was using this great empire to discipline a few tribes who had been faithless to his covenant was an audacious assumption. Israel put herself at the center of world history, and by so doing she made her God the God of all the world, and the mightiest empires of the world but devices in his plan for his chosen people.

Isaiah's explanation was persuasive in those days when Israel had "gone a whoring after foreign gods."[11] But what was to be said when the good king Josiah, who put away the abominations, was brought back dead in a chariot? Was it chastisement that Jerusalem should be a heap of ruins and that the Ark of the Lord should have disappeared? Could it be that Yahweh allowed the righteous to suffer? Job confronted the problem on an individual level, and his only answer in his sore affliction was to bow before the inscrutable will of the Almighty. In Babylon another prophet, known as the Second Isaiah, saw the problem in terms of the trials of the whole nation. "Comfort, comfort my people, says your God. Speak tenderly to Jerusalem, and cry to her that her warfare is ended, that her iniquity is pardoned, that she has received from the Lord's hand double for all her sins."[12] Double! What is the meaning of suffering which exceeds chastisement? This same prophet spoke of the servant who was smitten and afflicted and upon whom, despite his innocence, had been laid "the iniquity of

---

[10] Ps. 22:1.
[11] Ezek. 23:30; Lev. 17:7; Hos. 4:12, 9:1.
[12] Isa. 40:2.

us all" and "by [whose] stripes we are healed."[13] The suffering of the innocent thus might minister to the redemption of the guilty. The "servant" in the mind of the prophet may have been a personification of Israel, but Christians have always seen in this figure a foreshadowing of Christ.

But in any event, what of the fate of the guilty? Must they forever expiate their crime? The answer here was the proclamation of divine forgiveness that sounds throughout the Old Testament: "Though your sins are like scarlet, they shall be as white as snow; though they are red like crimson, they shall become like wool";[14] "Let the wicked forsake his way, and . . . return to the Lord, that he may have mercy on him, and to our God, for he will abundantly pardon."[15]

Besides precipitating such questions and answers, the Babylonian captivity gave a new quality to Judaism. Since the Temple was destroyed, Jerusalem inaccessible to the exiles, and the priesthood scattered, piety was focused upon the Torah, the Law, which was to be comprised in the first five books of the Old Testament, called the Pentateuch. The Law was now elucidated and amplified, and religion consisted of obeying its precepts. This great body of exegesis eventually became the Talmud, the civil and canonical law of the Jews for ages to come.

Two points in the Law were especially stressed. The first was the keeping of the Sabbath. The redactor of the creation story in Genesis represented God himself as observing the Sabbath, for he created the world in six days and rested on the seventh. The other point was a new emphasis on the importance of circumcision as a sign of the covenant. This rite had not distinguished the Jews from their earlier Semitic and Egyptian neighbors, but it did differentiate them at the outset from the "uncircumcized Philistines," as it now did from the Babylonians, and as it would later from the Greeks and the Romans. Such emphasis on the Law and the re-

[13] Isa. 53:5.
[14] Isa. 1:18.
[15] Isa. 55:7.

moteness from the Temple necessitated the institution of some other place for public worship and instruction in the Law. The synagogue was the answer; our earliest evidence of its existence comes from Egypt in the late third century before Christ.

The duration of the Babylonian captivity has traditionally been reckoned as seventy years (more precisely, it was seventy-two) dating from the destruction to the rebuilding of the Temple in Jerusalem. But the turning point in the fate of the exiles came with the rise of the Persians and the capture of Babylon by their king, Cyrus, in 538 B.C. The Jews regarded the Persians as liberators, and as a matter of fact the conquerors were comparatively liberal. They respected the languages of the subjugated and were not disposed, in this period at least, to encroach upon their religions. Cyrus decreed that the Jewish exiles might return to Palestine and that the Temple there might be rebuilt. The reconstruction, promptly commenced, was completed under his successor, Darius, in 515 B.C. Not all the exiles went back to Palestine: a colony of Jews remained in Babylon far into the Middle Ages. Nehemiah became the leader of those who did return, and under him the people rebuilt the walls of Jerusalem. Ezra, another leader, imposed upon the Jews in Palestine the rigorous devotion to the Torah that had developed in Babylon. To preserve religious purity, those who thus adhered to the Law were not to marry with those who did not.

Alexander the Great

Persian ascendancy ended with the victory of Alexander the Great at the Battle of Issus in 333 B.C., which introduced a new era in the relation of the Jews to the world about them. Alexander envisioned the unity of mankind. He certainly proposed to blend at least the cultures of the Greeks and the Persians. This meant orientalizing the West and Hellenizing the East; inevitably the Jews were involved.

Alexander had been the pupil of Aristotle and knew Hellenism in all its aspects. One of the characteristics of the Hellenic spirit was curiosity. The Greeks were interested in everything in the world about them—the stars, the plants, and the human body, in physics as well as medicine. They were interested in more than appearance; they sought to discern the relations of things. The Greeks discovered geometry. They inquired as to the nature of things, the nature of nature, the nature of God. The Hebrews desired to know only God's will. There were philosophers among the Greeks who saw in the cosmos a principle of order and who defined beauty in terms of harmonious proportions.

Little wonder that Greek philosophers discovered a rationale for the ideal of the unity of mankind! The Stoics taught that there is already such a unity. Men, endowed with reason, participate in the rational order of the universe and are capable of resolving their differences in a reasonable way by the concourse of minds rather than the clash of arms. Men, being rational, are able to perceive that there is a moral order in the cosmos, the law of nature, the norm for all the laws of men. According to this philosophy, the gift of reason has been conferred upon all men regardless of race; the distinction between the Hellenes and the barbarians had come to be that between the cultivated and the uncouth, not that between the Greeks and non-Greeks. Social status was a matter of indifference, for all men were created equal. There was once a Golden Age with no slavery, property, or war. The existence of these institutions is due to a fall of man, which did not, however, obfuscate his reasoning capacity. Since man participates in the order of the cosmos, he should be considered a citizen of the cosmos, a cosmopolite. Such ideas were profoundly to affect Christian thinking.

For the cultivation of another Greek ideal, that of the good life in which enlightened men converse together, there was need for the *polis*, a city like Athens, in which to gather. For the Greeks, the city was not so much a fort as a forum, a place of beauty, whose high places were not capped by ramparts, but crowned by temples of incomparable grace. Such cities were introduced into the Levant, cities adorned not only with temples and gardens, but also with gymnasiums, theatres, and hippodromes. When cities of this type arose in Palestine, they created a problem for the orthodox Jew, who looked askance at the gymnasiums where athletes ran naked.

But Hellenistic culture and Judaic culture were so complex that there were many points of convergence as well as of divergence between them. The Stoic picture of the Golden Age from which man had fallen, comported well with the account in Genesis of the fall of Adam and Eve. The Stoics, thinking in pantheistic terms, equated the divine with the principle of rationality in the cosmos. Their assumption of a law of nature, valid among all men, was easy to reconcile with the ethical demands of the Ten Commandments and to translate into a law of God. Aristotle, interested in natural science and causality, considered God to be the first cause of whatever is and the prime mover of whatever moves. The Platonists called God the ultimate intelligence, ordering the universe. Such descriptions are not alien to the picture of the Hebrew God who wills, acts, and speaks. The Stoic belief that all men were created equal was remote from Hebraic speculation, but no other people had such a burning sense of indignation against injustice to the common man as had the Jews. For example, when King David, in order to marry Bathsheba, placed her husband in the forefront of the battle where he was slain, the prophet Nathan told the king the story of a rich man, who, to feed his guests, took not from his own abundant herd, but seized the one ewe lamb of a poor man. David adjudged this rich man deserving of death, and the prophet thundered, "You are the man!"[16] There is no scene comparable to this in the literature of antiquity.

The discrepancy between Hellenic and Hebraic attitudes was indeed sometimes less than the discrepancy between varieties within the separate cultures. Among the Greeks, for example, the

[16] II Sam. 12:7.

Epicureans denied immortality, the Stoics believed that at death the individual soul is absorbed into the world soul, and the Platonists believed in the immortality of the soul as distinct from the body, which perishes. Among the Hebrews we shall later meet the Pharisees, who affirmed the immortality alike of the soul and the body, and the Sadducees, who denied both.

Hellenic and Hebraic views as to property and poverty differed, but both had subsequently an important influence on Christian concepts. Some among the Greeks, like Plato in *The Republic*, regarded communal ownership of property as ideal, and the Stoics believed that in the bygone Golden Age no property had been private. Aristotle, however, recognized private property. The Cynics had a cult of poverty, chiefly as a device for insuring peace of mind. In those turbulent times, the man of wealth never knew whether he might not die a slave; he could attain composure by stripping himself in advance of all that he might lose. The ideal was to live simply, like a dog. The name *Cynic* came from the Greek word for dog. Tools should be reduced to the strictly utilitarian. A knife needs no jeweled handle, nor does a table require ivory legs. Among the ancient Hebrews, we find the holding of property by the tribe but never a cult of poverty. For them, prosperity was a mark of divine favor and poverty was either a chastisement or a trial of faith.

Greek philosophers rejected all the anthropomorphisms and immoralities of the gods of the Homeric pantheon, but retained the gods as allegorical figures. For example, the god Kronos was alleged to have devoured his own children. The philosophers said that Kronos was to be equated with Chronos, the god of time, who does obliterate that which he has brought into being. Similarly, the various cults of the Graeco-Roman world were spiritualized.

We have noted that in the case of war the Hebrews introduced the idea of the crusade fought for God, under God, and without giving quarter. The Greeks fashioned the concept of the just war, whose purpose it was to vindicate justice and restore peace and in which violence should be minimal. Plato protested against the ruining of wells and orchards and made a distinction among the enemy between the innocent and the guilty.

Greek and Jewish traditions and ideas had, in fact, so much in common that they could be fused at certain levels. The fusion with philosophic Hellenism took place most naturally among those Jews who had long lived in a gentile environment, and there were many. The Diaspora, the dispersion of the Jews from Judea, had begun centuries before Christ. We have noted the continuing colony of Jews at Babylon. At Elephantine in Egypt, there was a colony in the fifth century B.C., which died out in the following century, but others were established elsewhere. When he took Jerusalem, Pompey sold thousands of Jews into slavery to Rome. They proved to be poor slaves because they would not work on the Sabbath nor eat certain foods. But they made such excellent associates that many soon acquired their freedom and formed an influential group in the capital. By the time of the Christian era, the Jews had dispersed throughout much of Asia Minor and the Mediterranean area, where Paul met them in the course of his travels. It is said they numbered about a million in Egypt, with a heavy concentration in Alexandria. These Jews spoke Greek. Some of them still knew Hebrew, but for the majority the Scriptures were translated into Greek somewhere around 200 B.C. This version of the Old Testament is called the Septuagint, because it is supposedly the work of seventy scholars.

There flourished in the first century of the Christian era among the Alexandrian Jews a cultivated scholar named Philo, who Hellenized the Old Testament by the same device that the philosophers had applied to Homer, namely, allegory. In the Old Testament he found much of Greek philosophy. Philo saw no danger to Judaism in this, for he believed that Plato, having lived later than Moses, had derived from him all his ideas, and Philo continued to observe the Jewish Law. His attempts to reconcile Greek thought with Jewish teachings later helped to shape Christian theology.

The great clash between Judaism and Hellenism occurred when Hellenistic kings claimed divinity for themselves. This was a phase of the orientalizing of the West, which had first assimilated Eastern ideas and then imposed them on the East in an altered form. The Romans of the republican period looked upon the elevation of man to divinity as presumption. The Greeks called it *hybris*—meaning, very roughly, arrogance or insolence. Yet the Greeks did regard the founders of their city-states, long since dead, as having been gods on earth. In Egypt, the living Pharaohs claimed to be gods, and the Persians developed an elaborate ritual of prostration in the presence of their rulers. These elements were fused by the successors of Alexander into a form of emperor worship, which was eventually adopted by the Romans and then required of all in the empire. Here are the roots of the clash between Christ and Caesar. The Jews were confronted with the problem even before the Romans invaded Palestine.

The conflict came with the successors of Alexander in the East, the Seleucids, who became the rulers of Syria and, in time, of Palestine. Under Antiochus Epiphanes (his very name means "God made manifest") a determined effort was made to Hellenize Judea. A gymnasium was introduced in Jerusalem. Although the orthodox among the Jews scowled, others were willing to accommodate themselves to Greek practices. Even some priests would first officiate in their robes in the Temple and then run naked in the gymnasium. Then Antiochus began interfering with the priesthood, and in 167 B.C., meeting opposition, he defiled the sanctuary at Jerusalem by sacrificing a pig on the altar. The Jewish religion was interdicted on pain of death, and pagan sacrifices were required of the Jews. Following this development, a certain Jew who was on the point of complying with the new regulations, together with an officer of the king, was cut down by another Jew; and out of this conflict developed a war between the Jews and their Seleucid oppressors. The slayer was of the clan of Hasmon, whose members were known as Hasmoneans. It was they who led the revolt. These warring clansmen are also known as the Maccabees, after Judah, called Maccabeus (the "hammer"), one of their leaders. Ill-armed though they were, these bands of passionate Jewish warriors, in the spirit of Joshua and Gideon, drove the Seleucid forces from Jerusalem and eventually recovered the kingdom of David.[17]

The power of the Seleucids had already been declining, but the valor of the Maccabees is not to be discounted. They were inspired by a book purportedly written during the Babylonian captivity, but actually written following the desecration of the Temple by Antiochus' order. It relates the experiences of Daniel, who was cast into a den of lions because of his religious intransigence, and of three Hebrew youths, who were thrown into a fiery furnace because they defied an order of Nebuchadnezzar to bow down before his image. They had maintained that their God could deliver them (as indeed he did), but even if he did not, they would in no case bow down. The Maccabees well knew that in this cryptic story Nebuchadnezzar signified Antiochus Epiphanes, and that the deliverance of Daniel and the three youths foretold the deliverance of the Jews from his power. This Book of Daniel, the first in the apocalyptic literature, strongly colored the spiritual life of the Jews with its implied messages of hope and salvation, and it sustained the early Christians under persecution.

With Jerusalem freed, the Temple was purified and rededicated in the year 165 B.C., on the twenty-fifth of Kislev, which usually falls in December according to our calendar, the date the Jews still celebrate as the first day of Hanukkah. The religious objective had been achieved. The Hasmoneans were now not content but sought to extend and maintain a monarchical state. This involved, again, foreign alliances. The purists among the Jews, who recoiled from Hasmonean policy and who felt that the monarchy itself conflicted with the lordship of Yahweh, became known as the Pharisees. The party of the priests, who were Hellenizers and allied with the Hasmoneans, were the Sadducees. When in 103 B.C. Alexander Jannaeus, a Sadducee high priest of

[17] Elias Bickermann, *Der Gott der Makkabäer* (Berlin, 1937).

profligate and barbarous character, declared himself king, the Pharisees clamored for his death. He retaliated by crucifying eight hundred of them at a public banquet which he attended with his concubines. A bloody civil war ensued, which was checked only when Pompey ended the Seleucid kingdom and established Roman rule over Syria and Palestine in 63 B.C.

Herod the Great

After twenty-three years of continued political turmoil, the area of the old Maccabean kingdom was entrusted to a vassal king called Herod the Great, an Edomite. He was charming, astute, magnificent, and brutal. Although he was half Jewish and had a Hasmonean wife, he built Hellenistic cities throughout Palestine, with temples to the pagan gods. At Caesarea he built a city with an artificial harbor, later to be the Roman capital for the area. A string of fortresses within signaling distance of each other guarded the approach to Jerusalem.

But of all Herod's works none exceeded in magnificence the rebuilding of the Temple in Jerusalem. All that the art of Hellas could supply was lavished on the sanctuary of the Jews. One thousand priests were trained as stone-cutters, carpenters, and decorators, lest any impure hand sully the Holy Place. Because Herod was not of the priestly house, he refrained from entering the most sacred precinct; because he respected Jewish scruples he refrained from stamping his own image on coins. When the Temple was completed, after Herod's death, eighteen thousand men were out of employment. Its adornment was sumptuous, with golden doors, a figured Babylonian curtain before it, and a huge golden vine above the lintel. From the altar of incense, from the seven-branched candlestick, and from burnt offerings rose clouds of smoke. Animal sacrifices were daily performed, and the sacrificial altar was covered with reeking blood, guts, and flies. Removed alike from the splendor and the squalor was a room, empty and dark—the Holy of Holies, the dwelling place of the Most High, replacing the lost Ark of the Covenant—into which only the high priest could enter, once a year, on the Day of Atonement. This monument Herod had built less for the glory of God than for his own eternal renown, but within little more than half a century hardly one stone was left upon another.

Higher than the Temple, Herod constructed a palace and, at a still greater eminence, a citadel. Such was his scale of values—a temple, a palace, and a fort. But Herod is chiefly remembered for his slaughter of the babies of Bethlehem in an effort to eliminate a scion of the House of David who might contest his throne. The account is not incredible. Herod was a ruthless man who executed one of his ten wives, his mother-in-law, and three of his sons. (Augustus said that it were better to be Herod's sow than his son.) But it should be said in Herod's favor that by his respect for the religion of the Jews he prevented an insurrection and, as a consequence, an invasion by the legions of Rome.

But through the extravagance of his building he left the land impoverished and even more seething with disaffection than it was at his accession. Prior to his time, the Jews had been sucked into Rome's civil wars, and one hundred thousand of them had fallen in conflicts not their own. The death of Herod brought struggles for the succession. In the uncertainty that followed, riots in Jerusalem led to a massacre of three thousand. In Galilee, where Jesus was growing up, a certain Judas, mentioned in the Book of the Acts of the Apostles, headed an insurrection against the authorities, killing not only Gentiles but also pacific Jews. The Roman governor of Syria suppressed the uprising and crucified two thousand insurgents who infested the mountain fastnesses and the caves of the desert. From among their sympathizers emerged the party of the Zealots, who cried, "Yahweh alone is king." Among the other factions were the Sadducees, who fraternized with any rulers; the Pharisees, who kept the Law and awaited divine vindication; and, even stricter than the Pharisees, the Essenes, some of whom are presumably identical with the members of the Qumran community, recently disclosed through the finding of the Dead Sea scrolls. In the interests of purity, the members withdrew to the wilderness, like ancient Israel, and established themselves on the banks of the Dead Sea, there to await the triumph of God through the victory of the Sons of Light over the Sons of Darkness.

Rome dealt with the political problem of succession in several ways. In the northern portion of Herod's domain, two of his sons were established as vassal rulers with the title of tetrarch. One of them was Herod Antipas in Galilee. But in the south, Judea and adjoining areas were made into a Roman province under a procurator with headquarters at Caesarea. In Jerusalem, the high priest enjoyed practical autonomy in conjunction with an assembly of the aristocracy called the Sanhedrin, which could pronounce a fellow Jew deserving of death but had to refer his actual execution to Rome. From time to time the procurators came to Jerusalem, but they did not display as much understanding for Judaism as Herod had done. The best-known of them, Pontius Pilate, at one time sent Roman troops into Jerusalem bearing the image of the deified Caesar on their ensigns. A concourse of Jews rushed down to Pilate's headquarters at Caesarea to protest this desecration of the holy city. Pilate threatened a massacre, but when the Jews fell on their faces awaiting the sword, he gave in.

Messianic Hope

Many solaced themselves with the expectation of a national deliverer. This might be either an earthly figure, a king of the seed of David, a Messiah (an anointed one), or a heavenly being. As the latter he appears in the Book of Daniel, where he is called a Son of Man. In later Jewish apocalypses he is depicted also as a pre-existent heavenly deliverer. Throughout the entire history of Israel, when her fortunes on earth were most bleak, the hope for deliverance from heaven waxed strong. When the ancient prophets thundered doom at an unrepentant people, either they or their redactors tempered denunciation with the comforting assurance that God would forgive and restore. After centuries of blasted hopes, when the land was occupied by the unbelievers, the struggle took on cosmic proportions. The enemy on earth was viewed as the instrument of sinister forces in the heavenly places. The outcome would be that Yahweh would triumph over all foes and, having cast the demonic assailants into the abyss, would break the teeth of sinners, consign mighty kings to a valley of fire, and give the carcasses of their minions to the vultures. Such was the mood of Israel at the time Jesus was born.

1. OLD TESTAMENT SCENES IN JEWISH ART

1a

Contemporary graphic material illustrative of the history of Judaism in the period of the Old Testament does not go beyond artifacts and photographs of ancient sites, but an extensive Jewish art dating from the first centuries of the Christian era has been discovered in cemeteries and notably in the synagogue at Dura-Europos. This city on the Euphrates, with its heavy walls, was founded in 300 B.C. by Alexander's successors and served as a garrison until it fell to the Parthians in 114 B.C. They made of it a commercial center between East and West. The Romans took it in A.D. 165 and used it to guard their eastern frontiers until it was captured by the Persians in A.D. 256. Thereafter it remained unoccupied. During the siege, the Roman inhabitants constructed huge embankments on the inside in order to prevent the Persians from undermining the walls, thereby covering and preserving the adjacent buildings, including a synagogue, a Mithraeum, and a Christian church. The synagogue has been transferred to the museum at Damascus, whereas the Mithraeum and the church are now at the art museum of Yale University, under whose auspices the excavations were conducted.

The frescoes on the synagogue walls show clearly that in this period the Jews were not deterred from depicting Old Testament scenes by the commandment to "make no likeness of anything that is in heaven above, or that is in the earth beneath, or that is in the water under the earth" (Exod. 20:4). Three scenes are reproduced here. The first shows Pharaoh's daughter discovering Moses amid the bulrushes (Exod. 2:1-10). The second portrays Aaron (note that his name is given in Greek letters) and the institution of the Levitical priesthood (Exod. 28). In the center is the seven-branched candlestick looted from the temple at Jerusalem by the Roman Emperor Titus. The third illustrates the vision of Ezekiel of the restoration of Israel's dead (Ezek. 37:7-10).

The illustrations are reproduced from Carl H. Kraeling, *Excavations at Dura-Europos*, Final Report VIII, Part I (New Haven, Yale University Press, 1956), plates LX, LXVIII, and LXXI.

2. HEROD THE GREAT

We have noted that Herod respected Jewish scruples against images and particularly against representations of rulers with a claim to divinity, and that he therefore refrained from stamping his likeness upon coins minted in Palestine and from erecting public statues of himself in Jewish territory. Until the recent discovery of the colossal head reproduced here, the assumption has been that no likeness of Herod was extant anywhere. This bust was found at Memphis in Egypt where a large colony of Idumean mercenaries was stationed. Herod, we recall, was an Idumean. His shaven upper lip and his beard are characteristic of the Semitic peoples. The features suggest a man who could be ingratiating, sensual, and cruel. They do not correspond to those of any Roman, Greek, or Egyptian ruler of whom an undisputed likeness has been preserved. There is no one of the period around 30 B.C. whom this bust fits better than Herod. For a detailed description and discussion, see Harold Ingholt, "A Colossal Head from Memphis, Severan or Augustan?" *Journal of the American Research Center in Egypt*, II (1963), 125–44, plus XLIV plates, of which the one here is XXX, 2 (courtesy of the Boston Museum of Fine Arts).

3. THE GOLDEN CANDLESTICK

The spoils from the conquest of Jerusalem by Emperor Titus in A.D. 70 are portrayed on the underside of the commemorative arch still standing in Rome. Its condition has seriously deteriorated and a more faithful representation of its original state than a photograph could offer is afforded by this drawing by Pietro Santo Bartoli (1635–1700). It shows a procession of Roman soldiers in civilian attire, crowned with the laurel wreaths of victory. They are carrying three military standards. The spoils of the temple at Jerusalem, on our right, consist of the golden table for the shewbread crossed by the silver trumpets. To our left is the seven-branched golden candlestick, called the Menorah. It remained in Rome until the sack by the Vandals, whose king, Genseric, took it to Carthage in A.D. 455. When Belisarius, the general of Justinian, recovered northern Africa for the empire, the Menorah was returned to Jerusalem. It disappeared in the looting of Jerusalem by the Persians in A.D. 614. On the fate of the Menorah, see Steward Perowne, *The Life and Times of Herod the Great* (Oxford, 1959), p. 142.

II

The Ministry of Christ and the Emergence of the Church

At the death of Herod, Rome mourned the loss of a loyal administrator. The birth of Jesus went unnoticed. For more than a hundred years no Roman historian mentioned him. Our information about his life comes from the four Gospels of Matthew, Mark, Luke, and John, together with a few other references in the New Testament and a few inconsequential sayings called *agrapha*, culled from early documents. We do not even know the precise date of Jesus' birth. According to Matthew, it was some time before the death of Herod the Great in 4 B.C. Luke records that it was at the time of the census of Quirinius, which was in A.D. 6. But again, according to Luke, Jesus was thirty years old in the fifteenth year of Tiberius' reign—from August, A.D. 28, to August, A.D. 29. That would place his birth very close to the traditional beginning of the Christian era.

The details of his birth are given only in the Gospels of Matthew and Luke. They agree that he was of the lineage of David and was born in Bethlehem, the native town of David, though Mary and Joseph lived in Nazareth. They happened to be in Bethlehem at the time Mary was delivered because the census required that each man be enrolled in his own city, and Joseph had come from Bethlehem.

In the Gospel accounts, only Matthew and Luke mention the virgin birth of Jesus. Paul's writings give no indication that he had ever heard of it. Mark's Gospel commences only with the baptism.

According to John, the Word—the Greek *Logos*, the immanent reason of the Stoics—which was in the beginning with God, became incarnate in him.

Whether fact, legend, or myth, the birth stories enshrine two themes, celebration in heaven and rejection on earth. The angels sang, but because "there was no room for them in the inn"[1] the Saviour had to be born in a stable and cradled in the feedbox of a donkey. To be sure, according to the Scriptures, wise men came from the East to do homage to the new-born King of the Jews, but none came from among the rulers at Jerusalem. Indeed, King Herod "sought the child to destroy him."[2] Of his own people only shepherds gathered about the crib. As the Gospel of John says, "He came to his own home, and his own people received him not."[3] The birth presaged the Passion.

Childhood of Jesus

Jesus' childhood was spent in the midst of poverty. The parables of Jesus portray sparse living where the loss of a coin, or that of clothes by moths or tools by rust, was a household calamity. Joseph, the head of the household, was a carpenter, and Jesus may have learned this trade. The apocryphal Gospels relate that Jesus was able, when a board was too short, to lengthen it miraculously, but the canonical Gospels record no divine interventions to alleviate the lot of the small artisan. Jesus' early proficiency in the Law is indicated by the story in Luke that, when only twelve, he astonished the rabbis in the Temple at Jerusalem with his questions and answers. Of his youth nothing more is known.

What lay behind his resolve to embark upon the ministry of an itinerant rabbi we do not know. This began when in his thirtieth

[1] Luke 2:7.
[2] Matt. 2:13.
[3] John 1:10.

year Jesus was baptized by his cousin John, called the Baptist, in the River Jordan. John was a desert ascetic, perhaps from the Qumran community. He announced the coming day of God's wrath upon the Israelites, "a brood of vipers,"[4] who to be saved should mend their lives rather than rely upon their descent from Abraham. John predicted that one greater than he would come after him as the agent of God's judgment, and he saw that figure in Jesus.

The Teachings of Jesus

The first preaching of Jesus was indeed very much like that of John. Returning to his native Galilee, Jesus traveled about the countryside speaking to throngs on the hilltops or at the lakeside, in synagogues and in homes, saying to them, "the kingdom of God is at hand; repent."[5] The kingdom of God meant the rule or lordship of God. Of course, God is always Lord, but Jesus meant that God's lordship was not only present but would soon be made manifest by his dramatic entry into history.

In preparation for this event, Jesus, like John, declared that Israel should mend her ways and accept God's lordship here and now. Jesus demanded absolute loyalty to God: "Seek first his kingdom and his righteousness." With an absolute loyalty went an absolute trust: "Take no thought for the morrow. Be not anxious for food and raiment. Look at the birds of the air: they neither sow nor reap nor gather into barns, and yet your heavenly Father feeds them. Are you not of more value than they? And why are you anxious about clothing? Consider the lilies of the field, how they grow; they neither toil nor spin; yet I tell you, even Solomon in all his glory was not arrayed like one of these. But if God so clothes the grass of the field, which today is alive and tomorrow is

---

[4] Matt. 3:7.
[5] Mark 1:15.

thrown into the oven, will he not much more clothe you, O men of little faith?"[6]

These were amazing words in such a time and in a land of such poverty. Of all this Jesus was certainly not unaware. Yet to those who had little more security than the birds and the lilies he counseled trust in God and readiness to forsake even what little they had in response to the demands of his kingdom.

This did not mean that they should withdraw into desert caves. It did not necessarily mean giving up family life. Jesus gave his sanction to marriage, both by his attendance at the wedding at Cana in Galilee and by his direct word. He did not condemn all possessions. He excoriated the rich who "devoured widows' houses."[7] But to only one person did he say, "sell what you possess and give to the poor,"[8] because this man inordinately treasured his worldly goods. Jesus feared wealth because it might divert the owner from devotion to the kingdom of heaven. "Truly," he said, "it will be hard for a rich man to enter the kingdom of heaven." He decried striving for wealth as indicating a lack of trust. He deplored the hoarding of wealth by man, whose soul may, any night, be required of him.[9] This is no Cynic cult of poverty, no ascetic rejection of creature comforts, but the foregoing of the easy life because of an exacting obligation. There was no demand for universal and absolute renunciation, but the primary loyalty to the kingdom of God might entail the forsaking of goods and kin, of father, mother, wife, and child.

The Disciples

Jesus did call upon some to leave all and to follow him as traveling evangelists. According to tradition his initial band of

[6] Matt. 5.
[7] Mark 12:40.
[8] Mark 10:21.
[9] Luke 12:20.

disciples, called the apostles, numbered twelve. They were a motley group. Peter, the fisherman, the first to be called, was mercurial. James and John, sons of Zebedee, likewise fishermen, were called "sons of thunder," perhaps because they proposed to call down fire from heaven to consume a Samaritan village which denied hospitality to them and their Master. These two were ambitious and pressed upon Jesus the request that they should sit at his right hand and at his left when he came into his kingdom. The Apostle Nathanael had a contemptuous spirit, and when first told of Jesus asked whether any good thing could come out of Nazareth. Thomas was a doubter and Judas Iscariot a traitor. Andrew and Bartholomew were scarcely impressive, and Matthew, the publican—a Jewish collector of taxes for the Romans—had the most despised occupation in Palestine. Among them all, Matthew was probably the only one who could read and write. He had to, in order to record the taxes. He is the only one among the apostles to whom a Gospel is ascribed. Peter may have been illiterate, since his memoirs are alleged to have been taken down by Mark and made into the Gospel bearing Mark's name. The members of this band, far from prepossessing, were in time so enflamed by love, by loyalty, and by faith that they—the "offscouring of all things"—overcame the world.

The twelve were not the only disciples. On one occasion Jesus sent out seventy. There were also a number of women among his followers. One was a woman of the streets, who washed the Master's feet with her tears and wiped them with her hair. She is commonly identified with a woman from Galilee who was present at the Crucifixion and to whom the risen Christ appeared in the garden. Her name was Mary Magdalene.

Rejection

But, although Jesus had a following, in the main he was rejected by men. The majority of his contemporaries were alienated by his teachings. The Zealots, who sought to foment a violent revolution against Rome, scorned Jesus' spirit of non-resistance when he said: "You have heard that it was said, 'An eye for an eye and a tooth for a tooth.' But I say to you, Do not resist one who is evil. But if any one strikes you on the right cheek, turn to him the other also; and if any one would sue you and take your coat, let him have your cloak as well." "You have heard that it was said, 'You shall love your neighbor and hate your enemy.' But I say to you, Love your enemies and pray for those who persecute you."[10]

At the same time Jesus alienated the Sadducees, who, as already observed, denied the immortality of body and soul alike. They were Hellenists and condoned fraternization with their Greek and Roman masters; they were among the partisans of Herod Antipas, the tetrarch of Galilee, to whom Jesus once referred as "that fox."[11]

The Pharisees were the party with which Jesus had the most in common, yet conflict is often most acute between those most nearly akin. Jesus agreed with the Pharisees that Israel should keep the Jewish Law and leave vindication to God, but differed from them radically as to what was involved in the keeping of the Law. The Pharisees were the faction devoted to observance of all the accretions to the Law made over the years by zealous scribes and elders, such as the prohibition of eating an egg laid on the Sabbath.[12] When criticized for healing a man on the Sabbath, Jesus retorted, "The sabbath was made for man, not man for the sabbath..."[13] The Law, he said, that allows a son by giving to the Temple to evade responsibility for his parents is in flat contradiction to the commandment to honor father and mother. All the regulations about the washing of hands, pots, cups, and vessels he branded as the traditions of men, not the commandments of God. For man is not defiled by anything from without, but only by

[10] Matt. 5:38–48.
[11] Luke 13:32.
[12] Günther Bornkamm, *Jesus of Nazareth* (New York, 1956), p. 36.
[13] Mark 2:27.

thoughts that proceed from within.[14] Jesus, therefore, did not dissociate himself from those deemed unclean; least of all did he withdraw to preserve his purity in the isolation of the Qumran community.

At the same time, he insisted he had not come to destroy the Law and the prophets but rather to fulfill them through the demands of a higher righteousness. He went beyond the injunction not to murder and taught men to reject even anger, not only not to commit adultery but to eschew even lust. Positively, he enjoined love for all men, including enemies, personal and national. The motive behind this higher righteousness was simply loyalty to God rather than the hope of delivering Israel or of ensuring a personal reward.

The concept of reward is not absent from the Gospels, to be sure, but there is no neat equation between deeds and recompense, and there can be no deliberate accumulation of merits. All depends on God's grace. Those to whom reward is announced at the judgment will be taken by surprise and will exclaim, "Lord, when did we see thee hungry and feed thee?"[15] The laborer who is hired at the eleventh hour will receive the same reward as those who have borne the heat of the day.[16] God will reward those who have fed, clothed, and comforted the least of men as though each had been the Son of Man; and God's mercy is incalculable. He gives to one his due, to another unmerited bounty. Such concepts went counter to popular piety.

All the good people were scandalized because Jesus consorted with publicans, who increased their wages by extortion, and because he associated with prostitutes, even presuming to forgive their sins. In so doing he emulated the example of God, who does not withhold his benefits from the bad but sends his sun and rain upon the just and the unjust.[17]

[14] Mark 7:15.
[15] Matt. 25:27.
[16] Matt. 20:12.
[17] Matt. 5:45.

Once, on a visit to his native Nazareth, Jesus explained to a congregation why he had healed the sick at Capernaum, a predominantly gentile city, and not in his own hometown. He called to mind that there were many widows in Israel during a famine in the days of Elijah, but the prophet helped only a widow in the heathen city of Sidon, and there were many lepers in Israel in the time of Elisha, but the only one cured was Naaman the Syrian. Thus, from the evidence of the Old Testament he illustrated the fact that God's mercy was not confined to Israel or to those who followed the Law. The Nazarenes were so incensed by his words that they attempted to throw Jesus over a cliff. Somehow, he escaped.[18]

An affront to Jewish national pride offended even the people of no strong religious conviction, and every faction in Palestine was outraged by Jesus' prediction that the day would come when not one stone of Herod's Temple would remain upon another.[19] There were some, to be sure, who would have made him king, but only because they misconstrued his aims; and when they realized their mistake they were ready to cry "Crucify him!"

Rejected by men, did Jesus expect to be vindicated by God? Jesus had proclaimed that the kingdom of God was at hand. This meant, as has been observed, that the rule of God, already present and demanding immediate loyalty, was soon to be displayed in power. There would be a great manifestation, preceded by wars and rumors of wars, earthquakes and famines. The sun would be turned into darkness and the moon into blood, and the stars would fall from heaven. Then, the Son of Man would come on the clouds with great power and glory to gather his elect. All this would happen within that generation, though God alone knew precisely when.

What did Jesus mean when he said that some then living would see the kingdom of God? The disciples certainly thought he had in mind the expulsion of the Romans and the restoration of the kingdom of David and of the Maccabees. After the Crucifixion,

[18] Luke 4:23–30.
[19] Mark 13:2.

the disciples on the way to Emmaus felt their hopes had been utterly blasted. As Luke recounted, "we had hoped that he was the one to redeem Israel."[20] Again, when Jesus appeared to his disciples after the Resurrection, they asked, "Lord, will you at this time restore the kingdom to Israel?"[21]

They obviously believed him to be the Messiah, but did he think of himself in that role? When Simon Peter confessed that Jesus was the Christ (the Greek word for Messiah), Jesus commended him, yet strictly enjoined him and all the disciples to keep this a secret.[22] What sort of Messiahship was it that could not be proclaimed? Was the point to wait until the great day when the Son of Man would come on the clouds of heaven? Did Jesus believe that he was not only the earthly Messiah of the seed of David but also the heavenly Son of Man? The disciples did, and there are sayings attributed to Jesus in which the title plainly refers to himself: "the Son of Man has nowhere to lay his head";[23] "the Son of Man came not to be served but to serve."[24] But, again, there are passages in which the term seems to refer to another: "everyone who acknowledges me before men, the Son of Man also will acknowledge";[25] and, "whoever says a word against the Son of Man will be forgiven. And whoever speaks against the Holy Spirit will not be forgiven."[26] Jesus may actually have identified himself with the Son of Man. But it is also possible that the disciples, having made this identification by the time they composed the Gospels some decades later, attributed the expression to Jesus. Such questions elude historical solution.

But much more important is it to know what kind of Messiah, what kind of Son of Man, what kind of kingdom of God Jesus envisaged. The Zealots looked for a Messiah who would break the invader with a rod of iron. In the Book of Daniel and in other

[20] Luke 24:21.
[21] Acts 1:6.
[22] Matt. 16:20.
[23] Matt. 8:20.
[24] Mark 10:45.
[25] Matt. 10:32.
[26] Matt. 12:32.

Jewish apocalypses, the Son of Man was to reign after the enemy had been given to the flames. How utterly foreign is all this to the spirit of Jesus! Would loving one's enemies restore the kingdom to Israel? Might it not destroy any kingdom that ever was? When his followers sought by force to make Jesus a king he fled from them to the hills. He reproved the spirit of those who sought domination: "You know that the rulers of the Gentiles lord it over them. ... It shall not be so among you; but whoever would be great among you must be your servant, and whoever would be first among you must be your slave. . . ."[27]

Jesus may have thought of his role as unique in the redemption of Israel but feared the traditional titles for a redeemer, which were certain to be misconstrued. The total image that emerges from the sayings and deeds of Jesus conforms best with the picture portrayed by the prophet Isaiah of the Suffering Servant, "despised and rejected by men . . . with whose stripes we are healed," [28] and with the prediction of the prophet Zechariah of a king who would be "humble and riding on an ass," who would "command peace to the nations."[29]

Already rejected by many and not yet vindicated by God, what course had Jesus to pursue? He might have withdrawn to gentile territory; he did, in fact, make an excursion to Tyre and Sidon. But he then came back and went to Jerusalem, perhaps simply because as a loyal Jew he would not omit the Passover pilgrimage. But there are indications that he intended to precipitate a crisis. On the Sunday before Passover, he rode into Jerusalem on a donkey in reminiscence of Zechariah's prediction. Palm branches were strewed in his path by throngs shouting, "Hosanna! Blessed is he who comes in the name of the Lord."[30]

The next day Jesus went into the Temple. He saw there the money-changers who replaced the currency brought by the Jews from abroad with the Temple coinage, which alone was valid for

[27] Luke 22:25–26.
[28] Isa. 53:3–5.
[29] Zech. 9:9.
[30] Mark 11:9.

the purchase of animals for sacrifice. In blazing indignation against those who profaned the Holy Place, Jesus overturned the tables and dispersed the traffickers in sacrifice.[31] The excitement in Jerusalem must have been intense, for such an act might well be interpreted as Messianic and as a prelude to the great day of the Lord. But the priests, who practically ruled Jerusalem, could hardly view this gesture save as an affront to their authority. And the jubilant throngs of the first day of the week must have been chilled when nothing more happened on the second or the third day. Instead of calling down legions of angels to drive out the Romans, Jesus did nothing more dramatic than sit in the Temple and teach.

Plots

Still, for the moment, Jesus enjoyed such popular support that the Jewish authorities feared to seize him without having a specific accusation against him. The Herodians and the Pharisees thereupon contrived a plot. Only a common hatred could have united those two factions. They well knew that by Roman law Jesus could not be put to death by the Sanhedrin, and the only offenses that the Roman government would punish were civil and political crimes. No civil crime could be proved. There remained, therefore, the charge of sedition. The plotters came to Jesus with the incriminating question, "Is it lawful to pay taxes to Caesar, or not?"[32] If Jesus answered Yes, the Zealots would be alienated. If he answered No, he could be charged before the Roman procurator, Pontius Pilate, with sedition.

Jesus refused to be trapped. He asked to be shown a denarius, a silver coin minted outside Palestine and bearing the head of the Emperor Tiberius and an inscription declaring him the son of the divine Augustus. Strict Jews would not touch these coins. When, then, his questioners produced one, it was quite plain that

[31] Mark 11:15–17.
[32] Mark 12:14.

to this extent they were themselves guilty of apostasy. Jesus asked, "Whose likeness and inscription is this?" They answered, "Caesar's." Jesus then replied, "Render therefore to Caesar the things that are Caesar's and to God the things that are God's. His point was that if they compromised by carrying the coins, they should pay the tribute, but their supreme duty lay in unqualified loyalty to God. It was an embarrassing retort for the questioners, but at the same time incriminating for Jesus. It would both enrage the Zealots and displease the Romans and their faction.

On Thursday night Jesus dined with his disciples. He foresaw that on one pretext or another he would be condemned. He predicted that one disciple would betray him and all would fail him. Simon Peter asserted that though it meant death, he would not desert his Master, but Jesus predicted that before the cock crowed Peter would three times deny knowing him.

All four Gospels have accounts of the Last Supper, but the version given by the Apostle Paul is that which has served as the basis for the liturgy of the Church. These are his words: "For I received from the Lord what I also delivered to you, that the Lord Jesus on the night when he was betrayed took bread, and when he had given thanks, he broke it, and said, 'This is my body which is for you. Do this in remembrance of me.' In the same way also the cup, after supper, saying, 'This cup is the new covenant in my blood. Do this, as often as you drink it, in remembrance of me.' For as often as you eat this bread and drink the cup, you proclaim the Lord's death until he comes."[33]

Passion and Death

After the supper they went out to the Garden of Gethsemane, at the foot of the Mount of Olives. While the disciples slept, Jesus withdrew to pray: "Abba, Father, all things are possible to thee; remove this cup from me, yet not what I will, but what thou

[33] I Cor. 11:23–26.

wilt."[34] Then came an armed band from the priests, led by the traitor Judas, to arrest Jesus.

What secret did Judas betray? The usual assumption is that he disclosed the whereabouts of Jesus, but that should not have been necessary because he taught daily in the Temple. Judas may have disclosed the Messianic secret and thus have provided a ground for the accusation of sedition. The first hearing was before the high priest. When Jesus was taken in the garden, all the disciples fled; but Peter, the boldest, followed and stood in the courtyard of the priest's palace. Presumably he could hear the examination. Caiaphas, the high priest, asked Jesus, "Are you the Christ?" He answered, "I am."[35] Caiaphas tore his mantle, declaring this to be blasphemy, and Jesus was pronounced deserving of death.

In the meantime, by the light of a fire someone recognized Peter as a follower of Jesus. He denied it. A second and a third time the point was made and he swore that he never knew the man. At once the cock crowed and Peter went out and wept bitterly. The account of this episode in the Gospels is unique in the literature of antiquity. The Greeks and the Romans would have treated the remorse of a rustic as a joke. Christianity had introduced a new sensitivity.

Since the priests could not pass sentence of death, they delivered Jesus to Pilate. We read that Pilate asked Jesus, "Are you the King of the Jews?"[36] Jesus answered enigmatically, "You have said so," and would say no more. Pilate is represented as seeing through the guile of the accusers and as trying to save Jesus by utilizing a favor annually accorded the Jews at Passover: the release of one prisoner of their choice. He offered them either Barabbas, who in an insurrection had killed a guard, or Jesus, and they cried out for Barabbas. As for Jesus, they clamored, "Crucify him!" When Pilate sought to dissuade them, they pointed out that he who showed leniency to one claiming kingship was not Caesar's

[34] Mark 14:36.
[35] Mark 14:61–62.
[36] John 18:33.

friend. Pilate wilted and condemned Jesus to death by crucifixion, an ignominious form of punishment, preceded by scourging, and usually reserved in Roman times for slaves, common criminals, and rebels.

Jesus was scourged, crowned in mockery with thorns, and compelled to carry his own cross until, when he sank beneath the weight of his burden, another was impressed to take over. The place of execution was a hill outside Jerusalem called Golgotha, which means the place of a skull. And they crucified him between two thieves. The passers-by railed at him, and the chief priests mocked him, saying, "Let the Christ, the King of Israel, come down now from the cross that we may see and believe."[37] And Jesus prayed, "Father, forgive them, for they know not what they do."[38] He was offered wine mixed with myrrh but he did not take it. Quoting the first verse of the twenty-second Psalm, he cried out, "My God, my God, why hast thou forsaken me?"[39] thus identifying himself with the age-old agony of his people. Then, with a loud cry, he yielded up his spirit. Late Friday afternoon he was laid in a tomb.

Resurrection

Early on Sunday morning, according to Mark's Gospel, certain women, including Mary Magdalene, came to the tomb and found it empty. There are several differing accounts of the re-appearances of Jesus after the Crucifixion. In one strand of the tradition he is said to have appeared first to the women at the empty tomb; in another it was at the shore of the Lake of Galilee. The Apostle Paul said that the Lord appeared first to Peter; the place is not mentioned. Subsequently, according to Paul, the Lord showed himself to the twelve apostles, then to five hundred brethren at

[37] Mark 15:32.
[38] Luke 23:34.
[39] Mark 15:34.

once, to James, the Lord's brother, and finally to Paul himself.[40] The accounts of the Gospels describe the risen Christ as able to speak, to eat, and to be touched. Paul, in reference to his own experience of the risen Christ, says only this: "He who had . . . called me through his grace was pleased to reveal his Son to me. . . ."[41]

But whatever the variations in the accounts, one point is plain. The disciples were sure that Christ crucified was Christ risen from the dead. Without this certainty there would probably have been no Christian Church. Heartbroken that their Master had been put to death as a common criminal, their hope shattered that he would restore the kingdom to Israel, his closest followers had dispersed. But, faith in his resurrection and the consciousness of his living presence brought them together again and averted the dissolution of the fellowship.

Early Christians

During the first few centuries following the death of Jesus, the Christian faith spread with phenomenal rapidity throughout most of the ancient world. What had been a small, local movement within Judaism was transformed into a far-reaching fellowship of many different peoples, well organized and with a distinctive worship. Less than three hundred years after the Crucifixion, Christianity had become the officially favored religion of the great Roman Empire.

The beginning of the infant Church, which was to grow with such remarkable vigor, is usually dated from Pentecost (the fiftieth day after Passover) following the death of Christ. On this occasion the disciples were gathered in an upper room when an exaltation of spirit seized them, as if tongues of fire had descended upon

[40] I Cor. 15:5–8.
[41] Gal. 1:15–16.

their heads.[42] To date the rise of the Church from this experience is somewhat arbitrary, for on this subject there can be no precision. However, the Church certainly then began to win converts. That day Peter preached the first Christian sermon; his message was to believe in the Lord Jesus, crucified, risen, and exalted to the right hand of God. The seal of admission to the new fellowship was baptism, accompanied by an intense emotional experience called the descent of the Spirit. In response to Peter's preaching that day, according to the Acts of the Apostles, three thousand were converted.

After the withdrawal of Christ from the earthly scene, the situation of the disciples was naturally changed. They had regarded Jesus as the Messiah who would restore the kingdom to Israel. Now he was considered to be the heavenly Son of Man who would come again in the very near future to inaugurate the kingdom of God. With joyous expectancy they awaited his coming, in the meantime sharing their possessions according to need, observing the Law and attending the Temple daily, and breaking bread together "with glad and generous hearts."[43] "Breaking bread" refers to a common meal called the *Agape*, or love feast, which included a celebration called the Eucharist, meaning a thanksgiving. These occasions looked backward in commemoration of the Last Supper and forward in anticipation of the returning Christ; they marked a fellowship of believers holding communion with the risen Christ. The meetings were held in private homes which for many years to come continued to serve as churches. A particular room might be arranged to serve as a baptistery.

Although the followers of Christ professed to be faithful Jews and continued to observe the basic Mosaic Law, they nevertheless held beliefs and engaged in practices repudiated by the orthodox. The successful preaching of the disciples and the dramatic miracles performed in the name of Jesus deeply concerned the authorities of Jerusalem. Shortly after Pentecost, Peter and John were

[42] Acts 2:2–3.
[43] Acts 2:46.

arrested and charged to be silent; but they answered, "Whether it is right in the sight of God to listen to you rather than to God, you must judge."[44] The blow next fell on Stephen. He was charged with blasphemy because he was alleged to have said that Jesus would come again and destroy the Temple and abolish the Law. When he refuted his accusers, "stiff-necked people, uncircumcised in heart and ears"[45] who resisted the Holy Spirit, Stephen was stoned to death. He was the first Christian martyr.

This sudden tragedy had far-reaching effects. In the face of the ensuing persecution, many of the disciples fled, and wherever they went, north toward Antioch or south toward Egypt, they preached the Gospel. (*Gospel* is the Old English form of the Greek word *evangelion*, meaning "good news.") The evangelist Philip moved into Samaria and was followed by Peter and John. Mark, Peter's amanuensis, is traditionally credited with the evangelization of Egypt, and the disciple Thomas with that of India.

Apostle Paul

But the great sphere of missionary expansion was to be the gentile world to the west, and the apostle to this region was preeminently Paul, a Jew of the tribe of Benjamin (*Paul* is the Greek form of his original name, Saul), who had been a zealous Pharisee and a persecutor of Christians, and who, when Stephen was stoned, had stood by, consenting to his death. After ferreting out suspects in Jerusalem, Saul received authority from the high priest to go to Damascus to see whether there had been any Christian infiltration into that synagogue. But as he approached Damascus, "suddenly a light flashed from heaven about him. And . . . a voice [said], 'Saul, Saul, why do you persecute me?' "[46] That vision of Christ made Saul, the persecutor, into Paul the

[44] Acts 4:19.
[45] Acts 7:51.
[46] Acts 9:4.

apostle; the encounter, he later insisted, made him as much as the others a witness to the Resurrection of Christ.

Paul was to be the greatest theologian of the early Church—and one of the few epochal figures in all history; a figure second only to Jesus in the history of Christianity. He was admirably suited for the role of apostle. Although a Jew, he had been reared in the Greek city of Tarsus in Cilicia, in Asia Minor. He was able to address a mob in Jerusalem in Aramaic, the language of Christ, and he could address the Gentiles in Greek, in which language alone his letters survive. He was also a Roman citizen, which meant that he could not be scourged without trial and that he enjoyed the right of appeal to Rome. It also meant that he could be executed only by the sword and not by crucifixion.

Christ, for Paul, stood at the apex of history. In him culminated the covenants made by God with Noah, Abraham, and Moses. As the prophet Jeremiah had promised, there was a new covenant, not graven on stone like the Ten Commandments, but on the hearts of men; not a stricter law like that of the Pharisees, but rather a new dispensation superseding the Law altogether and embracing Jew and Gentile alike. For Paul this new covenant—this new testament—was realized in Christ.

Paul recognized that the Gentiles had a law of their own, the law of nature; but he saw also that they failed to obey it, just as the Jews had failed to keep the Law of Moses. Man is incapable of fulfilling such laws and thereby gaining God's favor, because all men have been corrupted by the fall of Adam. Salvation cannot be achieved in obedience to any law, but only through the mercy of God. This mercy is vouchsafed through Christ, who, being God's Son, renounced his equality with the Father and suffered himself to be born of a woman and die upon a cross,[47] that men might be reconciled to God and, through faith in Christ, share in his death and rise "to walk in newness of life."[48] But why then do not all men respond? Because God has predestined only some to be

[47] Phil. 2:7-8.
[48] Rom. 6:4.

saved. Paul thus introduced the doctrine of predestination, which was to be of vast import in later Christian thought.

Paul was the greatest of all missionaries. When the early Christian evangelists confronted the pagan world, a very serious problem arose. Should observance of the Jewish Law be imposed upon Gentiles who were converted to faith in Christ? Judaism itself was missionary but had not made great gains among the Gentiles, because it required them to accept circumcision and dietary regulations. For Paul this was no problem, because to his mind the Law was no longer binding, even upon Jews. But the original disciples, including Peter, had not passed through the inner struggle by which Paul had emancipated himself from the bondage of the Law. At first they were of no mind even to consort with the Gentiles. However, Peter's prejudices were broken down by a vision. He had objected to eating anything deemed unclean. But in his vision a voice told him that what God had made clean he should not consider impure.[49]

Peter understood this to mean not only that no meat but that no man was unclean in the eyes of God; and when, the next day, a Roman centurion invited him to come and explain the Gospel, Peter went and received this Gentile into the faith. When Peter returned to Jerusalem, he was taken to task by James, brother of Jesus and leader of the Church there, for breaking bread with the uncircumcised; but he defended his course so persuasively that his questioners exclaimed, "Then to the Gentiles also God has granted repentance unto life."[50] When ritual regulations and circumcision were no longer imposed, Christianity was relieved of a great handicap in its appeal to Gentiles of the Roman world.

But, by the same token, the breach with Judaism became irreparable, a situation that only worsened when the Christians abandoned the seventh day of the week as the Sabbath in favor of the first day, the day on which Jesus rose from the dead. Precisely when this change was made we do not know, but in the Book of

[49] Acts 10:15.
[50] Acts 11:18.

Revelation, the last in the New Testament, there is a reference to "the Lord's Day."[51] The Sanhedrin pronounced a curse upon the Nazarenes, as the followers of Christ were contemptuously called. The term suggested that Christianity had its rise not at Bethlehem in Judea, but at Nazareth in half-pagan Galilee.

The Christian Church survived precariously in Palestine until the great insurrection of the Jews, which led the Emperor Titus in A.D. 70 to besiege Jerusalem and destroy the Temple. Of Herod's great structure only part of the foundations remained standing. The Menorah, the holy candelabrum with its seven candlesticks, was carried off to Rome, where it is portrayed on the triumphal arch of Titus. A second rebellion, headed by Bar Kochba in A.D. 132–35, during the reign of Hadrian, led to the end of the Jewish state until the establishment of modern Israel. On the other hand, the synagogues, long since widely distributed throughout the Roman world, afforded Paul a port of entry in every city he visited. Although he was invariably rejected by the majority of the congregation, he almost surely made converts among Hellenized Jews.

Several other factors greatly assisted the spread of Christianity throughout the Roman Empire. The conquests of Alexander had introduced a new cosmopolitanism in the ancient world. Among other things a common language, Hellenistic Greek called the Koine, was used from Italy to India. It was the language used by Paul in his Epistles. Following the consolidation of Rome's conquests by Caesar and Octavian, the vast Empire enjoyed a period of peace—the Pax Romana—that lasted for three hundred years. The Mediterranean, cleared of pirates by Pompey, became a Roman lake. The superb roads that bound the Empire together were relatively free of brigands. Paul suffered shipwreck, exposure, cold, hunger, and "peril of robbers" on his journeys,[52] but still he was able to travel and preach through Asia Minor, Thrace, Greece, and Italy; had he not been put to death he might well have

[51] Rev. 1:10.
[52] II Cor. 11:23–27.

realized his wish to go to Spain.[53] Wherever he went, whether in the synagogue or the forum, Paul, thanks to the tolerance of Roman rule, was free to debate the cause of Christianity, provided he said nothing subversive of Rome's political authority.

Although this gentile world which Paul addressed, rejoiced in the benefits of the Roman peace, it was subject to a deep malaise. Political independence was gone. The city-states with their local loyalties were losing their political and economic autonomy and no longer commanded the passionate devotion of their inhabitants. Men felt themselves adrift in a world grown too large, and they craved consequently such intimate fellowship as might be found in religious cults.

Worse than loneliness was ennui. For many, life had lost its allure. The Roman peace may have contributed to this feeling, for peace as well as war has its vices. The capital battened on the exploitation of the provinces. Rome witnessed the rise of an aristocracy, idle, pampered, luxurious, and lascivious. The capital city also attracted a motley horde that included the dregs of the populace of the Empire. The mob clamored for bread and circuses, for staged combats of beasts with beasts—lions from Africa, tigers from India—of men with beasts, and of men with men. Artificial lakes were constructed large enough to float navies which engaged in actual combat. It is strange that there was so little protest from cultivated men. Seneca did protest that "man sacred to man"[54] should be killed for sport, but nothing was done to arrest the madness, which spread to the provinces. The Greeks, who had been content with their Olympian games, came also to have arenas, and a number were constructed in the provincial cities of Gaul and elsewhere. Freed from war, men let blood for amusement.

Such avid pursuit of excitement witnesses to a profound malady of spirit. There were those who explained the vicissitudes of life in

---
[53] Rom. 15:24.
[54] Seneca *Epistulae morales* 95.

terms of malign supernatural influences. The swift dislocations of the civil wars of Rome that preceded the great peace led many to wonder whether life was not subject to the whims of the goddess Fortuna, who disposes capriciously of men. The Greeks had long had the concept of Moira, fate, and Tyche, caprice, which can thwart even the gods. In the classical period, however, this fate did not destroy freedom. Man could react to fate. This is the very essence of Greek tragedy. Fate determined that Oedipus should unwittingly kill his father and marry his mother, but of his own volition he pursued every clue until the ghastly truth was established and then took the guilt upon himself and spared his city the vengeance of the gods.

But in the later period, the Greek Moira came to be combined with Babylonian astral determinism. Man's fate was believed to be ruled by the conjunctions of the stars; he must therefore seek to discover lucky days for such events as marriage, and in all undertakings take account of his horoscope. Juvenal tells of a woman who would not rub a salve on an itching eye until she had checked the position of the stars. To ward off possible malign influences on their lives, men also resorted to magic by means of charms and amulets.

But, merely to fend off evil is not so reassuring as to lay hold of life; hence the great appeal of the religions of redemption. Probably many of those who assuaged their disquiet through the games reflected little on the meaning of life, but some certainly began to be convinced that understanding and hope lay only in the beyond. Those so minded were hospitable to the messages of the Oriental cults, including Christianity, with their promises of salvation.

At one point or another, Paul met on his journeys the whole gamut of contemporary paganism. At Lystra in Lycaonia in Asia Minor, Paul, accompanied by Barnabas, cured a cripple. Immediately the populace assumed that Paul and Barnabas were gods in the guise of men. Barnabas was identified with Zeus, and Paul, who did the talking, with Hermes, the messenger of the gods. The priest of Zeus brought oxen to sacrifice to these divinities. At Ephesus, the capital of the Roman province of "Asia," Paul came into conflict with the fertility cult of Artemis (Diana), who was portrayed in silver statuettes with what appear to be many breasts. Paul asserted that these idols were no gods. The silversmiths, whose trade was threatened, thereupon stirred up a riot.

In Galatia, Paul had to deal with a type of religion that sought to avoid malign elements of the cosmos by observing special days, months, seasons, and years. At Athens he faced audiences avid for new ideas. Stoic and Epicurean philosophers who questioned Paul listened attentively until he proclaimed the resurrection of Jesus; then some mocked him, as might have been expected, for they did not believe in immortality. He might have had a different reception from Platonists, who believed in the continued life of the spirit.

Paul's journeys took him through Asia Minor and Macedonia to Greece. He desired to reach Rome, where there was a Christian congregation, by whom founded we do not know; not by Paul, obviously, and there is no evidence in the New Testament that it was founded by Peter. However, about A.D. 51–52 the Emperor Claudius expelled the Jews from Rome because of rioting occasioned by one "Chrestus," presumably Christus—a vague but evocative reference to the uproar caused by the intrusion of Christianity among Jews in the capital. Probably in consequence of that expulsion a Christian-Jewish couple, Priscilla and Aquila by name, migrated to Corinth where Paul met them. Perhaps they were the founders of the Roman Christian congregation.

Before continuing his westward course toward Rome, Paul went to Jerusalem to bring a contribution from the gentile churches to the poor of Jerusalem. While there, he was accused by the Jews of bringing Gentiles into the Temple, and in the ensuing riot he was arrested by the Roman authorities. As they were about to "examine" him by scourging, Paul insisted on his rights as a Roman citizen. As a security measure, he was then taken under guard to the Roman capital at Caesarea. The procurator of the province, Festus, might have released him had not Paul taken the case out of his hands by appealing to Rome.

Paul had confidence in Roman justice and had every reason to expect that Caesar's court would dismiss the charges, because hitherto Roman rulers had looked upon Christianity as a Jewish sect and had intervened in disputes between the two factions only to protect the weaker party from violence. Yet Paul's case at Rome, after long delays, ended in his execution under Nero.

4. A DENARIUS OF THE EMPEROR TIBERIUS

When Jesus was asked whether tribute should be paid to the Roman emperor, he asked to be shown a denarius. It could have been a coin like the one portrayed above, a denarius of the Emperor Tiberius, for according to the evangelist Luke, Jesus began his public ministry in the fifteenth year of Tiberius and, according to the pagan historian Tacitus, he was crucified in the reign of this emperor. The coin bears the inscription, TI[BERIUS] CAESAR DIVI AUG[USTI] F[ILIUS] AUGUST[US] IMP[ERATOR] VIII, meaning Tiberius Caesar, of the divine Augustus the son, Augustus Emperor VIII (that is, in his eighth year). The coin bears the claim that the deceased emperor known as Augustus was divine. This was the claim that neither Jews nor Christians would accept. Notice that the word "Augustus" was also a title applied to Tiberius himself.

5. JESUS AS PORTRAYED

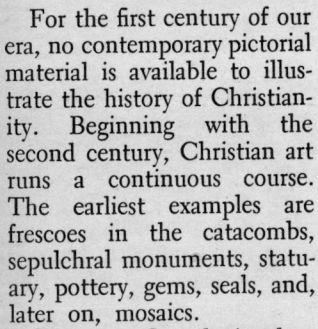

5a

5b

For the first century of our era, no contemporary pictorial material is available to illustrate the history of Christianity. Beginning with the second century, Christian art runs a continuous course. The earliest examples are frescoes in the catacombs, sepulchral monuments, statuary, pottery, gems, seals, and, later on, mosaics.

Jesus was first depicted as the Good Shepherd, a beardless youth. The type of the Good Shepherd did not originate with Christianity. New religions do not generally invent art forms, but take over earlier traditions and adapt them to their own ends. The figure of a deity carrying a sheep over his shoulders, dating back to one thousand years before Christ, has been found near Baalbek (Fig. 5a). Whether the animal is being carried for sacrifice or for protection is not clear. Jesus as the Good

Shepherd appears as a beardless youth, sometimes with cropped curly hair after the manner of Apollo, sometimes with long locks like Dionysus or Hermes Criophoros (Fig. 5b, a statue of the fourth century). Similar borrowing occurred in the contemporary cult of Mithras (cf. page 75f.). Hence the superficial resemblance of the above figure of Mithras (Fig. 5c) to that of Jesus, save that Mithras is dragging away the slain bull, whereas Jesus is carrying the live sheep. See David Talbot Rice, *The Beginnings of Christian Art* (New York, Abingdon Press, 1958), p. 65.

In the fourth century, the beardless type of Christ begins to be displaced by the bearded. This change has sometimes been described as the triumph of the Syrian over the Hellenistic type. Undeniably the Semitic peoples regarded the beard as a mark of virility, but the Greeks and the Romans were not all shaven. Among the gods, Zeus had a patriarchal beard. The poet Homer and the philosophers Socrates, Plato, and Aristotle were sculptured with beards. So, too, were some of the emperors and notably the two philosophers among them, Marcus Aurelius and Julian the Apostate (Julian's beard being so luxuriant that a wag suggested he should make it into rope). The beard marked the philosopher, and the bearded Christ is the true philosopher, the divine teacher, superior to the professors of Neoplatonism.

The illustration (Fig. 5d) is from the catacombs and dates from the fourth century. Christ's head is encircled by a halo and surmounted by the Chi Rho monogram in a form slightly different from the one in the fresco of the Virgin and Child (Fig. 6b). The letters to the right and left of the head are Alpha and Omega, the

5d

first and last letters of the Greek alphabet, signifying that Christ is the beginning and the end.

6. THE VIRGIN MARY AND THE CHILD

6a

Our earliest depiction of the Virgin Mary and the Child is very early indeed, dating from the first half of the second century. Though poorly preserved, the main outlines are clearly distinguishable. Above is the star; Mary wears the veil of a virgin; she is very plainly clad. Beside her stands the prophet Isaiah predicting that a virgin should bear a child. The reference is to Isa. 7:14, which had been

6b

incorrectly translated in the Greek version of the Old Testament. The Hebrew has the prediction that a young woman should bear. The word is *almah*, which the Greek rendered as *parthenos*, virgin. The portrayal from the cemetery of Priscilla at Rome (Fig. 6a) has a touch of realism in that the child is afraid of the prophet and is clinging to the mother.

The second example from the fourth century in the cemetery of Maius at Rome shows Mary on the way to becoming the Queen of Heaven, wearing earrings and a necklace. Again, she wears a veil. Her hands are uplifted in a pose assumed in prayer. One engaged in prayer was called an orant. The child is a diminutive adult, not because the early Christian artists were too unskilled to draw a child, but because the Son, having been the agent of the Father in the creation of the world, is older than his mother. To the right and to the left, we see the monogram of Christ, formed by combining the first two letters, Chi and Rho. Chi, the Greek Ch, has the form of the Latin X, and Rho, the Greek R, has the form of the Latin P. The normal form is the one on our left, which for the sake of symmetry has been inverted on the right.

7. THE WISE MEN

7a

The number of the Wise Men was variable in the earliest portrayals for the simple reason that the gospels specify only the number of the gifts and not that of the givers. In Fig. 7a, from the beginning of the third century, the number is two. In Fig. 7b, from about A.D. 300, the Wise Men are four. Another feature destined to permanence is the star. Usually, camels are depicted in the East, horses later on in the West. The Wise Men wear the Roman tunic and the flowing Phrygian mantle. Because of this similarity of attire to that of Mithras (see page 75f.), some have assumed that the early Christians thought of the Wise Men as priests of Mithras coming to acknowledge Christ's superiority. But one can scarcely assume so much purely on the basis of a likeness in dress. Fig. 7c combines the three Wise Men, who are depicted with their horses on the left, with Daniel in the lions' den, shown on the right.

8. THE SACRED MEAL

8

Frequent representations appear in the catacombs of a group varying in number seated about a table. Commonly in front of them are seen bread, fish, and wine. These scenes are susceptible of several interpretations. They may represent the common meal called the *Agape* or love feast, which members of the early Christian congregations ate together. This meal terminated in the Lord's Supper, called the Eucharist or Thanksgiving. But only bread and wine were required for this rite. Why then the fish? One reason may have been that in the gospel of John the symbolism of eating the flesh and drinking the blood of the Son of Man (Chap. VI) is introduced in connection with the account of the miracle of the loaves and fishes. Reminiscences of this miracle are very plain in many of these banquet scenes where baskets of loaves appear in front or at the sides, recalling the baskets of the fragments left over from the miracle. Again, the fish may have been included in the sacred meal because the fish itself was an important Christian symbol. The letters of the word for fish in Greek (*ichthys*) are the first letters of the words in Greek meaning Jesus Christ, Son of God, Savior. The fish rather than the cross was the sign of the Christian. The sacred meal might signify also the banquet that the disciples would eat with the Master in paradise.

The above fourth-century fresco from the catacomb of Peter and Marcellinus shows a group of six sitting about a table bearing bread, fish, and wine. Two persons or personifications with Greek names are addressed. The first is Irene, from the word *eirene*, meaning peace. The other is Agape, from the word meaning love. The inscriptions in Latin read, on the left, "Irene, give me warm [water]," and on the other, "Agape, mix for me," meaning that warm water is to be mixed with the wine, presumably for the celebration of the Eucharist.

9. THE EARLIEST EXTANT

9a

Discovered in the excavations at Dura-Europos, this church must be of an earlier date than A.D. 256, when the city was taken by the Parthians. The church was an adaptation of a private house. The foundations disclose a fair-sized room for purposes of assembly. A small room (now set up in the art museum of Yale University) served as a baptistry. In front is a niche overarching a baptismal font. On the back wall is a fresco (Fig. 9a), showing above, the Good Shepherd with a flock of sheep and rams and, below to our left, Adam and Eve separated and flanked by trees. Two serpents with heads erect are crawling below. The fig leaves of Adam and Eve resemble garments. On the side wall in the upper left hand corner (Fig. 9b), is the scene of Jesus raising the paralytic, who appears both lying on his bed and carrying it off. Further to the right, on a partially preserved ship, are some of the disciples. Somewhat lower down Peter is walking on the waves with his arm outstretched to grasp the saving hand of Christ. A still lower panel depicts the women coming to the tomb on Easter morning. The heads and busts of the first two women carrying torches are intact, of the third only the arm and a bowl. The remainder of the wall has space for two more women. On the bottom of the rear wall are five pairs of feet. The number five for the women is not taken from the canonical gospels, but from a harmony of the four made by Tatian, the Syrian, and called the *Diatessarion*, of which a fragment in Greek has been found at Dura. The two stars on the gables of the tomb are symbolic representations of the two angels. See Carl H. Kraeling, "The Christian Building," Yale University, *The Excavations at Dura-Europos*, Final Reports VIII,2 (1967).

CHRISTIAN CHURCH

9b

10. THE RELIGION OF MAGIC

In the world of the early Christians, there was widespread addiction to magic relying on incantations and amulets with bizarre symbols, mingling elements from diverse cults to ward off evil powers. Gnosticism was, to a degree, involved in this phenomenon. Among the extant gem amulets one is inscribed with the names of the seven archons of the Ophite system. Abraxas gems appear to have some connection with the school of the Gnostic, Basilides, since the Church Fathers say that his followers made much of a divine figure named Abraxas. The name was endowed with power by reason of its numerical value. Before the introduction of Arabic numerals, numbers were written by means of letters. In Greek, every letter represented a number. The sum of the letters in Abraxas adds up to 365, the exact number of days in the Egyptian year, which lacked the quarter day. This was also the number of the aeons in the system of the Basilidians. Some of the amulets bear the name Abraxas, frequently in conjunction with the cock-headed figure portrayed above. The symbolism is solar: the cock, which crows at dawn, stands for the sun. The uplifted arm with the whip is that of Phaeton driving the chariot of the sun. The significance of the serpent legs can only be conjectured. The word "Iao" is probably a corruption of the Hebrew name for God. These three letters are written in the proper Greek order from left to right, but the other two words are set in mirror script. If this were a seal for stamping an impression, one would expect all three words to be in mirror writing. Perhaps the other two words are set in the Hebrew word and letter order, for they are corruptions of Hebrew words. In Greek, they read *semes ilam*, for the Hebrew *shemesh olam*, the eternal sun.

Whatever may or may not have been the connection of these amulets and gems with popular Gnosticism, they certainly prove the prevalence of recourse to magic. The Christians did not deny the existence of the evil powers but proclaimed their conquest by Christ. For a recent critical treatment of the entire subject, see Campbell Banner, *Studies in Magical Amulets* (Ann Arbor, 1950).

11. AN EARLY CHRISTIAN LAMP

In the form of the sacred *ichthys* (fish), marked with a cross.

12. THE ROMAN ROADS

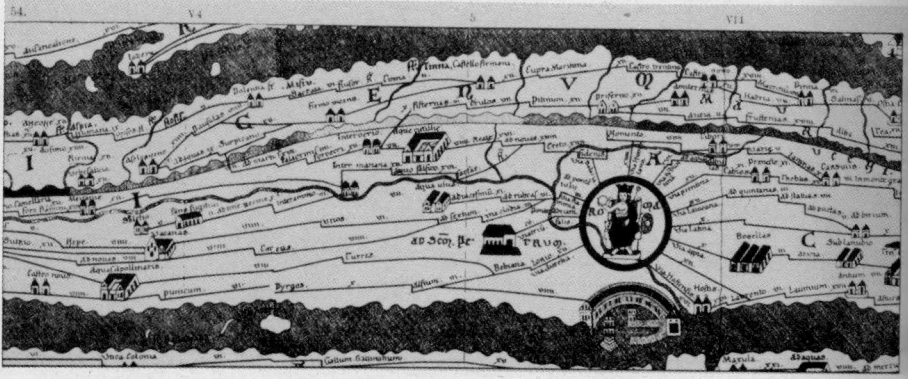

They facilitated the evangelization of the Roman Empire by Christian missionaries, among them St. Paul. A map of the road network is extant, dating from as early as the fourth century. The original is lost, but a careful transcript was made by a monk in the thirteenth century. This work went unnoticed until the sixteenth century, when it was published by Konrad Peutinger, after whom it was called the Peutinger Table. It is on a long scroll, reading horizontally, of which three sections are reproduced here. Fig. 12a shows Rome and its environs, Fig. 12b shows Constantinople and its environs, and Fig. 12c shows England.

12b

12c

III

Christ Against Caesar

For what reason had Rome altered her view of the Christians? Nero, to be sure, was not a rational man. Yet he apparently saw what wiser men failed to observe, that Christianity was a new religion. Writing some fifty years after the event, Tacitus tells us that, to divert the odium arising from the general belief that he had set fire to Rome, Nero

> blamed and savagely punished people popularly hated for their crimes and called Christians. The name was derived from Christ, who was executed under the Emperor Tiberius and the Procurator Pontius Pilate. Suppressed for a moment, this execrable superstition broke out again not only in Judea, where it began, but even in the city of Rome where all things base and shameful flow together and enjoy a vogue. Therefore, those were taken first who confessed, then on their testimony a vast multitude was convicted, not so much on the charge of arson as of hatred of the human race. A sport was made of their execution. Some, sewn in the skins of animals, were torn apart by dogs. Others were crucified or burned, and others, as darkness drew on, were used as torches. Nero devoted his gardens to the spectacle, provided a circus, and himself, in the costume of a charioteer, rode around among the crowd, until compassion began to arise for the victims, who though deserving of the severest penalties, were actually suffering not for the public good but to glut the cruelty of one man.[1]

Although the account refers to Judea as its place of origin,

---
[1] Tacitus *Annals* xv, 44, tr. R. H. Bainton.

there is otherwise no hint that Christianity was an outgrowth of Judaism. This recital raises other questions. What did the Christians confess? That they had burned the city? Under torture men will confess anything. Or simply that they were Christians? In that case, they must have been recognized as distinct from Jews, and merely to be a Christian must have been considered a crime.

But what is meant by saying that they were convicted of *odium humani generis*, hatred of the human race? With the emergence of Christianity in the pagan world, two intensely religious cultures came in conflict. The more fully a religion embraces all aspects of life, the more numerous are the points of conflict.

The Gods of Rome

The Greeks and Romans had deities for every aspect of living —for sowing and reaping, for rain, wind, and every weather, for volcanoes and rivers, for birth, marriage, and death—and they showed reverence for ancestors, for hearth and home. But to the Christians these gods were nothing, and their denial of them was deemed atheism by the pagans. By such blasphemy the gods would be incensed and would visit their resentment not only on the offender but on the entire community. Consequently, those who denied the gods were deemed to be not only atheists but enemies of the human race.

The Jews also denied the pagan gods, and they occasionally suffered severe persecutions. But, whereas the Christians were everywhere and were much more actively converting Gentiles, the Jews lived largely by themselves; their dietary laws and practice of circumcision further separated them from gentile life and, as we have seen, discouraged proselytism. More importantly, the Jews were tacitly exempt from participating in the cult of the deified emperor. If Christians claimed not to be Jews they would forfeit this exemption.

Again, the privilege of unrestricted expansion was accorded to

Judaism and other selected religions. The Roman government made a distinction between recognized and unrecognized religions, *religiones licitae* and *illicitae*. All the religions in the Empire were tolerated in the lands of their origin; and the government intervened only to suppress criminal rites, such as those of the Phoenicians, who cast children into the fires of Moloch. Rome even invited from the East, in 204 B.C., the introduction of the worship of Magna Mater, the Great Mother, in order to enlist her divine help against Hannibal. But the indiscriminate spread of religions was not permitted. Rome resisted the orientalizing of the West by Eastern cults, which infiltrated nevertheless and one by one became *religiones licitae*. Judaism enjoyed this status, but if Christianity was to be considered a new religion, it would have to be numbered among the *religiones illicitae*.

Another point of even greater moment was emerging. Although the Roman government was disinclined to impose a religion upon its subjects, the need was acutely felt for one common religion that, in addition to all local cults, would be practiced throughout the Empire and thus act as a cohesive force. This common religion was found in the cult of the deified ruler. Under Augustus, the worship of the emperor became the religious bond of the Empire. Although Augustus took pains not to claim divine status for himself, during his lifetime the worship of his *genius*, his divine spirit, became an established cult—a cult which for many actually did involve the worship of the emperor's person as a divinity. Upon his death, the Senate proclaimed Augustus a state deity.

Succeeding emperors varied greatly in their personal attitude to the cult. Tiberius wanted no deification for the emperor unless the Senate also were deified, though, as we have seen, on his denarius he called himself the son of the divine Augustus. But Caligula took the emperor cult very seriously and had the temerity to propose setting up his statue for worship in the Temple at Jerusalem. This was in the year A.D. 40. Philo, the Jewish philosopher of Alexandria, who happened to be in Rome at that time, remonstrated. Petronius, the Roman governor of Syria and Palestine, sent word that he would not enforce the order calling for emperor worship. He was ordered to commit suicide, but luckily before the instruction reached him the news arrived that the emperor had been assassinated. After that, no attempt was ever made again to require emperor worship of the Jews. They were the only people in the Empire to enjoy this immunity.

One can understand, therefore, why the Christians were eager to be accounted Jews by the Roman government, and why the evangelist Luke should insist that Christians were preaching nothing but Moses and the prophets, as if to say that those who believed in the risen Christ were the only true Jews. None but Christians, however, accepted this view. In the eyes of Rome, Christianity was a new religion, and now the fight that Judaism had waged against the deification of a human being, whether before or after death, was taken up by the Christians, though in a different form. For Judaism, the confrontation was between Yahweh and any "divine" ruler; for the Christians it was between Christ, in whom the one God became man, and Caesar, a man on the way, at least, to becoming a pagan god.

That this issue had become apparent by the time of Nero is very doubtful. Tacitus, who surely must have known that it was crucial in his own day, does not mention it for Nero's time. The emperors immediately succeeding Nero did not insist upon universal acknowledgment of their divine status. Vespasian made a joke of posthumous deification, and when asked on his death bed about his condition, replied that he felt as if he were about to become a god. At the end of the first century, however, Domitian went beyond all his predecessors and referred to himself as *dominus et deus*, lord and god. Christians could not, of course, accept such pretensions and flatly rejected the emperor cult. In consequence, Domitian struck at the nonconformists, and Rome became "drunk with the blood of the saints."[2] Our information on this score is derived to a large extent from the last book in our New Testament, the Book of Revelation, written about A.D. 95. Written in

[2] Rev. 17:6.

the midst of persecution, like the Book of Daniel, Revelation could employ only veiled imagery. Rome is there described as the new Babylon, the great whore seated upon the seven hills. Before she can be overthrown, the Lamb that was slain (a reference to Jesus) must cast the great beast into the abyss. Then will the new Jerusalem descend "out of heaven . . . as a bride adorned for her husband."[3] Before the first century elapsed, the issue between Christ and Caesar had become crucial.

The relation of the Church to the state naturally varied with circumstance. Whereas at the end of the first century, during the persecutions under Domitian, the Book of Revelation equated Rome with all the demonic powers, the Book of the Acts of the Apostles, written before Paul's death, played up Rome's protective attitude toward Christians. In the Epistle to the Romans,[4] Paul took a median position, asserting that government was instituted by God and entrusted with the sword to protect the good and punish the bad. He instructed Christians to obey the laws and pay taxes out of conscience rather than from fear. In other words, Paul endorsed the power of the state. But Christians refused to concede the state absolute power if its commands contravened those of God, and they applied to Rome the words of Peter to the Jewish authorities that God must be obeyed rather than men.[5]

The Early Church

But, in other respects the early Christians accepted many of the current political and social institutions, partly in the belief that with the imminent return of the Lord Jesus the whole order of society would be changed. Consequently, Paul advised no one to seek to alter his status, whether rich or poor, free or slave, mar-

[3] Rev. 21:2.
[4] Rom. 13.
[5] Acts 4:19.

ried or unmarried. Paul regarded marriage as honorable. Although he thought that unions should be contracted only within the faith, he advised that unions already contracted should not be dissolved if one partner became a convert and the other remained a pagan. And although the unmarried might better remain unencumbered and free, wholly to serve the Lord in the short interval before his return, they might marry if they could not control their desires. Paul thus countenanced marriage, but favored celibacy because of the particular circumstances.[6]

The organization of the early Church was at the outset somewhat informal. The various church functions were exercised by those endowed through the Holy Spirit with suitable qualifications, such as prophets (preachers), apostles (traveling evangelists), healers, teachers, administrators, and so on. Fortunately there were those who had the gift of telling who were so endowed.[7] In practice, this amounted to self-government by each local church, that is to say congregationalism, since the congregation endorsed the sagacity of its weightier members. Some persons were simply appointed. The Jerusalem church thus selected seven men to administer relief of the poor, presumably identical with those later called deacons. Pastoral care might be exercised by several persons, and there are indications that in certain churches a collegiate government was administered by men who were known as presbyters, or elders, because of their age, or as bishops, or overseers, because of their function. But only one person at a time could preside at the Lord's Supper, and it was perhaps out of this need that there arose the institution of a single bishop in one community.

Although local churches as self-governing units were congregational, still a conference of leaders meeting at Jerusalem issued decrees regarding the freedom of Christians from the Jewish Law.[8] This procedure suggests a presbyterian polity in which a collegiate

---

[6] I Cor. 7.
[7] I Cor. 12 and Rom. 12:6–8.
[8] Acts 15.

body has a measure of jurisdiction over several local congregations. Paul's supervision of all the churches of his foundation, in turn, corresponded functionally with the role of a modern bishop and thus suggests an episcopal polity. Thus, elements of the three main systems of government, as they are practiced today in Christian churches, may be traced back to the apostolic age.

Roman Views of Christians

The relation of Christianity to the Roman government in the early years of the second century is made abundantly clear in a document written by Pliny, the Roman governor of Bithynia in Asia Minor, to the Emperor Trajan between the years A.D. 111 and A.D. 113. He wrote:

> I have never been present at the trial of Christians, and I do not know what to ask or how to punish. I have been very much at a loss to know whether to make any distinction for age or strength, whether to excuse those who have renounced Christianity, whether the name itself, lacking other offense, or the crimes associated with the name should be punished. In the meantime this is what I have done. I have asked the accused whether they were Christians. If they confessed, I asked a second and a third time, threatening penalty. Those who persisted I ordered to be executed, for I did not doubt that, whatever it was they professed, they deserved to be punished for their inflexible obstinacy. There were others of equal madness who, because they were Roman citizens, I sent to Rome. Presently . . . more cases came to light. An anonymous document came in with many names. I dismissed those who said they were not or never had been Christians, and who in my presence supplicated the gods and placed wine and incense before your image, and especially cursed Christ, which I hear no true Christian will do.[9]

Pliny continued with further details but admitted that he could

[9] Pliny *Epistulae* 96, tr. R. H. Bainton.

discover nothing worse than a depraved superstition. The Emperor Trajan replied that Christians were not to be hunted out but, if brought to public attention, were to be handled as Pliny had indicated. Anonymous accusations—"the curse of the age"—were not to be considered.

Pliny's letter does not sound as if he were inaugurating a new policy. We may assume that the main lines of procedure date at least from the time of Domitian. Whatever its beginning, this policy determined the handling of Christians by Rome throughout the second century. Though Christianity itself was deemed a crime, suspects were not to be ferreted out and prosecution was to be instituted only when the existence of Christians came to public attention, presumably through popular denunciation.

The Christian Way of Life

This the populace was quite ready to provide. Sometimes Jews instigated persecution, because, although there were some Jewish converts to Christianity, the majority in the Diaspora observed the anathema pronounced by the Sanhedrin against the Nazarenes. Among pagans, the old charge of atheism was never dropped, and the conviction that Christians were guilty of hatred for the human race was reinforced by the increasingly apparent aloofness of the Christians from many aspects of the common life, so much so that Christians came to be called the "third race," neither pagan nor Jewish, but a race apart. The Christians gave some handle to the charge by their admission that they did not regard themselves as citizens of any country, because their citizenship was in heaven. "They live in their fatherlands as transients," wrote one unidentified Christian to a correspondent in the second or third century. "Every foreign country is their fatherland and every fatherland a foreign country."[10]

[10] *Epistle of Diognetus* v in *Apostolic Fathers* II (New York, Loeb Library, 1914).

Yet, as a matter of fact, in the main they did share in community life. They did not withdraw to isolated retreats, as did the Essenes, but since they remained in the midst of society, their abstention from certain common customs and activities was all the more conspicuous.

For Christians in the Graeco-Roman world, the friction was increased by their immersion into an urban culture. In the Hellenistic and Roman world, the Christians were so much associated with cities that the word for a man of the country, *paganus*, came eventually to mean pagan. Cities require contacts. Farmers slaughter their own livestock for meat, but urbanites must go to market for theirs. So, for the Christians there arose the question whether they might eat meat that had first been sacrificed to idols and afterward offered for sale in the public stalls. Paul had ruled that since the idol was nothing, the meat had not been contaminated. Yet he said that those who had scruples should refrain and, if they had none, they might still refrain out of regard for the conscience of another.[11] One can imagine the effect on the pagans if Christians rejected these meats.

Not only must the Christian not practice idolatry, he must not contribute to idolatry by assisting in any way in the making of idols. He might be a sculptor, but he must not carve images of the gods. He was restricted, therefore, to the decorative aspects of tombs or monuments, but even here he might carve a lion, a whale, or a bull—or gild any figure—only if it did not represent a god. Placing incense on the altar of the emperor was, of course, forbidden, but even celebrating his birthday was compromising, because this implied recognition of his divinity.

The schools presented a difficulty because they used as textbooks the works of Homer and Virgil with their stories of the pagan gods; and ordinary teachers did not allegorize these stories after the manner of the philosophers. Hence, early in the history of Christianity, the need arose for parochial schools. Hospitals as such were unobjectionable, but pagan hospitals were dedicated to

---

[11] I Cor. 8.

Aesculapius, the god of healing. Could the Christian lie in a hospital bed while the priest went down the corridors chanting to a god whom the Christians denied? Also, the Church discouraged interfaith marriages, and although Paul had advised against separation because of a difference of faith, after death the individual partners might be buried in different cemeteries.

Other current practices were rejected by Christians on ethical grounds. Gladiatorial combats, for example, were absolutely forbidden, although their seduction continued to be felt; as late as the early fifth century, Augustine tells the story of his friend Alypius, who agreed to attend a spectacle to please a companion, but resolved to keep his eyes shut. When the shouting began, his eyes popped open, and he was yelling above the rest. Any shedding of blood (*effusio sanguinis*) was abhorrent even in civil justice. The Christian could not assume the office of a judge who would have to pass sentence of death.[12]

The taking of life in war was unanimously condemned by all Christian writers of the period prior to Constantine, as far as such works are extant. They felt that war was incompatible with the injunction of the Lord to love one's enemies. There were other reasons as well. Late in the second century, Tertullian of Carthage, the first Christian theologian to write in Latin, took the legalistic stand that Christ, when he told Peter to put up his sword, had thereby disarmed every soldier. Tertullian did not concern himself with what would happen if the state renounced the sword. The outcome should be left to God; in any case, according to Tertullian, the consequences, whatever they might be, would be of short duration only, for he still believed in the imminent return of the Lord. Marcion, an influential if unorthodox Christian, of whom we shall hear more presently, regarded anything physical as repulsive, especially the gore of battle. Origen, a leader of the Christians at Alexandria in the early third century, believed that

[12] Bernhard Schopf, *Das Tötungsrecht bei den frühchristlichen Schriftstellern* (Regensburg, 1958).

triumphant Christianity would so change the quality of society that war would vanish.[13]

However, some Christians did serve in the army, regardless of the injunctions of Church leaders. Yet, whatever the exceptions, Christian abstention from military service was so notorious that Celsus, a pagan critic writing about A.D. 180, averred that if all men were like the Christians, the Empire would be overrun by lawless barbarians.

The Christians seemed strange to others also because, like the Cynics, they rejected luxury and personal adornment. Christian leaders admonished their flocks to refrain from attention to personal appearance. Women should not blacken their eyelids, rouge their cheeks, or perfume their bodies. Men should not pull out any hairs. Clothes should be undyed, for if God had wished purple clothes, he would have made purple sheep. Nor should there be any great distinction in costume for male and female. A simple white robe would do for both. Wigs should not be worn. If the presbyter laid his hand in blessing on a wig, whose hair would he bless? Delicate sheets do not induce sleep, tables require no ivory legs, nor do knives need jeweled handles. The Lord Jesus did not come down from heaven with a silver foot bath to wash the disciples' feet.

These various injunctions directly followed Cynic themes, but their point was different. The Christian was not seeking to outwit fate by renouncing everything before fate could take it away. He was denying the world, the more freely to follow the Lord. And, as Tertullian observed, he was in training for martyrdom. Tertullian demanded whether a foot that wore an anklet would bear the gyve of the torturer, whether the neck adorned with a necklace

[13] Roland H. Bainton, *Christian Attitudes toward War and Peace* (New York, 1960).

[14] Tertullian, *On the Apparel of Women.* Cf. similar passages collected by R. H. Bainton in *Early Christianity* (Princeton, 1960), chap. xiii, pp. 154–58.

would submit to the axe of the executioner.[14] To the pagan, such behavior made the Christians all the more appear to be a "third race." The impression was not dispelled by the fact that Christians led normal, even exemplary, family lives, and practiced agriculture and the handicrafts like the others in their communities. Despite their hospitality and philanthropy, despite their devotion to plague victims when pagans fled, despite so many proofs of Christian love for mankind, the belief persisted that they were haters of the human race. And herein lay the deepest reason for popular persecution.

Persecutions

During the second century the persecutions were sporadic and erratic. The first instance was under the Emperor Trajan, whose otherwise moderate policy has been noted. One of the victims was Ignatius, the bishop of Antioch in Syria, who was brought to Rome to die in the arena. On the way, his guards permitted him to visit Christian congregations whose members and bishops had not been arrested. One can easily surmise why Ignatius should have been taken and others left. He was certainly an aggressive Christian leader and, although extravagant craving for martyrdom was discouraged by the Church—whose counsel was "neither flee nor provoke"—Ignatius desired to be martyred in order that he might the more speedily be with Christ. He declared that if the wild beasts were not hungry, he would urge them on.

As Ignatius passed through Smyrna, he was received with honor by Polycarp, bishop of the congregation there. Not until some forty years later, when a mob clamored for his death, did Polycarp suffer a like martyrdom. An account of the event survives in a letter written by his own congregation immediately following the execution. In the arena, Polycarp was given an opportunity to save himself by recantation. The proconsul, following the procedure outlined by Pliny, told Polycarp to say, "Away with the atheists," meaning the Christians. But Polycarp pointed to the heathen in the stadium and shouted, "Away with the atheists." One would have supposed that this would have settled the matter, but the proconsul began again, saying, "Curse Christ." Polycarp answered, "I have served him eighty-six years, and he has done me no wrong; how can I blaspheme the king who saved me?" The proconsul tried once more: "Swear by the genius of Caesar." Polycarp replied simply, "I am a Christian." The proconsul threatened to throw him to the beasts. Polycarp answered, "Bring them in." The magistrate menaced him with fire, but Polycarp counseled him that the fire which burns for an hour is not to be compared to the fire of eternal punishment; and he was then burned to death. This was in A.D. 156. In his long life, Polycarp had served as an important link between the age of the apostles and that of the great Christian writers of the second century.

The greatest persecutors were not the worst emperors, but rather the better ones. Although he was a Stoic philosopher, the noble Marcus Aurelius took very seriously the popular rites performed for the welfare of the state. As a propitiation to the gods, he compelled criminals sentenced to death to slaughter each other in the amphitheatre. Before starting out to fight the Marcomanni, he called upon the priests of Rome to sacrifice oxen for the safety of his arms. Christians, who refused to take part in such practices, appeared to Marcus Aurelius as obstinate fanatics, dangerous to the public security.

A wave of persecution struck the churches of Lyons and nearby Vienne in southern France in A.D. 177. Mobs accused the Christians of incest and cannibalism. The accusations of sexual irregularity may easily arise against any disliked group that holds meetings in secret, and the Christians did not admit non-Christians to the celebration of the Lord's Supper. The charge of cannibalism was also connected with this rite because the pagans heard that the Christians consumed somebody's flesh and blood. Under torture some of the accused recanted, but they were then punished as criminals rather than as Christians. Yet some of those at the last recovered their courage and died for the faith. The fury was soon past and the congregation was able to reassemble.[15]

Such haphazard persecution advanced that which it sought to destroy. As Tertullian said, "The blood of the martyrs is seed."[16] The Church grew and growth brought new problems. In the first half of the second century we meet a phenomenon recurrent in the expansion of Christianity. First the Church must accommodate herself to the culture in which she takes root and in which she seeks to win converts; the Gospel must be couched in images intelligible to the heathen. The next stage is one of assimilation. The convert who is taken into the Christian community thereupon blends the old in his outlook with the new, perhaps to the enrichment, but almost invariably to the perversion of Christianity.

Gnosticism

This pattern was strikingly illustrated by the rise of Christian Gnosticism. Gnosticism was one of the religions of contemplation, which despised the world of matter and sought salvation by way of emancipation from the flesh. There was a great variety of Gnostic systems and ideas, but the core of the Gnostic myth was this: the ultimate is the great abyss of being, describable only by negatives —the unknown, the incomprehensible, the incommensurable, the unfathomable. This abyss is dynamic, and within its fullness (*pleroma*) differentiations arise by way of emanations. One of the emanations is Wisdom. She was filled with inordinate curiosity to understand the secret of the pleroma and in her distress gave off matter which, with the aid of the demiurge, was shaped into our visible world.

Here is the reverse of the Hebrew myth of creation, in which

---

[15] The records of the above persecutions are given in translation in E. C. E. Owen, *Some Authentic Acts of the Early Martyrs* (Oxford, 1927).

[16] Tertullian, *Apology*, 50.

the world was created good, and evil appeared later with the fall of man. In the Gnostic account, the fall of Wisdom came first and the creation followed in consequence. Hence, the material world was the result of the fall and, therefore, bad. Man is a composite being consisting of spirit imprisoned in matter, from which release is sought. At this point the role of Wisdom was reversed. Apparently penitent for her mischief, she became a redeeming principle, aiding man to liberate himself by communicating to him the illumination, or Gnosis, which enabled him to detach his spirit from the flesh, so that it might ascend until reunited with the pleroma. Not only matter is an impediment to salvation, but also time; salvation means deliverance from its weary cycles.

As an amalgam of popular Near Eastern beliefs and Greek philosophy, Gnosticism was quite ready to combine with existing religious systems, but it always conferred upon their mythology its own meaning. For example, Gnosticism absorbed Hebrew myths but completely reversed their values. Since the world is evil, Yahweh, who created the world, must be the evil demiurge. The serpent, who told Eve to eat of the tree of knowledge of good and evil, was a redeemer, for the knowledge of good and evil is precisely the saving Gnosis. All those persons commended in the Old Testament were evil servants of the evil Yahweh, and those reproved, like Cain, belonged to the illumined.

When Gnosticism was combined with Christianity, the result was no less a distortion. Gnostic Christians believed in Christ as the Redeemer, but since his function was to deliver man from the thralldom of the flesh, he could have had no flesh. It merely appeared that he had. His body was a phantom which only seemed to exist. Plainly, this view subverted the whole Christian doctrine of the Incarnation and the Crucifixion. The greatest fight in the early Church was to establish not the divinity, but the humanity of Christ. Again, the Incarnation was an event in time, but what the Gnostics sought was release from time; Gnosticism thus stripped history of all significance.

In the early decades of the second century, attempts were made to blend Gnosticism and Christianity by some distinguished intellectuals who felt that they were simply making a synthesis of all truth. The Christian Gnostics were Christian in that they gave Christ the supreme place of honor, even above Wisdom. But, what happened to the Hebrew background of Christianity in such thinking is apparent in the case of Marcion, the son of a bishop. Marcion was a Gnostic in his attitude toward the created world. It is bad, said he, and full of flies, fleas, and fevers. The God who made it, the creator God, could not have been the father of our Lord Jesus Christ, but was rather a malevolent demiurge. Marcion's contention meant that Christianity would have to sever itself from all its Hebrew antecedents and that the Old Testament must be rejected.

Creed and Canon

The spread of Gnosticism faced the still weakly organized Church with a grave crisis. What the Church believed to be the real truth had to be formulated, and what it did not believe had to be refuted; and those who were to be received in baptism must first be instructed in these matters. At baptism new converts were required to make a confession of their faith. The earliest version of their confession, called the Old Roman Symbol, developed later into what we know as the Apostles' Creed:

> I believe in God the Father Almighty; Maker of heaven and earth. And in Jesus Christ his only Son our Lord; who was conceived by the Holy Ghost, born of the Virgin Mary; suffered under Pontius Pilate, was crucified, dead, and buried; he descended into hell; the third day he rose from the dead; he ascended into heaven; and sitteth at the right hand of God the Father Almighty; from thence he shall come to judge the quick and the dead. I believe in the Holy Ghost; the holy Catholic Church; the communion of saints; the forgiveness of sins; the resurrection of the body; and the life everlasting. Amen.

Here, in direct contradiction to Gnostic precepts, it is asserted that God did create the physical world; that Christ was actually physically born; that he truly suffered; that this was at a definite point in history (under Pontius Pilate); and that he died a real death. By such affirmations the Church guarded the faith against perversions. This is by no means all that was believed, but this much had to be believed and its contrary rejected by those who professed Christianity.

On what authority did Christians base such definitions of their faith? First of all, they appealed to the authority of Scripture, meaning at this point the Old Testament, which contains the doctrine of God's creation of the world as *good*. But Marcion could not be convinced by the testimony of a book that the world is good. He argued that since the world is bad, the book is not good, and he collected all the passages in the Old Testament about the vindictiveness of God to prove that Yahweh's acts were contrary to Christian ethics. The churchmen replied that Marcion had made the dichotomy too sharp. In the Old Testament, Yahweh was not only wrathful but also "abundant in steadfast love," and in the New Testament, Jesus was not always tender, for he promised at the Judgment to send sinners into everlasting fire. The Church Fathers—this is the term used for the major Christian writers up to about A.D. 600—could not, of course, deny that elements of the Old Testament were incompatible with Christianity. The apparent contradictions were explained by allegory, after the manner of Philo. For example, the polygamy of the patriarchs meant that they were married to more than one virtue, and the slaughter of the Amalekites indicated the eradication of vices.

But, though the Old Testament gave support to certain Christian doctrines, there were others that it did not teach, and for these a Christian literature was necessary. Most of what was later included in the canon of the New Testament had been written during the first century: the four Gospels, the Acts of the Apostles, the letters of Paul to the various churches and to individuals

—Timothy, Titus, and Philemon. Two letters also bore the name of Peter, three the name of John, and one each the names of James and Jude. The Epistle to the Hebrews was anonymous. The Book of Revelation, as we have noted, was written by a man named John. Which portions of this material were written by the persons to whom they have been ascribed cannot always be ascertained; there is little question that virtually all of it came from the Christian community of the first century, with a few portions possibly dating from the second century.

Was all of it, and only this, worthy to be placed on a par with, or above, the Old Testament? The first man to address himself to that question was Marcion. His favorite apostle was Paul because he had so decisively rejected the Law of the Old Testament. Therefore Marcion made his canon include Paul's letters to the churches and the letter to Philemon, but not those to Timothy and Titus, and, as for the rest, only the Gospel of Luke. Why he chose that particular Gospel we do not know; perhaps it was more familiar in his native Pontus than were the others.

Christian leaders also drew up lists of what they considered authoritative writings, including the works in Marcion's canon, as well as the other books mentioned above. By about the middle of the third century, the collection represented in our New Testament was commonly recognized as the canon or rule of faith. There was controversy for a time only over a few books. John's Gospel made trouble because its dates for the death and resurrection of Christ differed from those in the other Gospels. In John's Gospel, Jesus died on the fourteenth of the Jewish month Nisan, the day the Passover lamb was slain. He did not live to eat the Passover supper, and this Gospel has no account of the Lord's Supper. But in the other three Gospels he did share with his disciples in the Passover meal and therefore must have suffered on the following day, which was the fifteenth.

Beyond that, there arose the question as to whether the Crucifixion or the Resurrection should be celebrated. The churches of Asia Minor, which followed the chronology of John's Gospel and which were called Quartodecimans (fourteenthers), commemorated the Crucifixion. The Roman Church, which followed the first three Gospels, celebrated the Resurrection. All four Gospels agreed that Jesus had died on a Friday and had risen on a Sunday; but, should the day of the week or the date of the month be observed? Romans and Asians disagreed, and as a consequence some Christians were feasting while others were fasting. The Roman Church established the practice of observing a fixed day of the week rather than a fixed day of the month, the first Sunday after the first full moon after the vernal equinox. The Asians demurred, and, about A.D. 190, Bishop Victor of Rome excommunicated their churches. The dispute eventually subsided and the Roman practice came to prevail in all churches.

While the controversy raged, there was a disposition to undercut the Asians by rejecting their gospel, but Irenaeus of Lyons, himself an émigré from Asia Minor to Gaul, preached peace and defended John's Gospel. There must be four Gospels, he asserted, just as there were four faces in the vision of Ezekiel, those of a man, a lion, an ox, and an eagle. This amusing argument became the basis for the symbolic representation of the four evangelists: a winged man for Matthew, a winged lion for Mark, a winged ox for Luke, and an eagle for John.

The Book of Revelation was accepted only slowly in the East, as was the Epistle to the Hebrews in the West. Athanasius, the bishop of Alexandria, who had lived in exile in Rome in the period after Constantine and who enjoyed the support of the Roman Church, served as a mediator. His Festal Epistle of A.D. 367 is commonly regarded as the first to define the canon of the New Testament as consisting of those twenty-seven books of which it is now composed.

The acceptance of these books meant the rejection of others, which are now called the New Testament Apocrypha. They consist of several gospels of Jesus' childhood, an account of his descent into Hades to release the spirits imprisoned by Satan, accounts of the travels of Peter, Paul, and other apostles, and reports of contests in miracles between Simon Peter and Simon Magus. In the last, Simon Peter caused a dried sardine to swim and a child at the breast to pronounce a pompous anathema on the other Simon, who displayed his powers by cavorting in the air.

This literature enjoyed a wide vogue, but the discriminating judgment of the Church Fathers prevailed over popular taste and excluded it from the canon. Nevertheless, scenes from the apocryphal gospels received wider pictorial representation during the Middle Ages than those from the genuine.

The authority of the books included in the canon of the New Testament depended in good part on their having been written either by an apostle or by a companion of an apostle. But such attribution did not automatically ensure inclusion. At the beginning of the third century, for instance, Serapion, the bishop of Antioch, was asked by his congregation whether the Gospel of Peter might be read in the church service. Without having read the book, he consented, assuming that anything by Peter would qualify. But, coming to examine the text, he found it to be Gnostic and promptly concluded that it could not have been written by Peter and should, therefore, not be read.[17]

If, then, the books of themselves did not establish the truth of doctrine, recourse must be taken to oral traditions. These, in turn, did not provide an infallible yardstick. The Gnostics claimed an oral tradition of their own, consisting of an esoteric wisdom, which they claimed Jesus had privately committed to certain of his disciples and which they, in turn, had transmitted to their successors. Irenaeus replied that if Jesus did have any such special wisdom to communicate, he would have entrusted it to those disciples whom he most trusted, and they in turn to their especial confidants. And surely those whom Jesus most trusted were those to whom he had entrusted the churches. By the same token, those in whom the disciples reposed the greatest confidence would have been those to whom they had passed on the churches. Therefore,

[17] Eusebius, *Ecclesiastical History*, VI, xii, 3–6.

to discover the true tradition one should turn to churches of apostolic foundation in which there had been an unbroken succession of appointed bishops.

The Church of Rome

Irenaeus pointed to the Church of Rome as the pre-eminent example, founded by the two martyred apostles, Peter and Paul, and presided over by a continuous succession of bishops known by name.

By the end of the second century, three sources of authority had emerged: the canon, the creed, and the oral tradition. The first two were interpreted in terms of the third. The Church was developing in its role as the custodian of all, and thus as the living source of authority. This development in turn had two aspects: the growth of the authority of the bishop as head of a local congregation or district, and the growing pre-eminence of the Church of Rome over other churches. As to the bishop, by the beginning of the second century his position had become more clearly defined, and the system of a single bishop in charge of a single congregation prevailed in Syria and Asia Minor. Ignatius and Polycarp were bishops in this sense. A maxim of Ignatius was, "Do nothing without the bishop."[18]

The early organization of the Church in Rome—which was to become the very seat of authority—is obscure. Although Clement of Rome is called in subsequent tradition the third bishop of Rome, in his letter to the Corinthians (written about A.D. 95) he makes no reference whatever to his own authority, nor does he clearly indicate that Rome had a single bishop. However, Clement is the first to enunciate the idea of the apostolic succession of church officers. By A.D. 185, the ideas of a single bishop in a church and of his apostolic succession were combined in the argument of Irenaeus. He traced the Roman succession to his own

[18] *Smyrnaeans* viii in *Apostolic Fathers* I (New York, Loeb Library, 1914).

time: Linus, Anacletus, Clement, Evaristus, Alexander, Sixtus (the sixth after the apostles), Telesphorus, Hyginus, Pius, Anicetus, Soter, and Eleutherus.[19] However, if Sixtus was the sixth bishop, Peter could not have been the first. This has been explained by placing Peter, as an apostle, in a special category; but, by this line of reasoning Paul could have been the first bishop. Peter is not definitely named as the first bishop of Rome until the Liberian Catalogue, compiled in Rome about A.D. 354. But this ascription rests on an earlier tradition. A letter spuriously attributed to Clement of Rome and dating from the third century has Peter say to the Roman congregation: "I ordain this Clement to be your bishop: and to him alone I entrust my chair of preaching and instruction. I bestow on him the power of binding and loosing, which the Lord bestowed on me, so that whatever he shall decree on earth shall be decreed in the heavens."[20]

Interestingly, this document does not mention either Linus or Anacletus. The lists of the Roman bishops originating in the East make Peter a founder of the Roman Church, but not her first bishop. That Peter was in Rome and suffered in Rome is as strongly attested as in the case of Paul. That he was the first bishop is rather a matter of faith than of historical demonstration. However, from the time of Nero's persecution, the Church of Rome was bound to be venerated as the church of the two apostolic martyrs. (Peter was placed above Paul because of the words of Jesus, that on Peter the Rock he would found his church.) By A.D. 185, as indicated by Irenaeus, the Church of Rome had attained pre-eminence as the custodian of the apostolic tradition.

The formulation of Christian doctrines and the strengthening of the Church organization had provided Christianity with necessary safeguards against such threats as those posed by Gnosticism. But

---

[19] Irenaeus, *Against Heresies*, III, 1–4.
[20] "Pseudo–Clement" I, 463–72, J.-P. Migne, ed., *Patrologiae Cursus Completus*, Series Graeca (Paris, 1857–66), tr. Shotwell and Loomis, *See of Peter* (New York, 1927), p. 163.

the attendant growth of the Church further altered her relations with the Roman government. In the first half of the third century, the emperors of the house of Severus, to unify the peoples of the Empire, pursued a policy of mingling the different religions, with a strong stress upon the Oriental cults. Septimius Severus, the first emperor of the house, who came to the throne in A.D. 193, married the daughter of the priest of the sun god of Emesa, in Syria. Alexander Severus was said to have in his private chapel statues of Abraham, Orpheus, and Christ (representing Judaism, the mystery religions, and Christianity). Septimius' successor, who was born in Emesa, had taken the name Elagabalus (Heliogabalus), as he was the high priest of the sun god Elagabal. With his accession, the cult of the deified emperor was divested of all the restrictions imposed by the Emperor Augustus and became unabashedly Oriental. Christians, like Jews, could never accept this. The Severi did not try to compel them, although in A.D. 202 Septimius Severus thought to check expansion of the two intransigent religions by prohibiting conversions to Judaism and to Christianity on pain of death.

Martyrs

We have a very moving account of a martyrdom in North Africa that resulted from this edict, as it was described by Perpetua, one of the victims. Perpetua was of the nobility, twenty-two years old, with a child at the breast, whom she was allowed to suckle in prison. Associated with her was Felicitas, a slave girl, who was with child and feared that she would not be able to die with the others because Rome did not execute pregnant women. As the day of the examination drew near, Perpetua's father came to undermine her resolution to die for her faith, saying, "Daughter, pity my white hairs! Pity your father, if I am worthy to be called your father. . . . Give me not over to the reproach of men! . . . Consider your son, who cannot live without you. Lay aside your pride and do not ruin us all." And Perpetua grieved for his sake. At the trial the procurator said to her, "Spare your father's white hairs. Spare the tender years of your child. Offer a sacrifice for the safety of the emperors." She answered "No." When asked, "Are you a Christian?" she said, "I am."

The jailer was kindly disposed and admitted friends to see the prisoners. "Now when the games approached, my father came to me worn with trouble and began to pluck out his beard and to throw himself on his face and curse his years, and . . . I sorrowed for the unhappiness of his old age." All the condemned prisoners prayed that Felicitas might not be left behind on the road to the same hope, and her pangs came upon her and she cried out. Then one of the jailers said to her: "If you cry out at this, what will it be when you are thrown to the beasts?" She answered, "Now I suffer what I suffer, but then another will be in me who will suffer for me, because I, too, am to suffer for him." She gave birth to a girl, whom one of her sisters reared as her own. When, later, the martyrs passed by the procurator's stand, they said, "You are judging us. God will judge you." They were then executed in the arena at Carthage.[21]

This wave of persecution was of short duration and not widespread. From the accession of Septimius Severus in A.D. 193, down to the persecution of Decius in A.D. 250, the Church in fact enjoyed an almost unbroken peace.

Mysteries

During this time, the Oriental cults, particularly the Mysteries, flourished as well. It appears that in the third century the Mysteries became the chief rivals of Christianity, so much so that in the latter part of the century the Emperor Aurelian attempted to establish the cult of the sun god as the state religion.

Judging from the writings of the early Church Fathers, Chris-

[21] For the record in translation, see E. C. E. Owen, *op. cit.*

tians were more concerned with the menace to their religion from Gnosticism and the older paganism than from the mystery cults; perhaps they did not see where the greatest danger lay. These mystery religions were so called because their rites were not disclosed to the uninitiated. Most of them had in common the dying and rising of a god. The chief deities were frequently in pairs, a male and a female, the one dying and the other aiding in the resurrection. In Palestine, Baal, who has been noted earlier, had a female partner called Ashtoreth. The Eleusinian Mysteries diverged from this pattern in that the principal pair consisted of a mother and daughter. The more common scheme was found in Babylon with Tammuz and Ishtar; in Syria with Adonis and Astarte; and in Asia Minor with Attis and Magna Mater, the Great Mother. In the Orphic Mysteries, the protagonists are Orpheus and his dead wife Eurydice, whom he follows into Hades, so as to bring her back to life. In the Egyptian religion, Osiris was dismembered by his brother but was reassembled by his wife and sister, Isis, to become the god of the dead and the judge of souls. His reproductive organs, however, were cast into the Nile, making it the bearer of fertility to the land of Egypt. Isis was portrayed in terms of poetic beauty as the radiantly fair nature goddess.

The dying and rising of the god usually coincided with the fall and spring equinoxes. All the cults had fertility elements, and even in Mithraism, which had probably no female deity, sculptures of Mithra slaying the bull sometimes show not blood but stalks of wheat issuing from the wounded flank. But such cults were more than devices for securing good harvests. In the performance of their rites, men were assured that, like nature, they, too, would be reborn after death, and that through union with the risen god they would themselves be made divine and thereby immortal.

Such union might be accomplished in various ways. In the Dionysian cult, the devotee killed and consumed with the utmost haste an animal supposedly inhabited by the god, who on the death of the animal would soon depart. In other cases, as in the religion of Magna Mater and in Mithraism, there might be a baptism in the life-containing blood of a goat or a bull. Inebriation and sexual stimulation might excite a state of ecstasy interpreted as being filled with the god. More refined methods of accomplishing the union included sacred meals of bread and wine or of fish; the witnessing of a dramatic enactment of the myth of the god; or sometimes, as in the Orphic cult, the employment of music.

Great as the conflict was between Christianity and the Mysteries, they did have in common certain aspirations and certain practices: the quest for redemption from mortality and evil, the closeness of association in intimate gathering places, the social fellowship in which slave and free, rich and poor were equal. Certain concepts could easily be refashioned and adapted to Christian belief and practice. Blessedness in the fields of Osiris could be transferred to the new Jerusalem, and security under the tutelage of Isis, the beneficent queen of heaven, could be transmuted into refuge beneath the folds of the robe of the *Regina Coeli*, the Virgin Mary, the Mother of God.

But, there were some respects in which those who came to Christianity from the Mysteries threatened to subvert the faith. They might destroy faith in God the Father, since their rites centered on a dying and rising saviour, with no higher god. A greater danger was that Christ might be regarded as a fertility god, dying and rising with the seasons, since indisputably he did rise in the spring.

Christian Feasts and Sacraments

For a time, some Christians in Asia Minor celebrated Easter on the twenty-fifth of March, the vernal equinox on the old calendar, the day on which Attis rose from the dead. The Church discouraged this practice, but in the fourth century it permitted the transferring of the celebration of Jesus' birth from the sixth of January to the twenty-fifth of December, the winter solstice and the birthday of the solar deity. The reason for the change was to institute a counter-attraction on this day when Christian converts were joining their pagan neighbors for the celebration. The danger was that the Christian festival would be too much like the one it sought to counter. In general, the Church was flexible at the periphery but adamant at the core. For instance, certain fertility symbols were allowed to become associated with Easter—eggs and rabbits—but the Church strongly insisted that Jesus be worshiped as a historical figure and not as the god of a vernal myth.

The sacraments also had to be carefully defined. The mystery cults held that to be immortal man must be united with the god; sometimes the union was effected through a sacred meal. In Christianity, the Eucharist served this end, not in any crude and magical fashion, but by a life-transforming union with Christ, so that man became a new creature. But it might be interpreted as an actual eating of the god, as it was in the Mysteries. John's Gospel appears to have been combating such a view when it reports Jesus as saying that one must eat the flesh and drink the blood, but then adds, "It is the spirit that gives life, the flesh is of no avail. . . ."[22]

Church Fathers

The period of comparative relaxation under the Severi enabled the Christian leaders to devote greater attention to the intellectual problems of Christianity. There were, naturally, differences of emphasis among the Christian thinkers concerning the relation of Christian teaching to the current philosophical traditions. Tertullian, who lived in Carthage, was the thinker least disposed to any blending of the classical philosophy with Christian traditions. "What," he exclaimed, "has Athens to do with Jerusalem?"[23]

Despite his disclaimer of any indebtedness to Athens, Tertullian

---
[22] John 6:63.
[23] Tertullian, *Prescription against Heretics*, vii.

was the heir and transmitter of the Greek intellectual tradition in that he had an acutely speculative mind and strove to systematize and define Christian beliefs. It was he who first coined the word Trinity and formulated the doctrine of three persons held together in the unity of one substance. He also introduced the word consubstantial, describing the relationship of the Son to the Father. In more common terminology one might say that the Son participates in the being of the Father.

The primary center of the fusion of Christianity and classical culture was not Carthage, however, but rather Alexandria, long a major center of Hellenistic Judaism. The two great Christian leaders there in the first half of the third century were Clement of Alexandria and Origen. They were not embarrassed by their debt to Greek philosophy. Clement was notably ready to appropriate the language of the classical tradition and to baptize the ideas of all the contemporary *isms*. For him, Christianity was the true philosophy and the true Gnosis, in the sense of knowledge or illumination. He classified Christians according to the stages of their illumination. At the same time, Clement was no Gnostic, for he did not turn the story of Jesus into a cosmic myth.

He used the language of the mystery religions: "Mysteries truly sacred! O light undefiled! In the flare of torches I behold the heavens and God. Being initiated, I become holy. The Lord himself inducts me, impresses his seal, leads with his light, and commits the believer to the Father, to be guarded forever. These are the Bacchic revels of my mysteries. Come if you will and be initiated. Dance in the chorus with angels around the unbegotten and imperishable only true God. And the Word of God will raise with us the hymn." But Clement did not turn Christianity into a fertility cult.[24]

For him, Christianity was the true poem and he waxed poetic in his description of the work of the Lord Jesus: "All things are suffused with light unsleeping, and the sinking of the sun is turned

---

[24] Clement of Alexandria, *Exhortation to the Heathen*, xii, tr. R. H. Bainton.

to rising. This is what is meant by the new creation, for the charioteer of the universe, 'the sun of righteousness,' visits equally all mankind, like unto his Father who causes his sun to shine upon all and distills upon them the dew of truth. He has changed the setting into the rising, having crucified death unto life, and having snatched man from destruction, has lifted him to the sky, transplanting corruption into incorruption and transferring earth to heaven."[25] But Clement was no mere rhetorician; he was appropriating Greek culture (*paideia*) to describe the education of the Christian.

What was true of Clement was even more true of his disciple Origen, a man of prodigious literary output, who by allegory, if need be, was able to incorporate the best of Judaism and Hellenism in the Christian synthesis.

The educated in the Church were the ones to effect the assimilation of the philosophical traditions of the ancient world. In the realm of arts, the common folk among the Christians took the initiative. As to music we can say very little. The Epistle to the Colossians speaks of psalms, hymns, and spiritual songs, but the texts and the music are lost. Early Christian art has been preserved in frescoes, sculpture, mosaic, and ceramics. Yet the great Church Fathers did not approve. Tertullian would allow only the depiction of a ship as a symbol of the Church, of an anchor suggesting the cross, and of the sacred fish. Clement of Alexandria deprecated adornment, in the Cynic tradition, as artificial. But the majority of Christians painted the catacombs and carved sculptured sepulchres, employing pagan art forms for the purpose, as the numerous illustrations from the catacombs testify. This divergence of views between the leaders and the common folk in the Church points to a wider phenomenon. A cleavage was developing within the Christian community between an elite on the one hand, from which came the bishops, the writers and more frequently the martyrs, and the anonymous congregations on the other. The leaders tended to be more rigorous and condemned participation

[25] *Ibid.*, xi, tr. R. H. Bainton.

in warfare and personal adornment. The flocks often did not heed their shepherds. The cleavage began to assume shape as a distinction between the laity and the clergy, who were expected to be preferably celibate and poor, abstaining from family life, business and politics, whereas the laity might pursue worldly vocations, including business. Whereas poverty had been universally extolled in the early Church and doubt entertained whether a rich man could be saved, Clement of Alexandria ruled that he might, provided he engaged in philanthropy, for which a measure of substance was indispensable. The general trend was toward a relaxation of rigor.

Forgiveness of Sins

During the first two centuries, the Church had looked upon three sins as forgivable by God, but never by the Church—the denial of the faith, sexual immorality, and the taking of life. The penalty for their commission was exclusion from the fellowship of the Church and deprivation of that sacrament which was the peculiar channel of divine grace, the Eucharist. Ignatius had called it "the medicine of immortality and the antidote of death,"[26] and Irenaeus had claimed that such a change took place in the elements after their consecration, that they were no longer to be regarded as common elements, and that "our bodies when they receive the Eucharist are no longer corruptible."[27]

Exclusion from the Eucharist thus imperiled salvation, and offenders so penalized craved a relaxation of such rigor. But, should the Church run the risk of sullying her purity by permitting the goats to resume fellowship with the sheep?

The first to accept repentant sinners as a matter of official Church policy was a bishop of Rome, Callistus, who readmitted penitent fornicators on several grounds: the Church is like the Ark

[26] Ignatius, *Ephesians*, xx.
[27] Irenaeus, *Against Heresies*, IV, xviii, 5.

of Noah in which there were unclean as well as clean beasts; the Church is like a field in which the tares were to be left to grow with the wheat; and finally, the Church of Rome is the heir of Peter, to whom Jesus had given keys both to bind and to loose. (This is the first recorded reference to this passage by a bishop of Rome.) Tertullian was aghast and exclaimed, "We do not forgive apostates, and shall we forgive adulterers?" But the ruling of Callistus won general acceptance.

Once those guilty of fornication and adultery were readmitted to the Church, the question arose whether apostates should not also be readmitted; apostasy had become especially widespread when the Roman government suddenly abandoned its policy of tolerance of Christians for one of systematic and universal persecution.

The new policy was the consequence of changing conditions within the Empire. The stable administration carried over from the second century was disintegrating, so much so that some historians date the fall of Rome not from the fifth century, but from the third. Anarchy threatened. The Roman legions gained increasing power and set up one military emperor after another. The cause of the trouble was in part economic. Taxation had become ruinous to trade and industry. In the republican period, the Romans had sustained themselves by their own labor on small farms, but the wars of expansion had brought hordes of slaves. During these wars and early in the Empire, the Romans lived on the spoils from the provinces. But these were eventually exhausted and there were no new conquests.

The emperors chosen by the legions were generals who had spent much of their lives defending the frontiers, rough fellows who settled problems of dissension or disagreement within the state not by pleas for tolerance, but by the sword. Like their contemporaries, they were religious and ascribed the ills of the Empire not to bankruptcy or bad administration, but to the neglect of the old religion under which Rome had grown great. Hence, without dropping the emperor cult, they stressed rather the worship of the ancient gods. So deep was the faith that increased religiosity would restore Rome to its ancient glory that in A.D. 212 the Emperor Caracalla had conferred Roman citizenship on all free men throughout the Empire, in order that there might be more persons qualified to offer acceptable prayers to the gods of the Empire.

Decius was the first emperor to demand universal worship of the old Roman gods. He was a general from the Danubian frontier, resolved to have no nonsense; the obstinate Christians appeared to him as enemies of the Empire, which had been abandoned by the gods because of their atheism. In A.D. 249, Decius decreed that all citizens of the Empire, male and female, Christian and pagan, prove their loyalty by offering public sacrifices to the gods; they would then be given certificates signed by local officials testifying to their compliance. Some Christians, with the connivance of officials, bought certificates without making the proper sacrifices. Some submitted and ran to the altars. Some were stalwart, and many perished. The fury ended in A.D. 251, when Decius, deserted by his gods, was killed in a battle with the Goths.

There arose then in a form even more acute the question of readmitting to the Church those who had been guilty of apostasy. They were numerous, sometimes as many as three-quarters of a congregation. During the long peace, as we have observed, many Christians had relaxed those disciplines that safeguarded the faith. Without adequate spiritual preparation they had been caught unexpectedly; like Peter in the courtyard of the high priest, they had denied the Lord and now wept bitterly. They were the more eager for restoration since the implications of exclusion from the Church were being even more clearly spelled out. Callistus, we observed, compared the Church to Noah's Ark, outside of which no souls were saved. Bishop Cyprian of Carthage said flatly, "Outside the Church there is no salvation"; and again, "He cannot have God as a Father who has not the Church as his mother."[28] Therefore a clamor arose for readmission.

[28] Cyprian of Carthage, *Ep.* lxxii and *On the Unity of the Catholic Church*, vi.

Cyprian pleaded for leniency toward the backsliders. Reversing Tertullian's question, "We do not forgive apostates, and shall we forgive adulterers?" he asked, "We forgive adulterers, and shall we not forgive apostates?"[29] At the same time Cyprian insisted on discrimination. Those who had bought certificates without having actually sacrificed were certainly guilty of dishonesty; nevertheless, they had made plain to the magistrates that they were Christians. Leniency should be extended to them, as well as to those who had sacrificed only after excruciating torture and who well might plead that their bodies, not their spirits, had given way. Those who had gone willingly to make sacrifices must receive the severest punishment.

To deal with these degrees of guilt, a graded system of penance evolved, in which the number of years of exclusion from the rites of the Church depended on the gravity of the offense. The concept of penance was developed as a sequel to baptism, which was believed to wash away all previous sins. Since baptism could not be repeated, martyrdom was regarded as a second baptism, a baptism of blood, remitting all sins committed since the first baptism. This was why some, like Ignatius, even desired and invited a martyr's death. For those who had sinned after their original baptism and who might not suffer martyrdom, penance was available. The idea was proposed in a writing called *The Shepherd of Hermas* written at Rome around the middle of the second century. The concept gradually evolved, in the popular understanding if not according to the official teachings of the Church, until by the Middle Ages penitential acts were considered to be more than evidence of contrition; they were held to be actually meritorious and could be checked off against offenses. How remote was this view from Paul's insistence that salvation is the sheer gift of God's unmerited grace!

---

[29] *Ibid.*, li, 20.

Neoplatonism

Decius' attempt to exterminate Christianity was repeated by his successors, particularly by Valerian. In A.D. 258, this emperor made a frantic effort to induce the gods to protect the Empire from its various foreign foes, but to no avail. He was captured during a campaign against the Persians in A.D. 260. The next emperor, Gallienus, abandoned the policy of persecution and issued in A.D. 261 what was in effect an edict of toleration. A plausible explanation of this move is that Gallienus' attitude was not that of a frontier general like Decius, but rather that of a cultured patron of philosophy, which was fashionable in his day in the form of Neoplatonism.

Plotinus, the leading figure in this school, flourished in Rome from about A.D. 244 to A.D. 270. For him, religion was a means of emancipating the soul from the things of sense, so that the soul might ultimately be united in ecstasy with the ineffable intelligence (*nous*). Yet, though he deprecated the physical world, he did not reject sacrifices to the gods. He did repudiate Christianity and even Gnostic Christianity. His pupil, Porphyry, rejected the entire biblical drama of creation, fall, incarnation, redemption, and judgment and wrote one of the most formidable criticisms to be directed at Christianity during the period of persecution. But the Neoplatonists were averse to using the arm of the state to compel religious compliance; as reasonable men, they felt it was better to show by arguments and refutations how preposterous were Christian teachings. The toleration during the reign of Gallienus was apparently part of the shift to this new mode of attack.

The anti-Christian literature of this period was fairly extensive, though only fragments remain. The Christians, involved in a struggle for survival, were not interested in conferring immortality upon the arguments of their opponents. Still, Christians could not reply to attacks against them without stating what these were; the Christian apologies contain therefore many quotations from pagan critics. We have only fragments of Porphyry's many writings against the Church, but they are extensive enough to show that he was well informed, acute, and a gentleman. He made no vulgar charges, but pointed rather to contradictions in the Scriptures; he asked, for example, how God could have made the light before he created the sun and the moon, or how could Christ say to his disciples that they would see him no more and at the same time that he would be with them always.

Celsus

The oldest of such literary attacks upon Christianity of which details survive was by Celsus, whose book *True Discourse* (*Alethes logos*, written about A.D. 180) has been very largely preserved in Origen's refutation of it, published some seventy years later. Celsus was drastic and caustic, though not so credulous as to repeat the popular charges of incest and cannibalism against the Christians. Yet he ridiculed and vilified every article of the Christian creed. God, he said, did not create the world. If he had done so, he would have made a better world, which would not have gone wrong. If it had gone wrong, however, God would not have been concerned to set it right. If he had been concerned, he would certainly not have selected Palestine as the locus; nor would he have saved the world through an illegitimate child, who gathered about him some of the worst rascals in the land and told them if they got into trouble in one town to run to the next. (The reference is to the words of Jesus, "When they persecute you in one town, flee to the next. . . ."[30]) What god would have selected as a disciple a man who would betray him? A robber chief would have had more insight. Jesus was crucified as a felon. He is said to have risen, but who saw him risen? Only a crazy woman and some other deluded persons. (Here the reference is to Jesus' appearance before Mary Magdalene in the garden and before the disciples.) The Christians

[30] Matt. 10:23.

claimed that Christ must have risen because he predicted his resurrection, but Celsus pointed out that the disciples could easily have inserted the prediction into the record.

The Christian claim that God would send fire to consume the heathen and leave the Christians unburned was silly, wrote Celsus. He repeated the usual charges that Christians stayed aloof from social and political life. We have noted his charge that no Christian would serve in the army, as well as his claim that if all were like the Christians, the Empire would be overrun by the barbarians. If Christians would not assume political obligations, said Celsus, then they should withdraw from society and have no families.

Christian writers produced extensive refutations of the charges made against them, whether by mobs, emperors, or philosophers. They replied that Christians were atheists only in the same sense as Socrates, who denied the gods but not God. Immoral the Christians were not, and their congregations stood out against the pagan world as beacons against a dark sky. Seditious they were not, though quite obviously they were guilty of civil disobedience. Their loyalty was to a higher law.

Answering Celsus' accusation that the disciples had falsified the records, Origen pointed out, among other things, that they would scarcely have been willing to die for a lie. Even more acutely he noted that forgers do not manufacture that which is to their discredit. Would Christians have recorded the betrayal by Judas and the denial of Peter, had they been seeking merely to ingratiate themselves with the pagan world? Deceivers they were not; deceived they might have been. A century later Athanasius, bishop of Alexandria, addressed himself to this latter possibility, specifically with regard to the resurrection. He argued not from the credibility of the witnesses, but from the experience of the Church. "Is he a dead Christ, who even now is revolutionizing the lives of men?"[31]

---

[31] Athanasius, *On the Incarnation of the Word*, xxx.

Christian Influences on Roman Society

Christianity was indeed transforming individuals and through them affected society so far that, after one more drastic ordeal, the religion of the persecuted was to become the religion of the former persecutors. Before passing on to that culmination, we may review the attitudes of Christians toward society and the Empire up to the beginning of the fourth century and summarize the reasons for the notable gains up to that time.

In the main, Christian attitudes to society carried on the lines already laid down by the New Testament. As for slavery, there was no change on the part of the Church and the amelioration of the legal status of slaves was the work of the Antonines under Stoic influence rather than that of the Church. Objection to sexual immorality, of course, continued unchanged. Paul's preference for virginity in view of the imminent end of the age was continued for the new reason that family ties would impede readiness for martyrdom. Political thought followed in the main the Pauline formula of obedience to the rulers ordained of God. The Roman Empire was appreciated as a force for order, restraining the chaos that would precede the last day. At the same time, the deified emperor was equated with Antichrist, and some Christians at their trials were truculent and contemptuous of their judges, reminding them of the judgment day when they would stand before the tribunal of Christ. A few bishops in Asia Minor, where Christianity was especially strong, saw a coordinate work of God in the coincident founding of the Christian religion and of the Roman Empire. The fusion of Church and state came about first in the kingdoms on the eastern fringes of the Empire. The first king to embrace Christianity was Abgar of Edessa, early in the third century. Toward the end of that century, prior to Constantine, came Tiridates of Armenia. The great missionary to Armenia was Gregory the Illuminator, after whom the Armenian Church is sometimes called the Gregorian. Throughout this whole period, the antagonistic views of the Book of Revelation toward the Empire found expression only in a poem of Commodianus, who looked to a Gothic invasion to wreak vengeance upon Rome, the persecutor.

If we inquire now as to the reasons for the success of early Christianity up to this point, we may adduce as a factor the breadth of the appeal. Those with a Jewish background would appreciate the monotheism and the high ethics. Those who came from the Mysteries would feel at home in the small associations. They would love the liturgy and rejoice in the resurrection and the promise of immortality. The educated would not be repelled, but rather attracted by the subtleties of Christian theology. After Plotinus, the great minds of the age were in the Church. The intrepidity of the martyrs sometimes converted the persecutors. The organization of the Church impressed even the emperors. The deportment of Christians belied slander and elicited reluctant admiration. When, after Constantine, the Emperor Julian tried to revive paganism, he testified to failure because people were seduced by the delusive gravity of Christian lives. The Christian apologists testified to the winsomeness of the Lord Jesus, more appealing than the image of a philosopher like Plato or of a general like Themistocles. Nevertheless, by the time of Constantine, the Christians could scarcely have numbered more than one-tenth of the population. Who then, in the year three hundred, would have thought it possible that in less than a quarter of a century Christianity would become the officially recognized religion of Rome?

13. THE GRAVESTONE OF TWO CHRISTIAN CHILDREN

This gravestone was found in a passageway of the Roman catacombs in 1911. The names Ulpius and Aelianus point to the period of Trajan and Hadrian, in the first half of the second century. The dove is the symbol of the Holy Spirit, which, in the gospel according to John, appeared in the form of a dove at the baptism of Jesus. The inscription reads: ULPIUS FILIO ULPIO QUI BIXIT ANNIS II MEN[SES] VI ET FELICITAS AELIANO FILIO QUI BIXIT ANNIS V MEN[SES] VIII. "Ulpius to his son Ulpius who lived two years and six months and Felicitas to her son Aelianus who lived five years and eight months." In the usual spelling *bixit* is *vixit*.

14. OCCUPATIONS OF

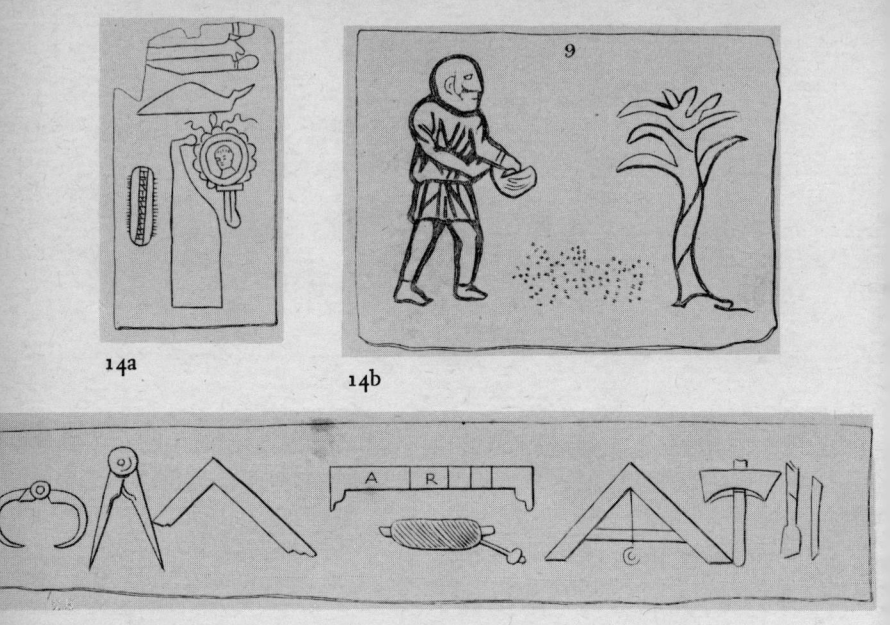

14a

14b

14e

The early Christians, accused of hatred for the human race because of their abstention from many aspects of the common life, were all the more eager to refute the charge by pointing out how much they were willing to do in fellowship with their pagan neighbors. This motive may account for the prevalence of representations of the occupation of the deceased on Christian tombs. The above examples are taken from gravestones in the Roman area during the first three centuries, though some may be from the fourth. The first (Fig. 14a) is from the tomb of a barber. At the top are the blades of his scissors, held together by a cord. On our left is his comb. His face is depicted in the mirror, which has both a handle and a loop for hanging. The other two instruments presumably served as razors. The second (Fig. 14b) is obviously a farmer and the third (Fig. 14c) a blacksmith. The fourth (Fig. 14d) is a carpenter with saw, adze, and chisel. The full inscription is not shown in the illustration. It memorializes a married couple, Bauto and his wife Maxima. The word *vivi* is meant to indicate what they had been doing while living. The fifth (Fig. 14e) commemorates a mason. His tools are calipers, compass, square, plumb line, level, mallet, and chisels. The sixth (Fig. 14f) represents a sculptor. The inscription reads: "Blessed god-fearing Eutropos, [rest] in peace. The son erected this." It is followed by the date. The name Eutropos appears again in small letters between the carved whales. Observe that, as a Christian, Eutropos was permitted to carve animal heads, but of course not idols. On our right is a dove with an olive branch, to the left a man with one arm raised in the attitude of prayer, his other arm holding a glass, perhaps of cold water.

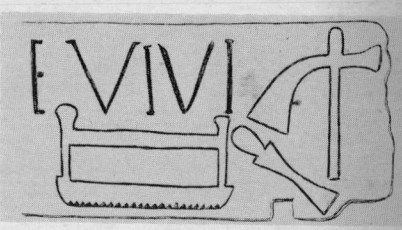

15. CHRISTIAN MARTYRDOM

15a

The theme of martyrdom in early Christian art was conveyed more commonly by allegory than directly. The frescoes in the catacombs allude to the sufferings of the martyrs and to their vindication through Christ by depicting the three Jewish youths Shadrach, Mesach, and Abednego, unharmed in the fiery furnace, and Daniel, unscathed in the den of lions (Dan. chap. 3 and 6). Their likenesses in the above example from the middle of the fourth century (Fig. 15a, from the catacomb *Sotto la Vigna Massimo*, Rome), though very poorly preserved, are unmistakable. Representations of the martyrs come at a later date and can hardly be regarded as portraits. The mosaics of Perpetua and Felicitas (Fig. 15b), from the archepiscopal church at Ravenna, may be dated from about A.D. 500, three centuries after the event. There is, however, historical verisimilitude in the costumes of Perpetua, the free woman, who is adorned, and in that of Felicitas, the slave girl, who is poorly clad.

We do have one sepulchral monument that depicts an actual martyrdom (Fig. 15c), or one that may thus be interpreted. The scene represents some form of public execution, for at the right stands the Roman lictor with his axe. In the central foreground, a woman is being held by hands and feet, both bound with rope. Behind her stands a figure whose face is not carved. He is the executioner who wore the mask of the god of death. His upraised hand holds a bent stick, another sign of the god of death. On the left, two men are shown approaching, carrying candles for torture. What we have, then, is a portrayal of the scourging and torture which preceded execution. The date is fixed by the headdress of the woman, which is in accord with the style set by the reigning empress. This places us in the reign of Gallienus. The victim herself arranged in advance for the monument, and in the inscription on our right

15b

15c

she expressly relieves her servants of any complicity that might endanger them. It reads: "Elia Afanasia (a corruption of Greek Athanasia, meaning deathlessness or immortality) erected this sarcophagus (misspelled sacofacus), lest her domestics Elpidus, Nidus and R (the name is not clear) should [suffer any harm]." Even to erect this monument was obviously dangerous. Yet the victim wished her sufferings at the hands of the law to be memorialized. What circumstance fits these details so well as the execution of a Christian? To be sure, the Emperor Gallienus issued an edict of toleration, but such mandates did not always stop local persecutions.

The Latin inscription may be reconstructed as follows: ELIA AFANASIA POS[U I T] SA[R]COFACUM NE SUIS DOM[ESTICIS] ELPIDIO NIDO RUF[O . . . DETRIMENTUM ESSET].

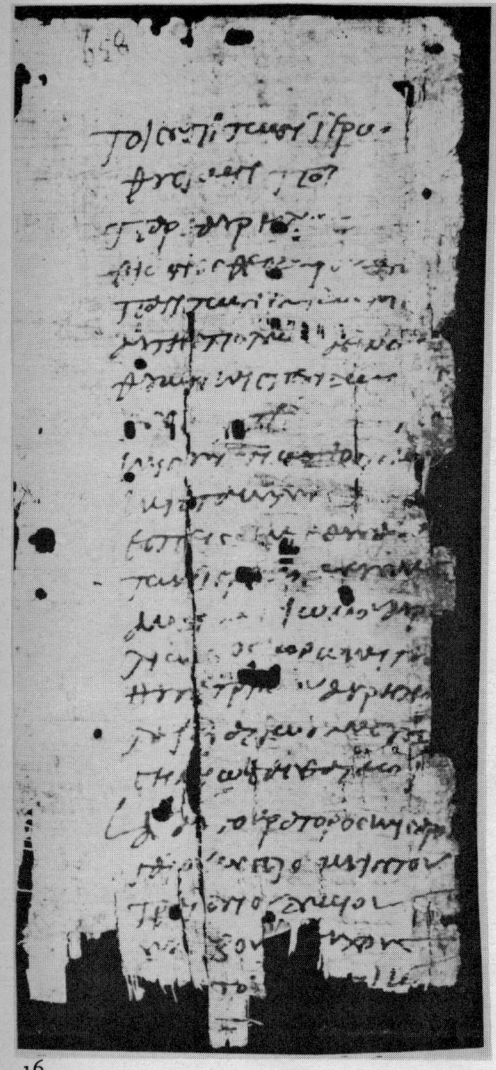

Τοῖς ἐπὶ τῶν ἱερῶν [καὶ
θυσιῶν πόλ[εως
παρ' Αὐρηλίου Δ.....
θίωνος Θεοδώρου μη[τρὸς
5 Παντωνυμίδος ἀπὸ τῆ[ς
αὐτῆς πόλεως. ἀεὶ μὲν
θύων καὶ σπένδων [τοῖ]ς
θεοῖς [δ]ιετέλ[εσα ἔ]τι δὲ
καὶ νῦν ἐνώπιον ὑμῶν
10 κατὰ τὰ κελευσθ[έ]ν[τα
ἔσπεισα καὶ ἔθυσα κα[ὶ
τῶν ἱερῶν ἐγευσάμην
ἅμα τῷ υἱῷ μου Αὐρη-
λίῳ Διοσκόρῳ καὶ τῇ
15 θυγατρί μου Αὐρηλίᾳ
Λαΐδι. ἀξιῶ ὑμᾶς ὑπο-
σημιώσασθαι μοι.
(ἔτους) α Αὐτοκράτορος Καίσαρος
Γαΐου Μεσσίου Κυΐντου
20 Τραιανοῦ Δεκίου
Εὐσεβοῦ[ς Εὐ]τυχοῦς
[Σεβασ]τοῦ (Παῦ)νι κ.
[.....]( )[
. . . . .

'To the superintendents of offerings and sacrifices at the city from Aurelius . . .thion son of Theodorus and Pantonymis, of the said city. It has ever been my custom to make sacrifices and libations to the gods, and now also I have in your presence in accordance with the command poured libations and sacrificed and tasted the offerings together with my son Aurelius Dioscorus and my daughter Aurelia Lais. I therefore request you to certify my statement. The 1st year of the Emperor Caesar Gaius Messius Quintus Trajanus Decius Pius Felix Augustus, Pauni 20.'

The Emperor Decius, in A.D. 250, required all citizens, perhaps the entire population of the empire, to sacrifice to the ancient gods. Commissions functioned in Egypt from June 12 to July 14, A.D. 250, in Smyrna on March 12, in Pamphylia on February 28, and at Carthage at an indeterminate date. Out of thirty-four names in the extant libelli from this village, one is Roman, eight are Greek, and twenty-five Egyptian. None is demonstrably Christian. Evidently, the pagans were also required to obtain certificates, and Aurelia Ammononous signs herself as the priestess of Petesouchos. There are more names of women than of men. Most of the signers have a double name, one component of which is Aurelius or Aurelia. The extra name was taken in honor of the Emperor Marcus Aurelius Antoninus Caracalla (popularly known by his last name), who had made an almost universal grant of citizenship to the inhabitants of the empire. The libelli follow a stereotyped form, with slight variations to meet individual cases.

This libellus is reproduced from a photograph supplied by the Classics Department of Yale University, where the papyrus is preserved. The above information about it is taken from Grenfell and Hunt, *The Oxyrhynchus Papyri*, pt. IV, *Theological Fragments*, no. 658, p. 49. For a discussion of the libelli, see John R. Knipping, "The Libelli of the Decian Persecution," *Harvard Theological Review*, XVI (1923), pp. 345–90.

17. MITHRAS

17

Mithraism was of Iranian origin. Mithras was the god of light and fire, greater than his associate the sun. From the body of a slaughtered bull, Mithras brought into being living things. The example here of a sculptured representation of the killing of the bull shows a dog in front and a serpent in the center, both ready to lap up the blood. A scorpion at the testicles will consume the semen. Franz Cumont, the first great investigator of Mithraism, interpreted the dog as friendly, the serpent and scorpion as hostile to vegetation, but Leroy A. Campbell, in his work *Mithraic Iconography and Ideology* (unpublished), believes that the serpent may represent the soul seeking rejuvenation through the life-giving blood of the bull and that the scorpion may symbolize the sign of the zodiac for the month which introduced the autumn rains. The inscription on the above monument reads:

Φλ. Γερόντιος πατὴρ νόμιμος τῶν τελετῶν τοῦ Θεοῦ εὐχαριστῶν ἀφιερωσάτω τῷ φ' ἔτει.

"Flavius Gerontios, authorized pater of the rites of the god, let him with thanksgiving consecrate [this temple] in the year 500." Dating according to the Seleucid era, the year 500 would correspond to A.D. 188. The name Flavius indicates that Gerontios' ancestors had been made Roman citizens in the period of the Flavian emperors, nearly two centuries earlier, since the enfranchised added to their own names that of the ruling house. The expression "authorized pater" indicates that the Mithraic cult had some form of consecration comparable to ordination. See Leroy A. Campbell, "Typology of Mithraic Tauroctones," *Berytus*, XI (1954), no. 101.

18. REDEMPTION AND RESURRECTION

18a

18b

18c

Early Christian art centered on the themes of redemption and resurrection. The figures commonly represented from the Old Testament were Adam, by whom humanity was corrupted, set over against Christ, the new Adam, through whom humanity was restored; Noah, with whom God made a covenant that the earth should be destroyed no more; and Moses, not as the giver of the law, which had been superseded, but as the savior of his people from thirst, who struck water from the rock. Christ appears as the Good Shepherd and divine teacher, but even more as the suffering redeemer and the victor over death. Yet, strangely the cross is extremely rare in early Christian art, and Christ is never depicted rising from the grave. The reason may be that in an age of persecution the cross was too overt and incriminating a symbol. It was suggested by the anchor, which had the form of the cross, save for its upward projection above the crossbar. Fig. 18a shows the anchor, with a dolphin as the sacred fish, the *ichthys*, twined about its stem. The word *ichthys* appears around the design in Greek letters, in mirror writing suitable for stamping an impression. Another and perhaps more important reason for not depicting the cross was that the piety of the early church centered not on the death but on the resurrection of Christ. And yet, we do not find any portrayal of Christ emerging from the tomb. Again, such a scene might have been too incriminating. But the theme was intimated through depictions of Jonah emerging from the whale. The connection may be sought in Matt. 12:14, where we read that, "as Jonah was three days and three nights in the belly of the whale, so should the Son of Man be three days and three nights in the heart of the earth."

When the cross gained prominence in Christian art in the fourth century, it was conjoined with a symbol of the resurrection, the laurel wreath used by the Greeks to crown the victor in the games and now by the Christians to symbolize Christ's victory over the grave. The sepulchral monument reproduced here (Fig. 18b) shows the cross with two of the guards at the tomb beneath its arms. Above is the wreath. The two doves on the arms of the cross are pecking at the laurel berries.

In our next two illustrations (Figs. 18c and 18d), the Jonah theme is likewise prominent. They are also of interest because they combine so many of the themes prevalent in early Christian iconography. In Fig. 18c (there are two versions of Fig. 18c, as there are also of Fig. 18d, the first being a photograph of the original work, the picture beneath it a drawing), the Jonah cycle is central. There are two whales, the one to swallow Jonah, the other to vomit him forth. Above the mast, the sun appears as a youth within a circle. Near him, to our right, Aeolus is blowing up the storm. Jonah, reclining under the gourd, is somewhat to the right and above the

184

level of the whales. Grouped around the Jonah cycle are small scenes on two levels. At the top, from left to right, we have the raising of Lazarus, then, after Aeolus, Moses striking water from the rock. The scene at the top center appears to depict the arrest of one of the martyrs, possibly Peter. In the corner, to the far right, there is a shepherd with his sheep. On the lower level, to the left, two men are carrying a pot. Above the whale, to the right, is Noah with his dove. Far right we have a fisherman in the midst of a snail, a lizard, a crab, two fish, and a crane. Beneath the fisherman's rod is a naked youth. A tree bears an apple. Whether these features are symbolic or merely decorative is difficult to say.

Fig. 18d has an orant in the center. At each end there is a representation of the Good Shepherd. In between, there are smaller scenes in two panels. At the top, from left to right, we have Daniel amid the lions, then someone reading a scroll. On the other side of the orant are Adam and Eve, with the serpent saving Eve the trouble of plucking the apple by proffering it to her in its mouth. Then, Noah and the dove with the olive branch. On the lower level, Jonah appears in three episodes, being swallowed by the whale, emerging, and reclining under the gourd. The sculptor has economized on space by using one body and one eye to serve two mouths of the whale, one to receive and the other to emit Jonah. By turning the picture sideways, the eye will be seen to shift over to serve the other mouth. The small Jonah emerging is about to land on the stomach of the much larger Jonah under the gourd. On the other side of the orant is the boy with the seven loaves that were multiplied in the miracle. This scene always suggested the eucharistic meal.

19. NOAH'S ARK

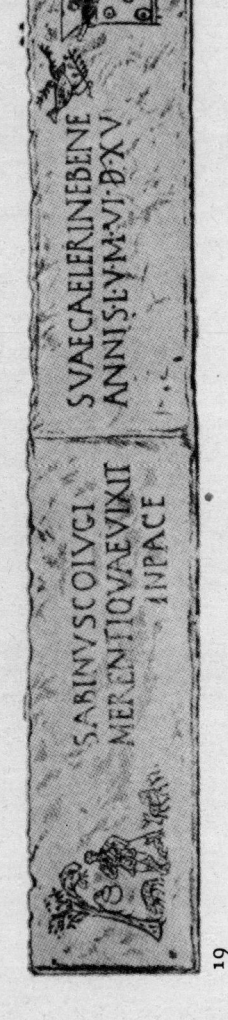

SABINVSCOIVGI | SVAECAELERINEBENE
MERENTIQVAEVIXIT | ANNISLVM·VI·D·XV
INPACE

For the early Christians, it was a symbol of the Church, outside of which no souls could be saved, just as no souls were saved in the flood, save those in the ark. This belief accounts for the eagerness of those who lapsed under persecution to be reinstated. This gravestone shows, on the left, the Good Shepherd, and, on the right, Noah receiving the dove carrying several olive branches. The inscription reads: SABINUS CO[N]IVGI SVAE CAELERINE BENE MERENTI QUAE VIXIT ANNIS LV M[ENSES] VI D[IES] XV IN PACE. "Sabinus to his wife Caelerine, the well deserving, who lived fifty-five years, six months, and fifteen days. In peace."

IV

The Christian Roman Empire

PROPAGANDA succeeded no better than persecution in dissipating Christianity. As the third century waned, the religious issue was becoming an ever more crucial concern of the Empire. To consolidate the power of the government, a universal religion was deemed essential, but Christians remained recalcitrant. Thus the alternatives had come to be: the secularization of the state, which was unthinkable; the extermination of Christianity, which so far had failed; and the adoption of Christianity by the rulers, in the hope that it would become the religion of the bulk of the population.

Persecution of Diocletian

Early in the fourth century, the Emperor Diocletian initiated a further attempt at extermination. He was another of those frontier generals like Decius, and associated with him were two men of the same provenance, his subordinates Galerius and Maximian. Like Decius, they also sought to restore the glory of the Empire by re-enlisting the favor of the gods under whom Rome had attained greatness. Diocletian believed he was personally under the patronage of Jupiter, Maximian under that of Hercules.

The persecution of the Christians began in 303 with an edict requiring that church buildings be destroyed and all copies of the Scriptures be consigned to be publicly burned. Christians lost their civil status and protection of the laws. Next, an edict was issued against the officials of the Church. A third edict was in effect an invitation to repent, but a fourth decreed death for all Christians. The roster of martyrs was so swollen that the days of the year no longer suffice for their commemoration. Diocletian retired as emperor in 305, but the persecutions in the East—spurred by Galerius, Maximinus Daza, and others—continued with only short respites until they were stayed in 324.

Diocletian's voluntary withdrawal was part of his valorous and imaginative attempt to avert civil war and stabilize the administration by decentralizing the government and setting up an orderly succession to the imperial office. The Empire was divided into two great districts, East and West, each to be administered by an official called an Augustus, with the aid of a subordinate called a Caesar. Correspondingly, there were two main imperial headquarters: Trèves (Trier) in the West near the Rhine, and Nicomedia in the East at the border between Europe and Asia. There were also two lesser headquarters: Milan in the West just south of the Alps, and Sirmium on the Danube, to guard the most menaced frontier. The Empire was further subdivided into about ninety-six provinces, so that no provincial commander could control too large a military force. These divisions incidentally survived in the administrative pattern of the Church, long after they had lost all political significance. Diocletian in the East and Maximian in the West were the first Augusti; they were to retire voluntarily at a given time, to be succeeded by their respective Caesars, Galerius and Constantius Chlorus, father of Constantine. The only dynastic element in the scheme was that Galerius and Constantius Chlorus were obliged to marry the daughters of the Augusti.

The Augusti did not have equal power; Diocletian retained supreme control from his headquarters in the East. When Diocletian retired, Maximian did likewise. The two Caesars became Augusti, Constantius Chlorus in the West, Galerius in the East. New Caesars were appointed, in the West Severus and in the East Maximinus Daza.

Constantine

The scheme seemed to be operating to perfection. However, on the death of his father, Constantine took command of the troops in Britain and Gaul and demanded recognition as his successor, reintroducing the dynastic principle. Galerius consented. Then Maxentius, the son of Maximian, undertook to succeed his retired father, killed Severus, ensconced himself in Rome, and demanded recognition. Galerius refused and instead appointed Licinius, who could find nowhere to exercise his authority save in Illyricum, in what is now western Yugoslavia. To complicate matters, Maximian had reclaimed the title of Augustus. Now there were six men undertaking to rule the Empire. The very disaster that Diocletian had sought to avert had actually come to pass. Intermittent civil war followed for a period of about twenty years.

The contenders in the East and in the West were reduced to one for each area by a series of elimination contests. The first of these took place in the West between Constantine and Maxentius. At the outset the religious issue was not paramount. Although Constantine and Maxentius were both pagans, neither was a persecutor of the Christians. Maxentius, in accord with the policy of Diocletian and his coterie, took as his patron Hercules, while Constantine placed himself under the tutelage of Apollo, or Helios, the sun god, and thenceforth placed the image of the sun upon his coins. Then Constantine took the astounding step of announcing his conversion to the Christian religion.

Thereupon, contrary to the advice of his military strategists, Constantine invaded Italy from Gaul and descended upon Rome. This could have been a rash move, for had Maxentius stayed inside the walls of Rome, he might have withstood a lengthy siege. However, he sallied forth instead, was attacked while crossing the Tiber over the Milvian Bridge, and was drowned. Maximian, having conspired against Constantine, had been apprehended and was granted his preferred mode of suicide. Thus, in 312 Constantine became the master of the West. He began at once to exercise paternal supervision over the affairs of the Church in that area.

In the East, the religious issue persisted. Diocletian, to be sure, did not meddle with it any more. He was tending his cabbages on his farm on the Dalmatian coast. But Galerius, shortly before his death in 311, admitted the failure of the policy of extermination. He issued an edict declaring that since Christians could not be recalled to the gods of their pagan ancestors, they might be permitted to worship their own God. He hoped that the Empire might gain some benefit even from the prayers to the Christian deity. Then Galerius died. Constantine had to deal next with Licinius.

The two met at Milan in 313 and agreed on a policy that placed all religions in the Empire on a par; each person might worship as he would, so that whatever gods there were might be propitious to the Empire. The edict embodying this decision did not give Christianity a preferred position and was not couched in Christian terminology; Licinius was still pagan. Yet a year later, in his victorious struggle with Maximinus Daza, who was still persecuting Christians in the East, Licinius appeared as their champion, only to change again and renew the persecutions in the final contest with Constantine a decade later. This struggle was terminated in 324 with a victory that made Constantine the sole ruler of the Empire. Under the standard of the cross he had conquered.

Why did Constantine embrace Christianity, and how fully did he understand what he had done? Politically speaking, his course must have appeared sheer folly, since Christianity can scarcely at this time have been the religion of more than one-tenth of the population in the West. A quarter of a century later, Bishop Eusebius recalled that Constantine mentioned having seen a vision of a cross in the sky bearing the legend "By this conquer." Another Christian author, writing earlier, said that Constantine had had a dream. The emperor himself testified to an experience of conversion, without mentioning either vision or dream.

However, there must be some truth in the story that Constantine believed the Christian God would guide him to ultimate victory. One might take him at his word and assume simply that he was converted, though one would have to add that evidently he considered Jesus to be a more powerful god than Hercules or Apollo. But, how deep was this conversion? Some have assumed that Constantine's faith sat lightly upon him, since he was not baptized until he lay on his death bed. But this was not unusual: the Church taught that baptism washes away all previous sins, and in Constantine's time the prudent usually postponed receiving the sacrament until all their sins had been committed. What makes the nature and depth of his conversion more difficult to evaluate are the ambiguities of his subsequent acts. He attributed his victory over Maxentius, for example, to divine impulse: *instinctu divinitatis* were the words carved on his triumphal arch at Rome. But which *divinitas*—Christ or Apollo? The symbol of Apollo remained on Constantine's coins even after his victory over Licinius, perhaps because it could be interpreted either as the actual sun or "as the Sun of Righteousness with healing in his wings." Definitely the Emperor gave up the claim to divinity, for when he was called upon to adjudicate in a Church dispute, he inquired why judgment should be asked of him, who also awaited the judgment of Christ.

Yet he stood in a peculiar relationship to God, calling himself "God's man," the instrument of the divine purpose. He believed God to be the Lord of history, who had revealed himself in Christ, especially through the Resurrection. Constantine described Christianity as "the struggle for deathlessness," that is, for that immortality assured to men by the resurrection of Christ. God's providential care for humanity, resisted by wicked men, had been vindicated by the martyrs, to whom Constantine now regarded himself as the successor. They by dying, he by fighting, had earned the title of *Victor*, which he now added to that of emperor.

His legislation gave to the Church privileges previously enjoyed by the pagan cults. Christian houses of worship, of course, were to be restored, and the Church was empowered to hold property as a legally constituted corporation. Manumission of slaves might take place in a church, as hitherto in a temple. The clergy, like the pagan priests, were exempted from municipal duties. The laws of Augustus penalizing the unmarried were repealed, reflecting, no doubt, the Christians' high regard for celibacy. The first day of the week was made a holiday. It was called, however, the Sun's Day, rather than the Lord's Day. (Curiously, this remnant of the solar cult survives among the Nordic peoples, including our own Anglo-Saxon forebears; we speak of Sunday, whereas Latin peoples call it the Lord's Day: *dimanche, domenica, domingo*.) Constantine's piety led to the abolition of crucifixion, but the laws against gladiatorial combat were not enforced and slavery was not abolished. Constantine effected no drastic changes in the structure of classical civilization.

As to the Church, he definitely avowed his adherence and called himself "a bishop, ordained by God to oversee whatever is external to the Church." Presumably he meant that he was not a priest and could not administer the sacraments; but there was little else ecclesiastical that he was not ready to do. Constantine did not impose his new-found faith as a state religion. Christianity was not the religion of the majority of his subjects, and Constantine was of no mind to force it upon the pagans; indeed, he himself retained for some time the title *Pontifex Maximus* of the pagan cults. "The struggle for deathlessness," he said, "must be free." What Constantine really did was to recognize a provisional religious pluralism; in the army, for instance, the pagan soldiers were allowed to use a vague prayer devoid of any Christian reference. Yet Constantine definitely announced himself as an adherent of the Christian faith and thus set the course for the development of the Byzantine Empire.

Constantine certainly hoped that the Church would prove to be a politically integrating force. He may not have been fully aware that Christianity was a factor that would correct cultural imbalances within the Empire. During the first three centuries after Christ, three unbalancing influences had been at work within the Roman world: the inscription of barbarians into the army, the militarization of the state, and the orientalizing of the court. As to the first, Christianity had not been identified with the barbarian newcomers; its strength lay in the centers of the old Roman population. Constantine, therefore, marching under the standard of the cross against the pagan Licinius, could pose as the champion of *Romanitas*, the heritage of Graeco-Roman civilization. Christianity worked against military dominance in government; Christians were concentrated in the most peaceful section of the Empire, remote from the threatened frontiers and, on principle, had long objected to participation in warfare. Finally, by denying the emperor's divinity, Christians eliminated the emperor cult with its Oriental associations. In favoring Christianity, Constantine—perhaps unwittingly—was favoring the old Roman, peaceful, republican elements in the body politic of the Empire.

For the Christians, the Constantinian era brought a radical change of attitude toward the Empire and toward their role as citizens. During the two decades of civil war in which the persecution of their religion was an issue, even those who would not fight could scarcely refrain from praying for the success of the arms of whichever contestant promised them toleration or favor; and when Constantine emerged victorious under the banner of the cross, Christians hailed him as the Lord's anointed. Their prevailing political philosophy in the new era was voiced by Bishop Eusebius of Caesarea, who picked up the theme voiced earlier only by a few bishops of Asia Minor: that the Empire and the Church, founded coincidentally, were two works conjointly designed by God for the redemption of mankind. The Church reconciled man with his Creator; the Empire achieved political unification by terminating the diverse kingdoms incited to war by demonic gods. Now Christians could confess one God, one Lord, one faith, one baptism, one empire, and one emperor. By his victory, they averred, Constantine had fulfilled the promise of Isaiah that henceforth swords should be beaten into plowshares and the nations should learn war no more.

Immediately after his victory over Maxentius, however, Constantine discovered that the Church, far from being the cement of the Empire, seemed likely to widen the existing cracks in its social structure. For Christianity was often bitterly divided within itself.

Donatists

The first dispute after Constantine's victory in the West occurred in North Africa and centered on the problem of discipline for those who had lapsed in the time of persecution. Following the persecution by Decius, the laity had been restored to the Church, after due penance. The question after the persecution by Diocletian had to do with the clergy, who in order not to imperil the lives of their flocks had complied with the edict to deliver up the Scriptures to be burned. The rigorists retorted that these *traditores* ("handers over" of the Scriptures, with the sense also of traitor) had abetted the destruction of the Holy Word and could never be restored to communion, let alone to office. This rigorist party acquired the name Donatists, after Donatus, whom they supported against the regularly appointed bishop of Carthage.

The rift was not confined to the religious sphere. In North Africa, there were three social strata. At the top were the landholding Latin aristocrats, often purer in their Latinity than the heterogeneous populace of Rome. Below them were the Punics, who, when Carthage had been demolished, were compelled to serve their new Roman masters on the land. They had their own churches and bishops, especially in Numidia. The third group were the Berbers, who antedated both the Punics and the Romans and lived on the steppes. The two submerged elements united to support the Donatists, precisely because the opposite, less rigorous policy was espoused by the local Latin nobility and by the Latins in Rome. The Berbers especially were anti-Roman. They had become Christian when Rome was persecuting the Christians; now they supported the branch of Christianity disapproved by Rome.

The case was brought to the attention of Constantine because a claim to property was involved. He had decreed the restitution of church buildings confiscated in the persecution. Which party had the rightful claim? Constantine referred the matter to the bishop of Rome, who decided against the Donatists. They would not submit. Constantine thereupon summoned a council of Western bishops, who met at Arles in Gaul in 314. This council also decided against the Donatists, but still they would not submit and appealed to the emperor himself. Violence flared. Constantine tried force without avail and then let events take their course. By the time of Augustine, a century later, the Donatists outnumbered the orthodox in North Africa. To reach a solution, three methods had been tried: reference to the bishop of Rome, to the emperor, and to the council of bishops. Though none had succeeded, Constantine was committed henceforth to the conciliar approach.

Arians

Then, there erupted in the East the Arian controversy, a dispute about the relationship of Christ to God. It arose at Alexandria in Egypt, where an aged presbyter named Arius contended that Christ the Son, although the highest of all creatures, was still a creature. He had a beginning of existence: "There was [a time] when he was not."[1] He had been made out of nothing; consequently, he had changed and was subject to change. The opposing party, led subsequently by Athanasius—then only a deacon and secretary to the bishop of Alexandria—affirmed that man's eternal salvation is imperiled if the relationship of the Son to the Father is not eternal and unchangeable. Behind the view of Athanasius lay the belief, held earlier by Irenaeus, that humanity and divinity are not so disparate as to be incapable of conjunction; the incarnation of God in Christ is the proof. If, then, God became man, man in a measure is able to become God. Christ is the forerunner and the mediator of this relationship; but this he can be only if, while fully

[1] Socrates Scholasticus, *Ecclesiastical History*, V.

human, he is fully, eternally, and unchangeably divine. If he were a creature he would be a subordinate god, and in that case why should there not be many more such gods, as in pagan polytheism?

Constantine was aghast. Clearly, he did not understand what all the "theological squabbling" was about, but he did know that it was disturbing the peace, for Arius stirred up even the dockhands in turbulent Alexandria. Moreover, a divided Christianity could not be the cement of the Empire. Constantine remonstrated with the bickering Alexandrians in a letter entrusted to his ecclesiastical adviser and emissary, Bishop Hosius of Cordova in Spain. The Emperor declared that he had embraced the Christian faith in order to consolidate the Empire. How grievously he had been disappointed by the earlier Donatist dispute in the West! In the East, whence the light of Christ arose, he had expected to find healing, but "O most merciful providence of God, what a wound did my ears receive when I learned that you were contending about mere words, points difficult to understand, and unprofitable in any case—squabbles, the fruit of a misused leisure." Thus, in effect, wrote Constantine to the contending Alexandrians.

The Alexandrians were not in the least quieted by being informed that their contention was "unworthy of men of sense," for they perceived that man's assurance of salvation depends on his relationship to Christ and on Christ's unaltered and unalterable relationship to God. The dispute could not be settled by an appeal to Scripture and tradition because support could be found in each for either party. The Athanasians could adduce the opening chapter of the Gospel of John, where Christ the Word was in the beginning with God. The Arians could cite the statement from the Epistle to the Colossians that Christ was "the first-born of all creation." Did that not imply that he was himself created? Among the earlier Christian writers, the Arians could refer to Tertullian, who had given the Son a beginning in time; and the Athanasians looked to Origen, who declared Christ's generation to have been timeless.

Council of Nicaea

When Scripture and tradition afforded no incontestable solution, recourse was possible only to the consensus of the Church. Constantine therefore summoned a council, which met at Nicaea in Asia Minor in 325. It is called the First Ecumenical (or universal) Council because it included bishops from the East and from the West. To celebrate the twentieth anniversary of his reign, Constantine invited the assembled bishops to dine with him. When those who had survived the great persecution filed between ranks of Roman soldiers to sit down with the emperor, one of their number wondered whether the kingdom of God had come or whether he dreamed. Here was another of those historic moments great with hope. But hope is seldom realized precisely as it is conceived. The council did not resolve Constantine's problems with the Church or the Church's own inner disputes. It rejected any subordination of the Son to the Father. The Greek word used to express their full equality was *homoousios*, meaning "of the same substance or being." The English equivalent (derived from the Latin) is "consubstantial." The Father and the Son were described as two persons sharing in one being or substance. With the Holy Spirit they constitute the Trinity.

The doctrine of the Trinity, as it was developed, is a formula that embraces a concept of great richness. It ascribes to God both unity and plurality: he is one and three. It ascribes to him both being and becoming: as the ultimate ground of being, he is static and changeless; yet there is in him an eternal, timeless process of generation, for the Son is begotten by the Father, and the Spirit proceeds from the Father alone (according to the Orthodox Church) or from the Father and the Son (according to the Roman Church). God is above time and within time; in the Incarnation and throughout the whole history of Israel and of the Christian Church, eternity impinges upon time. God is ultimate being, indescribable save by negatives, yet he has the personal characteristics of the God of Moses, the God who speaks. Christ is the very godhead become flesh, suffering and dying for the redemption of mankind. The doctrine of the Trinity was unifying, as indeed all orthodox Christian thought was unifying. The heretics were commonly dualists. In the second century the Gnostics had separated body and spirit. Now the Arians separated the creature from the creator. Later, as we shall see, the Nestorians tended to split the divine and the human natures in Christ.

But, although the Athanasians were able to unite God, as it were, they could not unite the Church. The Council of Nicaea pronounced in their favor. Constantine banished five dissidents, including Arius, and threatened with death anyone who did not deliver up his books to be burned. (The Emperor would not coerce pagans but felt differently about dissident Christians.) But, after the council had disbanded, Constantine discovered that the bulk of the population in the heavily Christianized area of Asia Minor had Arian leanings. He was mainly interested in concord and was willing to have the question reopened. Ten years later, in 335, a synod met at Tyre, and this time the Arians won: Arius was restored (though death cheated him of his victory) and Athanasius was exiled. But still the struggle was far from over.

Byzantium

In 330, Constantine had transferred the capital of the Empire from Rome to the mouth of the Bosporus at the site of the ancient fortress town of Byzantium, which he consecrated to Christ and which became known as Constantinople. There were good reasons for the move. The new capital stood close to the main focus of the Empire's trade; here might be established a bulwark to withstand enemies from the East and to check the inroads of migratory tribes from the steppes; and it was primarily in the East that Christianity had developed the strength to displace the moribund ideologies of the ancient world. Although the move was not meant to affect the Church directly, it did in fact leave the bishop of Rome heir to the mantle of the Caesars in the West.

Constantine died in 337, and the Empire was divided among his three sons. Constantine II received the provinces of the West; Constans held the middle—Africa, Greece, and Italy, including Rome; Constantius had the East. Each ruler adopted the religious view prevalent in his own territory. The West was Nicene, the East predominantly Arian. Constantine II and Constans were of the Nicene persuasion.

But, since they were fighting each other, the strength of the Nicene faction was divided and the Arians gained the ascendancy throughout the Empire. In 340, Constantine II having died, Constans was able to unify the Nicene areas and reverse the predominance. When, however, Constans in turn was assassinated in 350, Constantius, the Arian, ruled over the whole Empire. Then, as St. Jerome was to observe later, "The world groaned and was amazed to find itself Arian."[2]

Whichever contending party was victorious in the continuing Nicene controversy would banish the opposing bishops. Under Constantius the banished included Liberius, the bishop of Rome; Hosius of Cordova, who had been the ecclesiastical adviser of Constantine the Great; Hilary, the bishop of Poitiers in Gaul; and Athanasius of Alexandria. Pressures were exerted to break them down. Liberius at one time assented to the Arian position. Hosius, who was quite old, would never say a word against Athanasius, but became rather muddled over the creed. Hilary and Athanasius remained adamant. All of them, however, protested vigorously against imperial interference. "Let the emperor restrict himself to the empire," they said, "and learn from the bishops as to the Church."

---

[2] St. Jerome, *Against the Luciferians*, XIX.

Julian the Apostate

Then, with the death of Constantius in 361, the Empire reverted briefly to pagan rule under his cousin Julian, who has come down in history under the name Julian the Apostate. Although he had received Christian training as a youth, his religion was a curious blend of Neoplatonism and popular paganism in which the gods were conceived as emanations from the ultimate One. At first, Julian went back to the policy of religious neutrality promulgated in the Edict of Milan and allowed all the banished to return. (Thereby he aided unwittingly the eventual victory of the Nicene position, since the orthodox resumed their sees.)

Julian believed that Constantine had made a great mistake in adopting Christianity as the cement of the Empire, not merely because of its theological quarrels, but because Julian considered the faith to be on all counts incompatible with the Empire. Writing to the Alexandrians, he asked them whether their city had grown great on the precepts of the Galilean, who counseled turning the other cheek, rather than by the mighty deeds of their founder, Alexander the Conqueror. Moreover, Julian found Christianity incompatible with classical culture. Thus he forbade the Christians to teach the pagan classics and advised them to confine themselves to the exposition of the Gospels. Curiously, though he considered any form of Christianity degenerate, he deemed that of his own day to have been a further corruption of the primitive gospels, for the veneration of the bones of the saints, the exaltation of Mary, now called the Mother of God, and even the divinity of Christ, were in his eyes innovations. Yet, inadvertently he paid the Church a high tribute when he exhorted his pagan priests to imitate the sober deportment, the hospitality, and the philanthropy observed among the Christians.

The Christian State

Julian lasted as emperor only two years, from 361 to 363. The Arian-Athanasian controversy was then resumed until it was definitively resolved by the accession to the imperial dignity of the Spaniard Theodosius I, who was responsible for the final victory of the Nicene view. It was he who summoned the Second Ecumenical Council at Constantinople in 381, where the Creed of Nicaea was reaffirmed with slight modification. Theodosius did much more. He established what even Constantine had never envisaged: the Christian state. Heretics of every sort were forbidden to assemble and their churches were confiscated; they even lost the right to inherit property. As for paganism, once the official religion of the Empire, its rituals were proscribed, though its adherents were not treated violently or deprived of their civil rights. Half a century later, in 438, Theodosius II issued the Theodosian Code, which inflicted the penalty of death on those who denied the Trinity (the Arians) and on those who repeated baptism (the Donatists, who would not recognize Catholic baptism); in addition, it decreed that no pagans could serve in the army, lest their gods injure the Roman state.

What a change in the two and a half centuries since Celsus had charged that no Christian would serve in the army! What a change even in a century and a half, since the day when Origen accepted the charge and defended Christian pacifism! What an even greater change on the score of religious constraint! Tertullian in the days of persecution had asserted that religion admits of no constraint, and Constantine had declined to coerce the pagans. Yet he started those measures against the heretics that culminated in the Christian state of Theodosius I and eventually in the Theodosian Code.

Eastern Monasticism

As a state religion Christianity became to a degree secularized; the protest against this development led to the great monastic movement. The roots of monasticism, to be sure, reach back into the pre-Constantinian period. In Asia Minor, the first hermit of whom we have record came from the sect of the Novatianists; this sect, even before the Donatists, had separated from the Church in opposition to the laxity of the Church toward those who had weakened during the persecution under Decius. There is thus a connection between monasticism and sectarian rigorism. In the cities, during the persecutions, there had been groups of those dedicated to virginity and schooled for martyrdom. The whole penitential system encouraged heroic deeds of exceptional virtue to expiate sins. Above all, the threat of persecution kept alive the concept of the Church as a *militia Christi* fighting against the powers of darkness. When persecution ceased, these concepts were carried over into the monastic idea.

Still, despite the precursors, the great monastic exodus from society coincided with the era of Constantine: when the multitudes entered the Church the monks went to the desert. Here the battle was to be engaged with the demons who inhabit the waterless places. Anthony, generally regarded as the father of monasticism, withdrew into the Egyptian desert in 285 and remained there battling demons for twenty years.

The word *hermit* is derived from the Greek word meaning "desert"; the word *monk* comes from the Greek meaning "alone." But the term *monk* has come to be applied as well to those living in a community. Whether alone, however, or in groups, those who thus withdrew from the world did not do so on a family basis; to bring children into so disordered a world seemed to them irresponsible and in any case married life was deemed incompatible with unqualified dedication to communion with God.

Initially, monasticism was extravagant. The extravagances took the form of extreme castigations of the flesh intended to reduce the body to such enervation that sexual temptation would not arise. Another motive of spectacular asceticism was the spirit of competition: some of the early Eastern monks vied with one another to see who could stand longest on one leg without food or sleep, or who could remain the longest time on the highest pillar. But one should not let such extreme practices obscure the genuine holiness of the many. The significance of monasticism is not to be sought in its penchant for sleeplessness and flagellation or in its utter obliviousness to filth and vermin, but rather in its reaching for the infinite and its scorn for all those mundane pursuits on which men dissipate their days. Monasticism quickly passed from the eremitical to the cenobitic, so called from the Greek words *koinos bios*, meaning "the life in common." Pachomius, an Egyptian contemporary of Anthony, is credited with having been the first to introduce community living on an organized pattern. Codification of monastic practices in the East was the work of St. Basil, between 358 and 364, and in the West, a century and a half later, that of St. Benedict.

Monasticism soon came to have its impact on the world. Bishops began to be recruited, at times against their desires, from among those who had received monastic training. St. John Chrysostom, for example, who became first a priest at Antioch and later a bishop at Constantinople, had served his apprenticeship as a hermit-monk. When monks were thus transferred to episcopal sees, they tended to bring with them into the secular priesthood some of their monastic mores, particularly celibacy, though this became obligatory in the West only in the eleventh century and never in the East for the lower clergy. While monks thus went out into the service of the Church, bishops went on retreats to monasteries to replenish their spiritual energies.

St. Jerome

Once the early extravagances had subsided and monks began to live under stable and livable rules, the monastery began to assume tasks of enormous benefit to the Church and the world. The monastic cell became a study and the monks became scholars. The pioneer in this regard was St. Jerome (340–420), who began his monastic career as a hermit in the Syrian desert but found that he could exorcise his sexual temptations only by occupying his mind with a tough intellectual discipline. He took up the study of Hebrew and found it so effective that he could even venture to return to the world. At Rome, he became a teacher to Bishop Damasus and to a circle of high-born ladies on the problems of biblical exegesis. Hostility toward monks in Christian Rome—which, to Jerome's mind, in a measure still resembled Babylon—led him to withdraw to a monastery at Bethlehem, where his linguistic skills were put to use in translating the Old and the New Testament from the original tongues into literary Latin. The result was the so-called Vulgate, still in standard use in the Catholic breviary. Jerome illustrates again the tension between the classical tradition and Christian culture. Once, many years before, in a dream, the Supreme Judge had reproached him with being a Ciceronian rather than a Christian. He resolved to abjure the paganism of the ancient classics, but never divested himself of their elegant diction. He was to become the patron saint of the early Renaissance humanists.

Jerome's monastery was called upon quite unexpectedly to assume a new obligation. In the West, ever since Constantine's time, the Empire had been holding off the encroaching hordes of barbarians. Gaul was periodically threatened by the Franks and the Alamanni, and Britain by the Picts and the Scots, while Saxon pirates infested the surrounding seas. The provinces along the Danube, too, were harassed—and more than once overrun—by the Goths. Bickering between the Eastern and Western emperors weakened the Empire, and ruinous taxes sapped the strength and loyalty of the provinces. As the fifth century began, Rome was gravely threatened. Finally, in 410, a force of Visigoths under the leadership of Alaric took and sacked the eternal city.

For Jerome, the news was heralded by a stream of refugees heading eastward, who crowded into his cloister at Bethlehem in such numbers that only by stealing time from sleep was he able to continue his work on the Gospels. More than Rome itself was lost. The barbarians had also taken the Rhone cities, had pressed into the south of Gaul, into Aquitaine, and were poised for the assault on Spain when Jerome wrote a dirge bemoaning their attacks. Had he written but a few years later, he would have been forced to add that Spain, North Africa, and northern Italy, too, had succumbed to the invaders.

When Rome fell, Jerome was desolate. He, who had fled from Rome as from a Babylon, now lamented the rape of Rome the fair. The fall of the ancient seat of the Caesars affected the Mediterranean world quite out of proportion to the military significance of the event, for strategically the loss at the same time of the fortresses on the Rhine and the Danube was more crucial. But the sack of Rome shattered a dream. Since Virgil's *Aeneid*, men had believed that Rome would be eternal; the Christians of the fifth century could not know that her eternity would be achieved through the Church.

The Second Rome

The enormous losses meant, of course, the fall of the Roman Empire in the West. The imperial name was retained by the rulers of Byzantium at Constantinople, the second Rome. (Centuries later, at the time of the Crusades, the Byzantines still called themselves Romans; the Westerners they called the Franks.) This second Rome would hold out for centuries against the assaults of the barbarians. Then Byzantium herself was battered by new barbarians—the Avars, the Bulgars, and the Serbs—as well as by old enemies, the Persians. Finally, her sway even in the East was to be reduced: a new foe, the Arabs, arose, whom she was unable to hold in leash—in part because her strength had been sapped by internal dissensions caused by theological disputes.

The East had never fulfilled the dream of Alexander that all her peoples should be indistinguishably blended in the unity of mankind. In addition to Greeks, the Eastern Empire comprised among others Syrians and Copts. They, along with the Georgians and Armenians, with their diverse tongues, were to be alienated from the orthodox faith and from the Greeks of the Byzantine Empire. In addition, a rivalry of cities undermined the unity of the Empire. Usually Constantinople, supported by Antioch and Asia Minor, was ranged against Alexandria in religious controversies; when the two were deadlocked, Rome generally cast the deciding vote.

The controversy in which the Empire was embroiled soon after Nestorius became bishop of Constantinople in 428, concerned the relationship of the human and the divine natures in Christ. The Council of Nicaea had declared Christ to be of one substance with God. While affirming Christ's divinity, the Apostles' Creed emphasized his humanity. If, then, Christ was both God and man, how were the human and the divine related in him? The tendency on the part of those whose thinking about God and man was dualistic—and who therefore had difficulty in conceiving of humanity and divinity as conjoined—was so to emphasize the distinction between the human and divine natures in Christ as to make him virtually a split personality. This was the general trend of the thought of Nestorius. Specifically, he objected to calling Mary the Mother of God, for it would never do to think of God at the breast. Nestorius would call Mary only the Mother of Christ. His position, stoutly repudiated by Cyril, the bishop of Alexandria, was condemned with the concurrence of the bishop of Rome at the Third Ecumenical Council, meeting at Ephesus in 431.

Another solution to the problem was to unify Christ's person in such a way as to eliminate practically his human nature. This was the view of the Monophysites (from the Greek meaning "one nature"). Their concern was to ensure that the Son could never be at variance with the Father; and they therefore posited only a divine nature. This view—first propounded by Eutyches, a monk of Constantinople, in opposition to his bishop but supported by the see of Alexandria—was repudiated by the Fourth Ecumenical Council, which met at Chalcedon in 451. There, it was asserted that Christ was in two natures, inseparable and unconfused. He is of one substance with the Father as to his divinity and of one substance with man as to his humanity. From Rome, the pope concurred, and this has ever since been the position accepted by all the Orthodox Churches.

Nevertheless, it was not and never has been accepted universally. The Monophysite position was espoused by the Copts in Egypt and transmitted by them to the Ethiopians. In Syria, the Jacobite Church was Monophysite. However, Syria had also a Nestorian branch, which obtained a considerable following in Persia and still persists in modern Iran. (Persia, being in constant rivalry with the Greek Empire, preferred a form of Christianity unacceptable to the Greeks.) She sent missionaries to India and influenced the Mar Thoma Church, so called because of the supposition that India had been converted by the Apostle Thomas. At any rate, the connections of the Mar Thoma Church with Syria are undeniable, since her liturgical language is Syriac and her theology akin to that of the Nestorians.

The Nestorians pushed as far as China and left as their memorial (about 781) the Nestorian stone, with inscriptions in Chinese and Syriac. At first, Nestorianism enjoyed favor in the Mongol Empire. The mothers of several khans were Christians; as late as 1277, the leader of a Mongol embassy sent to England was a Nestorian Christian. Naturally, these Eastern heretics did not accept papal claims. One of the khans inquired how many horsemen and camelmen were in the pope's army. When Tamerlane (1336–1405) embraced Islam, the Nestorian Christians were annihilated.

The Church in the Kingdom of Armenia, caught between the Byzantine and Persian empires, preferred a form of Christianity unacceptable to either and became Monophysite. Their neighbors, the Georgians, however, remained loyal to the Greek Orthodox Church. The Armenians and the Georgians were thereby so divided religiously that they were unable to unite in a common struggle for independence from the Turks.

Religious rifts coinciding with regional and linguistic cleavages gravely imperiled the stability of the Empire after the middle of the fifth century. A solid front in the east against the Persians was indispensable to the emperors at Constantinople. Consequently, the imperial policy was oriented toward the conciliation of the eastern dissidents, the Monophysites, rather than the Nestorians, who had moved into Persia. The bishops of Rome resisted all concessions to the heretics and disavowed the attempt of the Emperor to conciliate them with an ambiguous formula.

Justinian

Such was the situation that confronted Justinian when he ascended the imperial throne in 527: the West had been lost to the barbarians, and much of the East—Egypt, Syria, Armenia—was disaffected by religious strife. He set out to mend both rents in the garment of the Empire.

In his first attempt, he came close to his goal. He brought down the Vandal kingdom in Africa, drove the Visigoths out of Andalusia in southern Spain, and expelled the Ostrogoths from northern Italy. For a brief time, the Mediterranean could once again be called *mare nostrum*, "our sea."

Then, Justinian applied himself to wooing the more moderate Monophysites, summoning a Fifth Ecumenical Council at Constantinople in 553. The Emperor sought to make peace with the Monophysites by hurling anathemas at the memories of three undistinguished Nestorians who had been overlooked in the curses pronounced by the Council of Chalcedon. Vigilius, the bishop of Rome, made a strong remonstrance but was cowed by violence. Then the western provinces of Istria and Illyricum, both in present-day Yugoslavia, foreswore communion with the Eastern Church. The attempt to unite the East religiously only divided the West within itself and failed to pacify the East. The Monophysite heresy still raged.

Byzantine Culture

But the greatness of Justinian lies neither in his western victories nor in his eastern diplomacy, but rather in this: that he gave a definitive form to Byzantine culture. It was an amalgam of Roman law, Christian faith, and Hellenistic philosophy channeled into theological speculation, in addition to an admixture of Oriental elements. Justinian codified the Roman law in the great *Codex Justinianus*, the Justinian Code, which in the East and West alike survived for centuries as the Roman law. The Christian element is very much manifest in the Code. It began with a section on the Holy Trinity and included rules governing the qualifications of bishops. Moreover, it penalized religious dissenters. Against heretics it repeated the penalties of the Theodosian Code. Pagans were forbidden under pain of death to offer sacrifices to the gods, and any convert to Christianity who lapsed into paganism was to be beheaded; the pagan university of Athens was closed. Jews, too, came under the Code's restrictions: they were forbidden to convert Christians and prevented from holding Christian slaves. The heretics were suppressed and the pagans died out. The Jews survived, to assume their difficult role as aliens in a Christian society. This whole system has been called Caesaropapism. Contemporaries did not call it that, and modern historians of the Byzantine Empire resent the term. They point out that the emperor was not a priest, that he was obligated by oath to introduce no innovations into the life and thought of the Church, and that he might be excommunicated by the patriarch. Time and again, emperors were excommunicated and sometimes driven to submission. The characteristic mark of the Byzantine Church-state pattern, we are told, was harmony, *symphonia*, in which the spiritual and the civil authorities supported each other. Yet, it must not be forgotten that the emperor controlled the election of the patriarch, and that even the decision of a church council was not binding without his consent. Moreover, if he did not think of himself as God, he aspired to be the visible icon of the invisible King, and the ceremonies of the court still had something of the aura of emperor worship.

As the system developed, the *symphonia* was generally achieved by a division of functions. The Church felt she could leave political administration to the Christian rulers of the state and devote herself to theology and enrichment of the liturgy in the sanctuaries and to the contemplative life in the monasteries. The whole of Byzantine society believed itself to be under the patronage of God and the Mother of God. The Virgin, like a Homeric goddess, would even enter the fray to throw a lance or sink an enemy ship. The emperor was the Lord's anointed, after the manner of David and Solomon. The temporal achievements of the empire were never attributed to sound finance, efficient administration, or military skill, but only to the favor of Heaven.

Nowhere is the unique quality of the Byzantine amalgam more manifest than in its art and architecture. Here the naturalism of classical art, the pure spirituality that Christianity inherited from Judaism, and an Oriental tradition of rich, nonfigurative decoration were fused into one of the most sumptuous arts of all time. It was in Byzantine art that Christianity first developed a characteristic style, in which representation of the familiar, physical world of human experience was sublimated into a suggestion of the world supernal, everlasting, and transcendental. Deliberately stylized figures set against glittering gold backgrounds of mosaic serve not so much to re-create a sensible image as to evoke a spiritual presence in an other-worldly atmosphere of resplendent grandeur.

The space within the dome, though contained, appears as illimitable and unfathomable as the sky.

When Justinian rebuilt Constantine's Church of Holy Wisdom, Hagia Sophia, and consecrated it in 538, he exclaimed that he had outdone Solomon, and perhaps he had. The dome, as the contemporary historian Procopius described it, hung as it were by a golden chain from heaven, a link in the hierarchy rising from the finite to the infinite and descending from the Creator to the creature. The mosaics, plastered over by the Turks in 1453 and uncovered in our own day, shone with dazzling brilliance. In them, Constantine and Justinian were portrayed, the one offering to the Mother of God a model of Constantinople, the new Rome, and the other a model of the Church of Holy Wisdom.

But the reign of Justinian was only a golden interlude for the Roman Empire. When his grip was loosened, the Visigoths repossessed the whole of Spain, the Vandals resumed sway in Africa, and the Lombards took over large portions of Italy (though not Rome or Ravenna, the seat of the emperor's exarch). In the East, Constantinople was besieged by the Avars, while the Persians overran Syria, Palestine, and Egypt. Jerusalem was sacked in 614. A solid front composed of Greeks, Copts, Syrians, and Armenians was never more essential, but theology—ostensibly, at any rate—stood in the way. A formula had to be found to satisfy the Monophysites without simply conceding their entire position. Since their main interest was to exclude the possibility of divergence between the Son and the Father, the bishop of Rome, Honorius by name (625–638), gave his support to the view that Christ, having two natures, yet had only one will. This view is called Monothelite, from the Greek words meaning "one" and "will."

The gesture was futile and soon became politically irrelevant, for a great storm was swirling in from the Arabian desert that in little more than a century would sweep across the southern shore of the Mediterranean and up to the very Pyrenees. The central figure was Mohammed, who appeared about the year 610 as the prophet of Allah. Profoundly influenced by Hebraism, he had no penchant for sophisticated theological speculation. Like the Jewish sect known as the Rechabites, who would touch no wine, he forbade the use of alcoholic beverages, but at the same time so far reacted against Christian asceticism as to revive the polygamy of the Old Testament patriarchs. The Jewish concept of the chosen people was now transferred to the Moslems. The sons of the prophet, confident that Allah would deliver the unbelievers into their hands, embarked upon an astonishing career of conquest and conversion.

Their way was facilitated by divisions among the Christians. Quite possibly the dissenters from the Eastern Church were the readier to accept the rule of Islam because it appeared to them to be so closely related to Christianity: Mohammed accepted the virgin birth and the role of Christ at the Last Judgment. More inducive to submission was the comparative religious liberty the Moslems accorded to Jews and Christians alike, upon the payment of taxes. Whatever the reasons, the sons of the prophet overran Syria, Palestine, Egypt, North Africa, Spain, and at length Armenia. Southern Italy and Sicily were to be at times in their hands. In all these Christian areas the Church survived—except in North Africa, where the old Punic and Berber elements may have renounced the Christian faith for the same reason that they had earlier embraced heresy, out of opposition to Rome; the diocese of St.Augustine in what is now Algeria was wholly lost to the faith. In the lands where Christianity had arisen, the Church found itself under the heel of the infidel.

When the effort to win back the Monophysites had lost its political significance, now that they were in the territory conquered by the foe, the Monothelite concession was repudiated by the Sixth Ecumenical Council, held at Constantinople in 680 and 681. Bishop Honorius of Rome, who had sponsored the view, was anathematized as a heretic. (This action does not invalidate the modern claim that the popes are infallible; they are preserved from error by the Holy Spirit only when they speak *ex cathedra*, that is, officially and to the entire Church. Honorius had spoken only privately.)

The Moslems again attacked and besieged Constantinople in 718. They were repulsed by the Emperor Leo III, called the Isaurian. But, while he hoped to restore political peace, he was responsible for another cataclysm, which shook the empire. This upheaval, like so many previously, was basically religious, although social, economic, and political factors were also involved. Specifically, it concerned the veneration of sacred images or icons, by then an established practice in the Eastern Church. When Leo launched an attack against the images in an edict of 726, he may have been influenced by the somewhat puritanical Isaurian bishops who interpreted strictly the second of the Ten Commandments. The bishops of Isauria advocated iconoclasm—the breaking of images, including the crucifix. Early Christian practice could be adduced for their position; as we have already noted, the early Church seldom used the cross as a symbol, and the crucifix scarcely appears in Christian art before the close of the fourth century. Leo must have been moved by conviction, for to stir up another theological controversy in an empire already rent by religious dissension was highly impolitic. And a full-blown controversy it became: riots broke out in Constantinople, and unrest spread as far as Greece and Italy. Leo and the succeeding iconoclastic emperors had the support of the army, but were vigorously resisted by the populace and especially by the monks. The iconoclasts denounced the icons as pagan idols, but their deepest aversion was not so much to paganism as to the use of physical forms to represent spiritual concepts.

The reply to those who favored the images was formulated most clearly by John of Damascus, a great theologian, who living under Moslem rule was in a position to speak freely, without fear of retribution from the Byzantine emperor. John, of course, appealed to the images mentioned in the Bible—the brazen serpent in the wilderness, the lions in Solomon's Temple—but his primary argument was from the Incarnation and the Eucharist. If God himself in Christ became flesh, then the flesh cannot be evil and, if Christ is bodily present in the bread and wine, then sensory aids to religion are not to be rejected. John then moved to educational considerations. The images, said he, are the books of the unlearned, lifting them up from the symbol to that which it signified. At the Seventh Ecumenical Council, meeting at Nicaea in 787, the images were restored, but with the qualification that the icons must be paintings or sculptures in low, but not in high relief. If the thumb and forefinger could be held on the nose of an image it was unacceptable. For the churches of the Byzantine tradition the sculptures of Chartres in the West thus became impossible.

The Byzantine Empire was to continue as a bulwark against Asiatic hordes for another six centuries. The Church contributed alike to its weakness and its strength. Certainly, the theological controversies precipitated the splintering-off of the non-Greek elements from the Greek core. In the conflict with Islam, this debilitated the Empire. On the other hand, the Greek nucleus, after being divested of all alien elements, developed a remarkable toughness and resilience, not the least because this people considered itself to be the custodian of the true orthodox faith and of a Christian classical culture. And, if the Byzantines did not convert the Arabs, they did, in the course of time, transmit to them the classical heritage that the Arabs in turn were to pass on, by way of Spain, to the whole of the Christian West.

The Slavic Peoples

The great sphere of Byzantine missionary activity, however, was in the Balkans and in Russia. Around the middle of the ninth century, the brothers Cyril (baptized Constantine) and Methodius, Byzantine monks of Slavic origin, undertook missions to Bulgaria and Moravia. Adapting the Greek alphabet, they translated the Bible and the liturgy into the Slavonic tongue. This Old

Slavonic liturgy has been able to serve as a focus for pan-Slavistic movements, even after the rise of a large variety of Slavic languages. But the Slavs have not been ecclesiastically united. The Serbs, the Bulgarians, and later the Russians have been oriented toward Constantinople, even though they became later ecclesiastically independent of the patriarchate, whereas the northern Slavs, the Croats, the Slovenes, the Czechs, the Slovaks, and the Poles, having been converted from the West, have been incorporated into Western Christendom under Rome.

The nominal conversion of Russia is usually dated from the even more nominal conversion of Prince Vladimir in A.D. 1000. He is said to have investigated the various religions. He did not like Judaism because he would have to give up pork, nor Mohammedanism because he must renounce alcohol, though he had no aversion to polygamy in Paradise. Christianity deprived him of the least. The liturgy of the Greek Church was breath-taking and to adopt the religion of Constantinople would offer political advantages.

The Russian Church was the daughter of the Byzantine, but in a number of respects the Byzantine pattern was not immediately transferred and could not be. Caesaropapism, if the term may be used, is possible only when there is a Caesar and an empire. Russia had no empire and her princelings were scarcely Caesars. In early Russia, as still earlier in the West of the Middle Ages, the Church led the state. The churchmen, coming from Constantinople, were the only educated class. They undertook to advise the princes and to instruct the people. Monasticism, which had become contemplative in the Byzantine Empire, became active in the Christianizing of a pagan people. The monastic ideal centered on the figure of the humiliated Christ, called the kenotic Christ. *Kenotic* comes from the Greek word meaning "empty." The reference is to St.Paul's statement that Christ emptied himself of his equality with God and became a servant.[3] Even so, the monk

[3] Phil. 2:7.

should empty himself of riches and renown and devote himself unstintingly to works of service and mercy. The ideal of St.Francis was anticipated by centuries in Russia.

Thus, the Church and the monasteries were the greatest integrating and civilizing forces in the life of the people. One is tempted to venture the suggestion that the Church is disruptive when the state is strong and integrating when the state is weak, though this may be qualified by saying that the Church can take the lead only on her own terms. Another point is that when the Church is confronted by an overwhelming task in society, she is much less rent by dissensions of her own. The absence of theological controversy in Russia had, however, another root. The Russians lacked the speculative interest of the Greeks.

Further differences were inherent in the fact that the Russians did not take over the Greek language for their liturgy but used the Slavonic instead. In structure, the Russian Church did not have an independent head. The only patriarch was at Constantinople. The Russian Church was governed by his subordinate, called a metropolitan.

This situation continued during the first period of Russian Church history, called the Kievan, because the ecclesiastical center was then in Kiev, in the south of Russia. The subsequent history is marked by successive moves to the north. The next center was Moscow, and the reason for it was the Mongol invasion, which was resisted and eventually completely repulsed by the princes of Moscow, who in the process developed a centralized government that alone could provide a counterpart to the Byzantine state. Moscow was made the capital in 1300 by Ivan I and the metropolitan began to be subordinated to the crown. With the fall of Constantinople in 1453, Ivan III married Zoé Paleologus, the daughter of the fallen emperor. Moscow was called the Third Rome, and the double eagle was adopted as her symbol. The liturgy of the Church was developed and the finest artists employed in icon painting. This was done partly as a device for magnifying the ruling class, for the patriarchs of the Old Testament

20. ST. NICHOLAS OF MYRA

20

This icon of St. Nicholas is introduced here to show the heavy black crosses that characteristically appear on the robes of the Eastern bishops, but he is worthy of mention more particularly because he became our Santa Claus. In the reign of Diocletian he became the bishop of Myra in Asia Minor, but sometimes he is called St. Nicholas of Bari because, after his cult had become popular in the West, his remains were transferred to Bari in Italy.

21. CONSTANTINE'S

21a

Fig. 21a depicts the battle at the Milvian Bridge, as shown on the Arch of Constantine. In honor of Constantine's victory over Maxentius, the Roman Senate erected this triumphal arch, which stands to this day. The inscription on it reads: IMP. CAES. FL. CONSTANTINO MAXIMO P. F. AUGUSTO S. P. Q. R. QVOD INSTINCTV DIVINITATIS MENTIS MAGNITVDINE CVM EXERCITV SVO TAM DE TYRANNO QVAM DE OMNI EIVS FACTIONE VNO TEMPORE IVSTIS REMPVBLICAM VLTVS EST ARMIS ARCVM TRIVMPHIS INSIGNEM DICAVIT (The Senate and the People of Rome dedicated this notable arch of triumph to the Emperor Caesar Flavius Constantine the Great, the piously happy Augustus, because, inspired by the deity and by the greatness of his own mind, he, with his army, avenged the republic on the tyrant, as well as on his entire faction, at one stroke, by justly taking up arms). Observe that "inspired by the deity" (or, "by divine impulse") may be taken either in a pagan or in a Christian sense.

The coin of Constantine with the monogram of Christ (Fig. 21b) is extremely important in dating the conversion of Constantine at about the time of his victory over Maxentius, in October, 312. The coin was minted in 315. The monogram of Christ may be seen within a small circle fronting the crest of Constantine's helmet. The monogram consists of the first two letters of Christ's name in Greek: the ch in Greek, called "chi," has the form of our letter X, and the Greek letter r, called "rho," has the shape of our letter P. Constantine is in military armor, his right hand on the bridle of his horse. The left hand is holding a shield embossed with the figures of a wolf and and of Romulus and Remus (not clear in this reproduction). From behind the shield rises a staff with a small crossbar surmounted by a

CONVERSION

21b

sphere. This is the royal mace or sceptre, symbolizing the imperial authority of Constantine, and possibly the cross as well.

22. ST. PETER'S BASILICA AT ROME

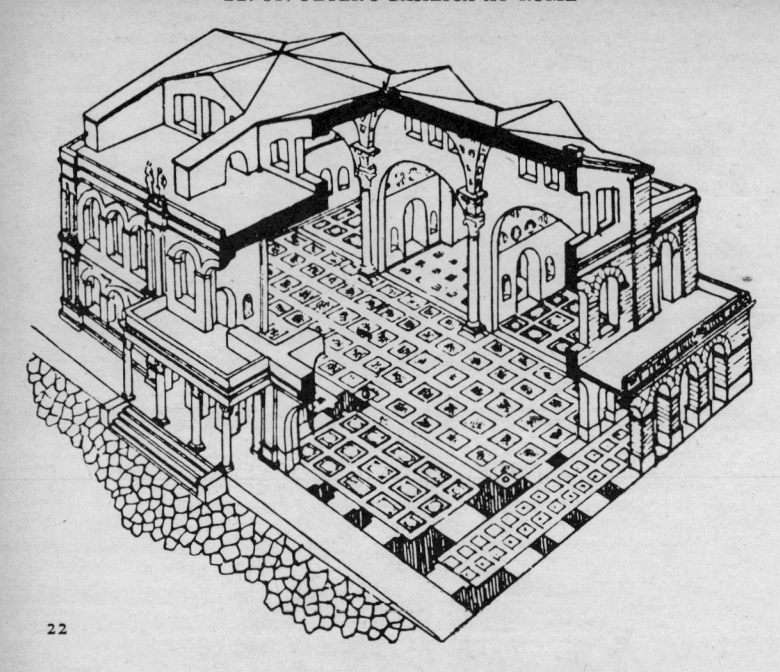

22

Constantine was a great builder of churches. The most famous of his constructions are the Church of the Holy Sepulchre at Jerusalem and St. Peter's in Rome. St. Peter's was built of wood and lasted until the Renaissance, when it was deemed unsafe and was demolished to make place for the present edifice. However, enough drawings of the original structure remained to make possible the above reconstruction. The church was of the basilica type, borrowing from the architecture of Roman public buildings.

23. THE TRINITY

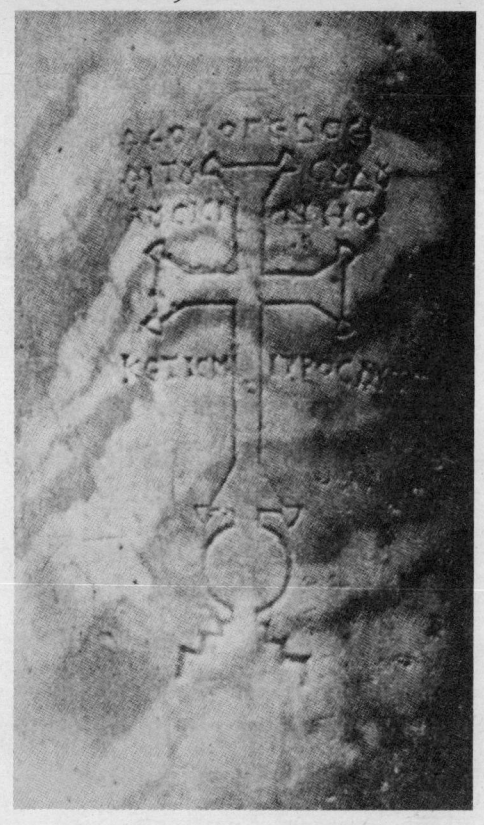

The earliest symbol of the Trinity was simply the triangle. In the graffiti it is sometimes hung from an arm of the cross. In this example, it serves as a base for the cross; triangles also terminate the arms and the upright of the cross. Below the pedestal triangle is a circle, in this case probably signifying the circle of the earth. It rests, in turn, upon stairs. This illustration is on the alleged tomb of St. John at Ephesus. The inscription reads:

ΘΕΟΛΟΓΕ ΒΟΕΘΙΤΟ
ΣΟΥ ΔΟΥΛΟΥ ΣΙΣΙΝΗΟΥ Κ[ΑΙ] ΕΤΙ Σ[ΙΣΙΝΗΟΥ]
ΜΙΤΡΟΣ Μ[....]

"O thou seer of God (the word is theologos), aid thou thy servant Sisinios and his mother." It predates the reign of Justinian in the sixth century, but it is uncertain by how much.

24. THE FLIGHT OF ATHANASIUS

24

This miniature is from a ninth-century manuscript that purports to illustrate the burning of the Orthodox who had been set adrift on the Bosporus in a flaming ship, but in this picture there is no hint of flames. The art historian, Kurt Weitzmann, points out that the miniaturists, whenever possible, repeated earlier treatments of their themes and sometimes misunderstood what they were copying. If, then, a picture does not fit its subject, one must determine exactly what is portrayed and try to match it with an historical incident that would correspond more closely. In this instance we see a bishop with a few companions in a small boat, corresponding exactly to the situation of Athanasius on one of his flights from Alexandria. Twice under Constantius and once under Julian, he had escaped the hand of the emperor by sailing up the Nile. The early church historian Theodoret relates (III, 5) that, in A.D. 362, Athanasius, condemned to death by Julian the Apostate, sailed up the Nile. He had recourse to a ruse, turning back after a while and sailing downstream. The imperial officer, meeting him and not recognizing his quarry, demanded, "Where is Athanasius?" "Not far away," replied the bishop truthfully. The officer made haste upstream and Athanasius and his companions glided back into concealment in Alexandria. (Cf. Kurt Weitzmann, "Illustrations for the Chronicles of Sozomenos, Theodoret and Malalas," *Byzantion*, XVI, 1 [1942], pp. 87–134.)

25. ST. JEROME

25a

25b

No contemporary portrayal survives, but in later centuries his life received graphic representation in various editions of his works. These two are from an Italian Renaissance translation of his life and letters (Hieronymus, *Vita et Epistolae*, italice a Matt. de Ferrara [Ferrara, Lorenzo Rossi, 1497]). The first is captioned, "St. Jerome wrote many books." He certainly did: not only the Vulgate translation of the Bible, but a volume of letters, biographies of noted Christians and treatises on monasticism. The second drawing (Fig. 25b) shows him, accompanied by his faithful lion, conversing with Marcella who, together with her mother and sister, assisted him in his work on the Scriptures. He is pointing derisively at critics who took a dim view even of his talking to a woman.

26a

No illustrative material of the lives of the early monks is extant, save for modern-day photographs of their desert caves; but, in later years, their lives, abundantly embellished by legend, were frequently illustrated. Unhappily, the extravagant and the eccentric lend themselves best to the graphic. The prototype of these ascetics was John the Baptist, who lived in the wilderness, clothed in camel's hair, and ate locusts and wild honey. His portrayals typify the ideal of the early monastics. He is commonly shown pointing with his finger, because it was he who pointed to Christ as the Lamb of God. The above drawing (Fig. 26a), from a tenth-century miniature, is a stereotyped depiction.

26b

26c

One motive for monasticism was penitence. St. Macarius, one of several of the same name, was alleged to have been so contrite for having killed a mosquito that for penance he lived six months in a swamp, stung by venomous insects (Fig. 26b). On his return, the brethren recognized him only by his voice, as his skin resembled that of an elephant.

For a time, sex became an obsession with the monks who had withdrawn from the world and thereby from female companionship. The monk above (Fig. 26c), to dispel his temptations, has resorted to the drastic expedient of burning away his fingers. The left hand has been reduced to a stump, and on the right hand only the thumb and one finger remain.

27. THE NESTORIAN MONUMENT

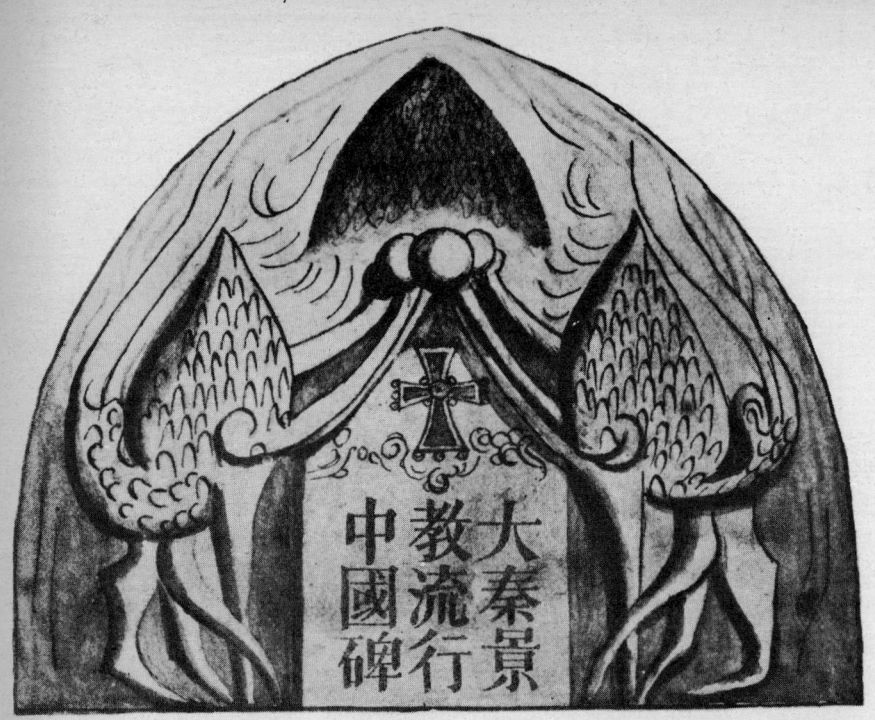

27a

The Syrian Nestorians in China erected in A.D. 781 a monument that towers well above the height of a man. It is crowned by the design reproduced here (Fig. 27a). Note the cross at the center. The entire face is covered with Chinese characters (Fig. 27b), which relate how the true Lord, uncaused, profound and still, brought into being the earth and gave to heaven its frame. He disclosed his separate godhead, that is, he sent to earth his Son. The darkness was dispelled and the light was spread abroad until

> Our brightest Truth then came to T'ang;
> Its Scriptures spoke in T'ang's own tongue;
> Its monasteries in grandeur rose;
> To save both quick and dead forth sprung
> Its ship. All blessing straight arose;
> The myriad regions had repose....

The inscription on the side (Fig. 27c) is written in the Syriac

景教流行中國碑 卅四

更効景門，依仁施利，每歲集四寺僧徒，虔事精供，備諸五旬，餒者來而飯之，寒者來而衣之，病者療而起之，死者葬而安之，清節達娑，未聞斯美，白衣景士，今見其人。願刻洪碑，以揚休烈。詞曰：真主无元，湛寂常然，權輿匠化，起地立天分

身出代救度無邊，日昇暗滅，咸證真元。○赫赫文皇道

冠前王，乘時撥亂，乾廓坤張，明明景教，言歸我唐，翻經建寺，

存歿舟航，百福皆作，萬邦之康。○高宗纂祖，更築精宇，

language. It gives the date and the names of various persons involved. Some names are given both in Syriac and in Chinese characters. The

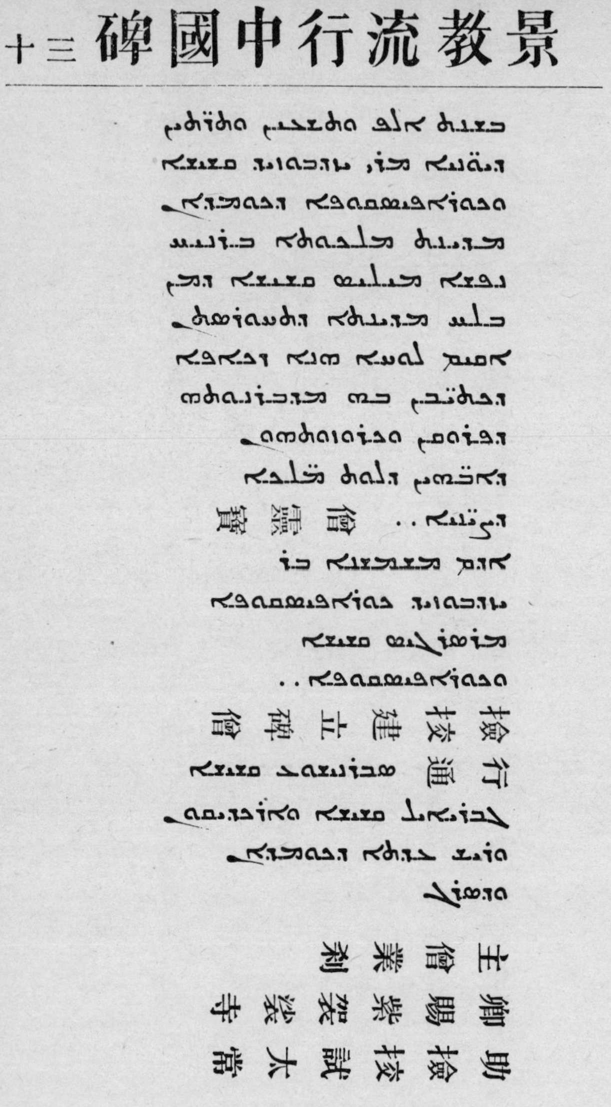

十三 景教流行中國碑

ܒܫܢܬ ܐܠܦ ܘܬܠܬ ܡܐܐ
ܘܬܫܥ ܕܝܘܢܝܐ ܡܪܝ ܝܙܕܒܘܙܝܕ
ܩܫܝܫܐ ܘܟܘܪܐܦܣܩܘܦܐ
ܕܟܘܡܕܢ ܡܕܝܢܬܐ ܡܠܟܝܬܐ
ܒܪܗ ܕܡܝܠܣ ܩܫܝܫܐ ܕܡܢ
ܒܠܚ ܡܕܝܢܬܐ ܕܬܚܘܪܣܬܢ
ܐܩܝܡ ܠܘܚܐ ܕܟܐܦܐ ܗܕܐ
ܕܪܫܝܡܢ ܒܗ ܡܕܒܪܢܘܬܗ
ܕܦܪܘܩܢ ܘܟܪܘܙܘܬܐ
ܕܐܒܗܬܢ ܠܡܠܟܐ ..
ܕܨܝܢܝܐ 僧 靈 寶
ܐܕܡ ܡܫܡܫܢܐ ܒܪ
ܝܙܕܒܘܙܝܕ ܟܘܪܐܦܣܩܘܦܐ
ܡܪ ܣܪܓܝܣ ܩܫܝܫܐ
ܘܟܘܪܐܦܣܩܘܦܐ ..
行 檢
僧 校
建 業
立 秦
碑 試
僧 太
常
ܣܒܪܝܫܘܥ ܩܫܝܫܐ ܘܓܒܪܐܝܠ
ܩܫܝܫܐ ܘܐܪܟܝܕܝܩܘܢ
ܘܪܝܫ ܥܕܬܐ ܕܟܘܡܕܢ ܘܕܣܪܓ

主 僧 業 剎 寺
鄉 賜 秦 裟
助 紫 試 太
 袈 常

27c

monument still stands on its site at Shen-Hsî. (Cf. James Legge, *The Nestorian Monument of Hsî-An Fû* [London, 1888].)

28. ARMENIAN CHURCH ARCHITECTURE

The Church of Odzoun in Armenia of the late sixth or seventh century shows the characteristic features of the cupola, suggesting the Byzantine dome but resting upon the Roman type of basilica. The interior of Armenian churches is dark, symbolizing the withdrawal of the Church from the world. Evidently this one was deemed too light, for a window on the wall facing us has been blocked in.

29. JUSTINIAN

29a   S. Vitale; Scala

When the Emperor Justinian overthrew the kingdom of Theodoric the Ostrogoth in Italy (A.D. 554), the mosaics of Biblical scenes put up by the Arians in the church of S. Vitale at Ravenna were allowed to remain, except those to the glory of Theodoric, which were replaced by mosaics in honor of Justinian and his redoubtable empress, Theodora. In Fig. 29a, Justinian presents a bowl to the churchmen on the right. One holds a cross, the other a book (perhaps a Bible or a lectionary), and the third a censer. The name of the one holding the cross is inscribed in bold letters above his head: MAXIMIANUS. He was the archbishop of Ravenna, an appointee of Justinian, energetic and statesmanlike. He helped to compose a schism in Illyria, and built, with incredible speed, the church of S. Apollinarius at Ravenna. His portrait here is sometimes hailed as the first instance of a genuine likeness of a Christian ecclesiastic. To the left from Justinian stand his bodyguards. Observe the Chi Rho monogram on the shield.

Alinari–Art Reference Bureau

The mosaic of Theodora and her suite (Fig. 29b) is interesting artistically because all the figures face front, but appear to be moving as in a procession to our left. The illusion is created by the hand holding open the curtain, by the gesture of Theodora proffering the bowl in that direction, by the turning of the faces and the leaning of the bodies on our right, and not least by the lively pace of the Three Wise Men embroidered on the hem of Theodora's robe. Justinian and Theodora wear round halos, which were commonly reserved for the dead, while the living were given square halos. Just as some of the Roman emperors in the pagan period claimed divinity prior to death, so now the Christian emperor and his empress lay claim to sainthood while yet alive.

30. HAGIA SOPHIA

A cross-section of the church of Hagia Sophia at Constantinople. Built by the Emperor Justinian in the sixth century, it is still standing today. "Perhaps," writes David Talbot Rice, "the greatest of the innovations that characterized Sancta Sophia was the conception of the building as an interior—in contrast with a classical temple like the Parthenon or even a basilica like the old St. Peter's or Santa Maria Maggiore at Rome. . . . It is the interior that is Sancta Sophia's real glory; there worldly thoughts are lost sight of and the soul is, as it were, wafted to the skies above. As with Christian teaching, it is the inner life that is of real importance, not the outward façade, and the whole decoration of the interior of the building was conceived to support this idea." (David Talbot Rice, *Art of the Byzantine Era* [New York, Frederick A. Praeger, 1963], p. 56.)

31. A MOSAIC IN HAGIA SOPHIA

Marburg–Art Reference Bureau

The great church of Hagia Sophia is adorned with mosaics of dazzling brilliance, covered over for centuries by plaster applied by the Turks after their capture of Constantinople in 1453. They respected Christianity enough to take its images seriously and therefore to conceal them from the view of True Believers. The present-day Turkish government has permitted the mosaics to be uncovered; the church itself is now a museum. The tenth-century mosaic above shows Constantine on the right presenting to the Virgin Mary a model of the city bearing his name, while on the left Justinian presents a model of the church itself. The inscription next to Justinian reads:

ΙΟΥΣΤΙΝΙΑΝΟΣ Ο ΑΟΙΔΙΜΟΣ ΒΑΣΙΛΕΥΣ

"Justinian the illustrious emperor." That next to Constantine reads:

ΚΩΝΣΤΑΝΤΙΝΟΣ Ο ΕΝ ΑΓΙΟΙΣ ΜΕΓΑΣ ΒΑΣΙΛΕΥΣ

"Constantine among the saints the great emperor." The abbreviations on either side of the head of the Virgin Mary ΜΗΤΗΡ ΘΕΟΥ stand for "the Mother of God."

32. ICONOCLASM

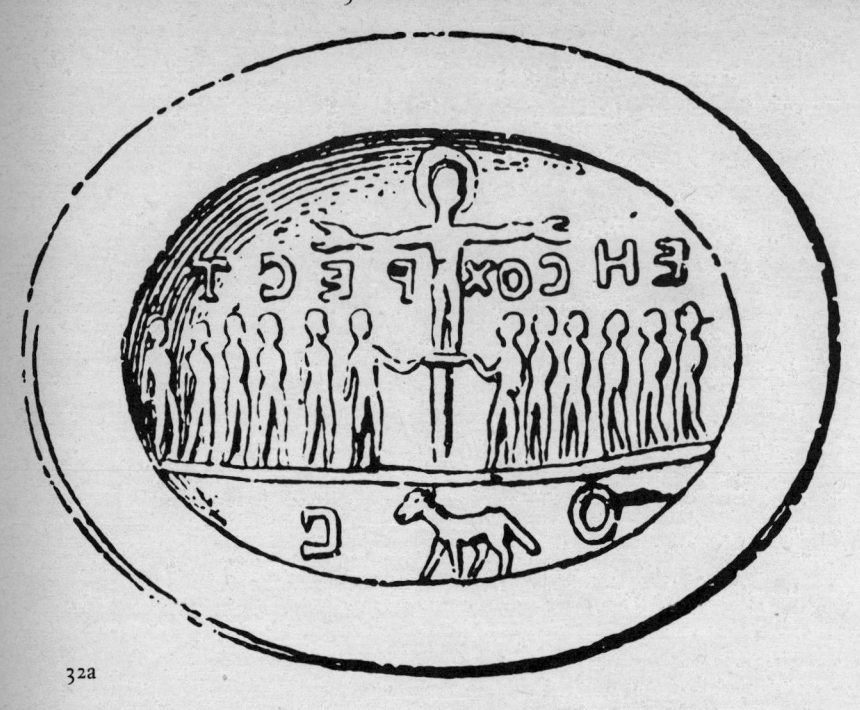

32a

The iconoclasts were correct in their contention that the image worshippers were innovators, for the first example of the crucifix, that is, the image of the body of Christ on the cross, cannot be earlier than the middle of the fourth century (Fig. 32a), because Christ has a halo of which the earliest example is dated A.D. 340. This is a seal, with its letters engraved in mirror script, for the stamping of impressions. The transliteration of the name Jesus is very unusual: E-Ā-SO (A as in ale). The name Christ takes the form *Chrestos*, which appears also in the writing of Suetonius, a pagan historian. On either side of Christ stand six apostles. His feet appear to rest on a pediment, as they do not in Fig. 32b, which dates from the fifth century. (For a discussion of Fig. 32a, see Franz Dölger, *Das Fischsymbol*, IV [Münster, 1947], Taf. 209, fig. 13.) In Fig. 32b, Christ is beardless, his feet neither nailed nor supported. Beneath on the left are Mary and John, and on the right possibly the soldier who pierced the side of Christ, although no lance is shown. On the left, Judas hangs from the branch of a tree, his money bag at his feet and the thirty pieces of silver strewn on the ground. On the tree a dove feeds her fledglings.

32b

32c

32d

In Fig. 32c, dating from the sixth century, the thieves are held by nails as well as by thongs. Christ is nailed to the cross, but whether he is also strapped is not clear since he is draped. Since Monophysitism was influential in this area, the covering of the body may be an instance of the Monophysite influence, even though this picture originated in Syria. Christ is bearded, as he is in the Syrian tradition. The soldier who pierced the side of Christ is given his legendary name, Longinus, written in Greek characters; the inscription above the cross, however, is in Syriac. The word *melka*, meaning king, is clearly legible. On the other side of the cross is the soldier who gave Christ the sponge soaked in vinegar. On the far left stand Mary and John; to the right are the three Galilean women. Beneath the cross, soldiers dice for the garment of Jesus. Above the sun and moon appear, alluding apparently to the eclipse at the time of the crucifixion (Mark 15:33). The sun has a spot, the moon a face. The arms of the cross are of unequal length, to fit the space of the picture. Fig. 32d is a drawing showing the iconoclasts commencing their work of destruction: the head of one of the thieves has been knocked off. Bishop Nessus (his name is written over his shoulder) exhorts his followers to complete the demolition. Note that in this instance the moon is a crescent and the sun has a face.

33. RUSSIAN CHURCH ARCHITECTURE

The Church of the Intercession on the River Nerl shows the characteristically Russian development of the bulbous or "onion" dome. It was built in the twelfth century.

No finer example of this genre can be chosen than "The Trinity" of Andrei Rublev, dating from the fifteenth century. It is called the Old Testament Trinity because it does not directly represent the Father, Son, and Holy Ghost, but rather the three angels who appeared to Abraham at the oak of Mamre. Abraham's house and the tree are shown in the background. Christians believed that the Holy Triad had made an appearance to the Patriarch in the guise of these three angels. Just as the Father, Son, and Spirit chose to disclose themselves in this oblique way so, it was felt, the artist too should avoid the anthropomorphism of direct representation, which the Eastern Christians found so objectionable. A Russian synod, meeting in Moscow in 1667, decreed: "To represent the God of Sabaoth on icons with a gray beard, with His only Son in His lap, and a dove between them, is exceedingly absurd and unseemly, since no one has seen God the Father. For the Father has no flesh, and it was not in the flesh that the Son was born from the Father before all ages. . . . This birth, before all ages, of the only begotten Son from the Father should be understood by the mind, and must not be and cannot be represented on icons."

Rublev employed a circular composition to symbolize the unity of the Trinity, the circumference of the circle passing through a point above the head of the central angel and below the feet of the other two. The figures are nearly identical, but nevertheless individual. The Father is on the left. His colors are of an indefinite hue since He is ineffable. The Son incarnate is given the traditional colors with the purple chiton and the blue cloak. The Spirit is clad in green, symbolizing the vitality of youth. Leonid Ouspensky comments: "This icon with its inexhaustible equilibrium of composition, majestically calm figures of the Angels, light, joyous summer colors, could be the creation only of a man who had stilled in his soul all agitation and doubt and was illumined by the light of the knowledge of God." (Leonid Ouspensky and Vladimir Lossky, *The Meaning of Icons* [Boston, 1952], pp. 203–07.)

35. THE TRINITY

35

This example from the beginning of the thirteenth century illustrates the type of representation to which the Russian Church objected: God the Father portrayed so literally that even his toes appear on the pedestal of the cross. Such anthropomorphism evolved only gradually in the West. At first, the presence of God was indicated by a hand emerging from the clouds, sometimes darting rays of light from each finger. From the twelfth century onward, first the face, then the bust, then the entire figure began to appear. A second feature objectionable to all of Eastern Christendom was the dove of the Holy Spirit linking the Father and the Son, in accord with the teaching of the Western Church that the Spirit proceeds from the Father *and from the Son* (*filioque*). This constitutes a point of divergence between the Orthodox and the Catholic churches to this day. In the corners of this illumination are the symbols of the evangelists. In the second century, the Church Father Irenaeus had already likened the four gospels with the four figures mentioned in the vision of Ezekiel 10:14. (On the iconography of the Trinity in the West, see M. Didron, *Christian Iconography* [London, 1851].)

were depicted wearing the robes of the Russian rulers. Active monasticism was extoled by displaying the good deeds of St.Sergius. One would not suggest, however, that the icons were merely a device of imperial propaganda. Where is spirituality more finely conveyed than in the contemplative detachment of the three angelic figures in Rublev's Trinity?

Ivan IV, in 1547, took the title of Czar or Tzar, derived from Caesar. Ecclesiastical independence of Constantinople was declared thereafter and the Russian Church came to have its own patriarch, who became increasingly subservient to the Czar. The more the connection with Byzantium was severed, the more the Byzantine pattern was transferred, and even exaggerated, for the term Caesaropapism applied better to Moscow than to Constantinople.

V

The Conversion of the Barbarians

BARBARIAN invasions were taking place in the West coincidentally with the events in the East, which we have traced thus far to the year 800. We must now turn back and pick up the parallel history in the West. Notice has already been taken of the fall of Rome in 410, of the first barbarian inroads, of the partial recovery under Justinian, and of the subsequent defeats under his successors. This course of events calls for a delineation in greater detail, with special reference to the role of the Church in Christianizing and civilizing the Western peoples.

The differences between the developments in the East and the West invite both reflection and speculation. The East held out against alien assaults for a thousand years longer than the West but did so by sacrificing some of its territory. At the same time, the effort simply to hold the line led to rigid conservatism. The West, at the outset, was overrun by the barbarians. There followed a long period of disorder and cultural retardation until the old and the new had assimilated each other. Then came a time of richly varied efflorescence. It was followed, to be sure, by an era of diminished élan after the high Middle Ages because the rhythms of history do not permit a sustained loftiness. One cannot help wondering what might have happened if the Byzantine Empire had been overrun by Asiatic hordes. Perhaps there might have resulted a different kind of Asia. To be conquered is not necessarily the ultimate calamity.

But to those who are conquered it must appear so, and the emotional impact of the fall of the eternal city on the spirit of the West was, indeed, devastating. To weather the shocks of history man must have a philosophy of history. Almost every philosophy of history in that age was religious and, for the pagans, the natural explanation of the disaster was the wrath of the gods at the success of Christianity. Prior to the fall of Rome, when the Danubian provinces were being invaded, the Christians were able to make a countercharge based on the pagan type of reasoning. In the late fourth century, the inhabitants of those provinces were still largely Arian in their faith because they had embraced Christianity in order to curry favor with the emperors at a time when the emperors were Arian. Now that this territory was being ravaged, the orthodox saw the cause in God's displeasure at the spread of heresy. Such was the explanation offered by St.Ambrose (340–397), the bishop of Milan, a slightly older contemporary of St. Jerome and St.Chrysostom. But, when the very citadel of Christian orthodoxy fell, the spread of heresy could no longer explain why God had suffered the inroads of the barbarians.

St.Augustine

The problem had to be confronted anew and the man who essayed an answer was St.Augustine (354–430), the bishop of Hippo, a little town in North Africa. His was a rich and seminal mind, which gathered up the strands from Christian traditions and classical antiquity alike and wove them into a new fabric destined to influence profoundly the thought of the Church, during the Middle Ages and even the Reformation. He had no simple answer for anything. The problem of history was set by him into the context of the nature and destiny of man, the character and the purpose of God, the redemptive role of Christ, and the function of Church and state.

Augustine's view of the nature of man was expounded in his

Confessions. This is the first full-length autobiography in Christian history and the first spiritual autobiography in all history—at any rate in the Western world.[1] In classical antiquity, autobiography was used as an apologia by public figures like Isocrates, Demosthenes, and Cicero to justify their careers; and though Marcus Aurelius concerned himself with the inner life, he did not cast his *Meditations* in the form of a life story. Christianity made the pilgrimage of the soul for the first time more important than the conquest of a province. The *Confessions* of St.Augustine exceed the personal dimension, however, for in describing his own tortuous course he analyzed all mankind. He was himself an illustration of man's corruption, redemption, and continuing imperfection.

Augustine was born to a pagan father and a Christian mother, Monica. He was reared as a Christian but was not baptized. The account he gives of his youth provides the most penetrating probing of the nature of sin since the New Testament. He inferred from his observation of infants that even before he could speak he might well have been livid with jealousy of other children. He remembered that as a boy he had robbed the pantry. This was surviving infantilism—feeding on demand. As a youth, he was guilty of sexual irregularity. This was surviving animalism. The next sin was vastly more troublesome to explain. With some comrades he raided an orchard of green pears. Why pluck unripe fruit? He says he would not have done it had he been alone. This was the bravado of the mob. The boys chuckled over the chagrin of the owner. This was glee over wanton destruction, of which not even an animal would be guilty. Then Augustine records his pleasure in going to a theatre to enjoy weeping over an unreal situation. This was flight into illusion. How different is all this from the earlier Christian rating of the chief sins as idolatry, adultery, and homicide!

As a young man, Augustine became a teacher of pagan rhetoric at Carthage. He had contracted a union with a girl whom he could

[1] Georg Misch, *Geschichte der Autobiographie*, I *Altertum* (Leipzig, 1907).

not marry because she was beneath him in status, and by her he had one child whom they called Adeodatus, "the gift of God." During these years of his youth in Carthage, Augustine went through great spiritual turmoil. In the course of his studies, he came upon a book of the writings of Cicero, which reawakened in him an intense desire for truth; but the truth did not appear to him to rest in Christianity and he stoutly resisted his mother's persistent attempts to draw him into the Church. Instead, he embraced the creed of the Manichaeans, a religion of Persian origin. The Manichaeans were even more extreme than the Gnostics in condemning matter as evil. They considered it so evil, in fact, that they deemed it a crime to give birth to children and thus to imprison new souls in bodies; having sexual relations was bad, but having children was worse. In years to come, St. Augustine reproached himself that during the fifteen years he had lived with his concubine they had had but one son, uninvited but loved for his own sake.

Already disillusioned by the all too simple Manichaean explanation of evil in terms of matter, he encountered evil in the form of intractability on the part of his students at Carthage. Instead of mastering the technique of discipline, he fled from the snarl and, against his mother's wishes, set sail surreptitiously for Rome, together with his concubine and son. Here he had difficulty in collecting student fees and, instead of vindicating his rights, withdrew to a post at Milan, where he was joined by his mother and some former African students.

Still, he was groping for a solution of his spiritual problem. Neoplatonism, studied in the Latin translations of Plotinus by Victorinus, now attracted him with its doctrine that evil is simply the absence of good; he was even more attracted by the experience of intense spiritual exaltation which it induced. While at Rome, he underwent a brief period of skepticism, though he says he never doubted God and immortality. Yet evidently he doubted himself, since he was helped by the argument that the very fact that one could doubt one's existence presupposed one's existence.

Ambrose was at this time in Milan, and Monica, ever determined to see her son baptized, sent Augustine to the famous bishop. Ambrose was a remarkable figure whose qualities were the very reverse of Augustine's; whereas Augustine retreated from embarrassing situations, Ambrose was audacious. Ambrose was no subtle thinker, no analyst of man's inner states. His apprenticeship had been in the public service of northern Italy. When an episcopal election was pending at Milan, he sought to keep the peace, lest the Arian and the Nicene factions should break each others' skulls. As he walked down the aisle of the church, a child's voice cried out, "Ambrose for bishop." As an unbaptized Christian, he protested his unfitness for the office, but the congregation advanced him from baptism to the bishopric in a week.

Ambrose was bolder and more influential as a bishop than he had been as a civil administrator. In 385, when the dowager Empress Justina demanded one basilica in Milan for the use of the Arian Goths among her troops, Ambrose and his congregation ensconced themselves in the basilica and withstood a siege, maintaining their morale by singing the hymns which he composed. In the face of such intransigence, the Empress capitulated.

On another occasion, Ambrose defied the authority of the emperor. Theodosius I, the vindicator of orthodoxy, had been guilty of an act of impetuous barbarism. An imperial officer had been killed during a riot at the hippodrome in Thessalonike. In revenge, Theodosius ordered seven thousand of the populace assembled in the amphitheatre to be massacred by his troops. When the emperor presented himself thereafter at the portal of Ambrose's church, the bishop forbade entry to a man whose hands were thus imbrued with human blood, and the emperor was driven to do penance. By these forthright actions Ambrose set important precedents for the development of an independent Church in the West.

Such a man was Ambrose. But he was more than a dauntless guardian of the faith; his eloquence was celebrated, and Augustine, himself a professor of rhetoric, went to church to observe his technique in oratory. As he listened, he was smitten by something exceeding eloquence. Here was a man who grappled with the problems of faith and who showed that one could be intellectually honest and a Christian at the same time.

In the meantime, his mother had prevailed on Augustine to dismiss his concubine. Lacking the stamina to resist his mother, he sent his faithful companion of so many years back to Africa. Monica then arranged a marriage for him with a girl too young for wedlock and, while waiting for her, Augustine formed another irregular union. At this time he heard of the Egyptian monks and was amazed that these illiterates had such control over their passions while he, a professor of rhetoric, could not master his incontinence. Coincidentally, his confidence in Neoplatonism was shaken by the discovery that the Neoplatonist Victorinus had joined the Church and made a public confession.

Augustine now turned to the New Testament in earnest. The "sickness unto death" invaded him and one day he went alone into a garden. He tore his hair and beat his breast, reflecting as he did so that his hand thus obeyed his will whereas his heart would not. (Even in such a crisis he was an inveterate analyst.) From next door he heard the voice of a child at play, crooning *"Tolle lege"* (Take up and read). He went to a bench where there was a copy of the New Testament and, opening the thirteenth chapter of Romans, he read: "Not in reveling and drunkenness, not in debauchery and licentiousness, not in quarreling and jealousy. But put on the Lord Jesus Christ and make no provision for the flesh, to gratify its desires." This was for him the experience comparable to that of Paul on the road to Damascus. Some time thereafter, together with his son Adeodatus, Augustine was baptized by Ambrose.

Then, with his mother and son, he set out to return to Africa. Monica died en route, Adeodatus shortly after arriving in Africa. Severed thus from all family ties, Augustine became first a monk and then, in 396, the bishop of Hippo, where he commenced his mighty career as administrator, pastor, and theologian.

Augustine's self-analysis enabled him to revive the thinking of the Apostle Paul as no one had done in the preceding centuries. But every revival tends to be an exaggeration, and Augustine spelled out more sharply the implications of Pauline thought. Man, said Augustine, has been so corrupted by the fall of Adam that he is bound at some point to sin. Even his virtues are tainted by his desire for self-aggrandizement. And sin is not merely the absence of good, as the Neoplatonists said, but rather, as with the Hebrews, it is a rebellion against the majesty of God. The only cure lies in the miracle of God's grace, vouchsafed through Christ and conferring upon man forgiveness, restoration, and healing. Yet this healing is never complete. Sin remains with man to the portals of the grave. Perfection in this life is impossible. Augustine had once thought otherwise, but the years had erased every vestige of illusion, and now he could no longer hope for a perfect society or a warless world.

Augustine developed also Paul's teaching on predestination, which is not the view that man is predetermined to do wrong but that he is predestined either to blessedness in the life to come through God's mercy or to the punishment merited by his sins. This dualism between the chosen and the rejected, formulated with sharper rigidity than by Paul, was in Augustine's case devoid of sociological or even ecclesiastical consequences, because he saw no way of distinguishing in this life the one from the other. The Church he recognized as a mixed company of tares and wheat, which meant that the Church is much less distinguishable from the world at large than if it were a community of saints. The line of demarcation is further blurred since, as the Church is not wholly good, so the world is not wholly bad. The pagans are capable of virtues of a sort: discipline, industry, courage, fidelity, magnanimity. Augustine recognized natural law, and when he was asked whether a Christian might accept an oath of fidelity from a pagan retainer who swore by his own gods, he answered yes, on the ground that the principle of fidelity is valid, even though the gods be false.

With this body of presuppositions, Augustine confronted the problem of the fall of Rome. For him, there were two major questions: first, why had God suffered this to happen; and, second, should Christians have recourse to war to repulse the barbarians? In his *City of God*, Augustine dealt with both.

Why had God allowed this to happen? Certainly not because of the spread of the Christian religion. Rome had been subject to calamities even before the advent of Christianity. Rather, Rome's calamities were the nemesis of her crimes. As classical authors had themselves admitted, there was a virus of corruption in the Roman bloodstream, manifest in the murder of Remus by Romulus and in the ruthless destruction of Carthage. Augustine, as an African, felt a deep sympathy for the rancor of his Punic and Berber compatriots against the indignities inflicted upon them by Rome. The curses of all the conquered reverberate through his pages. He recalled that when the Romans invaded Spain, the Spaniards flung themselves and their families over cliffs, rather than submit to the barbarism of the conquerors. From the pages of an ancient historian, Augustine lifted the excoriations of the Greeks against Rome and quoted the remark of a Briton, "The Romans make a desert and call it peace." With the Jews, Augustine saw Rome destined for the apocalyptic woes. But, then came the retort that Rome had conferred great benefits upon the conquered. To be sure, he answered, but at what price of blood? Again came the rejoinder that God must have approved of the Roman Empire, since he sent his Son to be born at the very time of its inception. At this point there was no lyricism in Augustine over the synchronism of the Empire and Christianity as conjoint works of God for the redemption of mankind, as Eusebius had assumed, for what, demanded Augustine, are great empires without justice if not robbery on a grand scale? To his mind, the nexus of corruption was broken only with the conversion of Constantine to Christianity and, if the rulers of the Empire were Christian, then he would say, let their sway increase.

In all this argumentation, Augustine seems to be saying that

Rome had fallen because of the sins by which she had risen to greatness. But the argument would appear to have broken down, inasmuch as the disaster had been deferred so long that not pagan but Christian Rome was paying the penalty. Augustine then set the entire question into a wider frame from which all moralism was removed. After all, said he, every empire deserves destruction because dominated by the lust for power, and it is no more moral when rising than when falling, but God, according to his sovereign will, allows empires to rise through a blending on their part of self-discipline and arrogance, only to bring them down in his own good time. As the prophets of Israel had seen, God may allow the Assyrian to swagger and may even use him as the rod of his anger, only to inflict in the end chastisement upon his tool.

But, if God brings down nations because of their crimes, ought they not in that case be brought down, and should one try to save them? Should the barbarians be resisted? Yes, wrote Augustine, because, after all, Rome's Empire enshrined a certain good. The Roman peace had facilitated the spread of the Gospel, and the Roman order did afford the possibility of the administration of justice. Even though Rome had been reared by blood, she was not to be relinquished to bloody barbarians. When Boniface, the Roman general in Africa, having lost his wife, wanted to become a monk, Augustine exclaimed, "For God's sake not now!" With the Vandals on the point of crossing the Straits of Gibraltar, the general must fight.

Was it right then for a Christian to take arms? Here Augustine adapted to Christian ends the classical code of war as finally formulated by Cicero, who had stipulated that war is legitimate only under the auspices of the state. Its object is to vindicate justice and restore peace. Violence must not be wanton. The justice of war is to be determined by the ruler. The code of humanity is to be observed. Good faith is to be kept with the enemy. Prisoners and hostages are to be respected. Such was the view of Cicero. Augustine added two points: the motive for war must be love, and this was possible, he believed, because killing of the body does not entail the death of the soul; and, if the war is to be just, one side must be unjust. Augustine was thus the father of the war-guilt theory.

Finally, he had three codes of conduct for three classes. First were the rulers, who should determine the justice and assume the direction of the war. Second were the subjects, who should fight at the behest of rulers, but never otherwise; in private relations there should be no self-defense. Third came those dedicated to religion, who should abstain from war entirely—the priests because they serve at the altar, the monks because non-resistance is one of the counsels of perfection.[2]

By exhorting Roman rulers thus to stem barbarian anarchy, Augustine made quite clear that he envisaged a society embodying, to a certain degree, Christian ideals. This society was focused on two institutions, the state and the Church. The purpose of the state was to maintain justice, defined as giving to each his due, which for Augustine meant primarily the rights of life and property. The state itself, however, need not be just in order to be a state, which is a community bound together by a common object of love. From that point of view a robber band could be a state, and to Augustine's mind great states commonly were robber bands on a grand scale. Yet the state may be at least an approximate instrument of justice, particularly if administered by Christian rulers; and those rulers need the direction of the Church—a point of view which suggests the social role the papacy sought to play in the Middle Ages. He was the more ready to assign a role to the Church in society because he envisaged for mankind a long span of time on earth; unlike the early Christians, who expected the speedy termination of the historical process through the return of Christ, Augustine projected the end indefinitely into the future. The role of the saints as judges of the world in the great assize on the last day was then transferred to the Church on earth.

Church and state were the more closely associated because each was thought of as a mixed society, embracing saints and sinners.

[2] Gustave Combès, *La Pensée Politique de St.Augustin* (Paris, 1927).

If the Church was to direct the state, the state was to uphold the Church, even to the point of using coercion in the interests of the true faith. A particular problem confronting the orthodox Church in Augustine's day was its conflict with the Donatist sect. In North Africa its members had become more numerous than the Catholics and often violently attacked Church buildings and priests. Augustine was at first strongly opposed to any use of coercion, until the state stepped in and by fines and imprisonment constrained the Donatists to attend the Catholic churches. Many declared that they were voluntarily converted by what they then heard. Hitherto, they explained, they had been forcibly restrained by their own leaders from hearing the truth of the Catholic faith; now that force had countered force, the scales were removed from their eyes. Augustine declared that he could not resist such testimony and proceeded to justify constraint as a work of love, like the saving of a life by the amputation of a limb. He did not regard the state or the Church as a corporate body of which a heretic was a gangrenous limb, to be removed by the death penalty. That analogy was, however, to be used in this sense centuries later, to justify the Inquisition.

Augustine gave virtually definitive shape to Catholic teaching on another great ethical problem. His views on sex and marriage were profoundly affected by his revulsion against the Manichaean avoidance of procreation. This is precisely the primary purpose of marriage, said he. Ideally, he believed, there should be no sexual relations save for procreation, though he knew of no married couple who practiced such restraint. The physical act of sex, he held, is not sinful; yet, even though the intent be propagation, there is a sinful concomitant in that the excitation of passion dissipates rational control. This sin, however, is venial when within the marriage bond. Augustine came close to wishing that God had devised some other expedient for procreation, yet recognized that marriage is ordained by God, though continence is superior. His attitude was developed in opposition to those who sought to enjoy sex without progeny at all. His view, originating in opposition to the

Manichaeans, has profoundly affected subsequent Catholic thinking.

In the realm of theology, one of Augustine's great contributions was to seek to make the traditional doctrines intelligible by analogy, for example the doctrine of the Trinity. He began by pointing out that, if one had never seen a cow, one could never conceive an image of a cow through unaided reason, merely by looking at the tracks on a meadow. But, given a cow, the tracks take on meaning. Similarly, one would not arrive at the doctrine of the Trinity by examining the psychological structure of man with its threefold pattern of memory, intellect, and will, but when the doctrine of the Trinity becomes manifest by revelation, then the threefold structure of man gives a clue to the understanding of the threefoldness in the unity of God.

Augustine drew richly from the past. On the classical side, he took over from Cicero his love of truth, his concept of the just war and his attention to literary style; from the Stoics he appropriated the doctrine of the law of nature and the harmony of the cosmos; and, from the Neoplatonists, their ecstatic vision of God. On the Judeo-Christian side, he gave greater depth to the Hebrew philosophy of history. In the Christian tradition he espoused the teaching of the Apostle Paul on grace and predestination and had also a deep feeling for the ethics of the Sermon on the Mount, including its pacifism in private life. His views on Church and state, war and peace, sex and marriage, tolerance and constraint, have made their impact afresh on each succeeding generation in the Western Church, whether Catholic or Protestant.

Barbarian Invasions

Augustine died in 430, while the Vandals were besieging Hippo. The barbarian invasions were to last for six hundred years. There were three waves: we have noted that of the continental Germans in the fifth and sixth century and that of the Saracens in the seventh and eighth century; after these, there came the invasion of the extra-continental Germans, the Scandinavians and the Vikings in the ninth and tenth century, as well as that of the Magyars, who were not altogether repulsed until about the year 1000. Modern historians debate which invasion was the most destructive of classical civilization. To contemporaries, the worst invasion was the one they experienced themselves. For us, today, it is not so important to differentiate among them as to remember that for more than half a millennium Europe was in a state of siege. At the same time, the degree to which the ancient culture was actually disrupted can be exaggerated.

The first wave led to the breakdown of the universal empire and the establishment of independent kingdoms. We have observed the Vandals in Africa, the Visigoths in Spain, the Franks in Gaul, and, first the Ostrogoths, then the Lombards, in Italy. In the fifth century, the Angles and Saxons invaded England. This situation was not altogether unprecedented. The barbarians had been making inroads for a long time. Throughout the imperial period they had been first recruited into the Roman armies and afterwards settled on the land. There were barbarian factions at court. Eudoxia, the empress in the days of Chrysostom, was the daughter of a Gothic chieftain, and Alaric, who sacked Rome, was opposed by the Roman general, Stilicho, also a barbarian. More significant was the settlement of barbarians *en masse*, with the granting of local autonomy. Constantine settled some 200,000 Sarmatians. The so-called barbarian invasions really constituted the breakdown of controlled immigration.

Culturally, the invaders were not savages; they were not nomads but agricultural folk who sought new lands because of pressures upon them by other peoples from the east. In the arts they were far from primitive. The Visigoths introduced into Europe techniques and motifs, which they themselves had borrowed from the Scythians and Sarmatians, of bizarre, decorative designs with an exuberance of geometric forms: wheels, rosettes, and spirals, together with cloisonné work and the bejewelling of coffers.³ Nor were the barbarians slow or inept in appropriating classical and Byzantine art. Theodoric, the Ostrogoth, built the church of S.Apollinare in Classe at Ravenna with its gorgeous mosaics, wherein Roman, Byzantine, and Teutonic elements are blended. The Magi bearing gifts to the infant Jesus wear Germanic trousers. When Justinian recovered Ravenna, he replaced all mosaics glorifying Theodoric with others exalting himself and his empress, Theodora. But the mosaics of biblical scenes were allowed to remain. Since these Goths were Arian, art historians seek to detect in the portrayals some influence of the Arian view of Christ as subordinate to God, but the mosaics disclose nothing obviously Arian and, had they done so, they would have been removed by the orthodox Justinian.

In the field of law, the Germanic peoples observed the principle of compensation in lieu of castigation. For murder the perpetrator had to pay the family of the victim. Mutilations had a graded scale of compensation. The highest price was for an eye or a foot, next for an ear. Teeth were rated according to their prominence. Fingers brought twice as much as toes, and even fingernails rated a shilling each. This whole system of commutation is important because, centuries later, it provided a basis for the ecclesiastical practice of penance and indulgences.⁴

With regard to morals, Salvian, a Christian, claimed in the fifth century the barbarians were more chaste than the nobility of the Empire, and he lauded Gaiseric, the Vandal, for closing the brothels of Carthage.⁵ But Salvian probably knew better how bad the Romans were, rather than how good were the Vandals. At any rate, when we encounter the barbarians within the Empire at a later date, their sexual behavior was not superior to that of the older population. On the score of cruelty, there was little to choose between the barbarians and the Romans. Did not the

³ Sartell Prentice, *The Voices of the Cathedral* (New York, 1938), p. 54.
⁴ Carl Stephenson, *Medieval History* (Rev. ed.; New York, 1961), p. 64.
⁵ Salvian, *On the Government of God*, tr. Sanford (New York, 1930), VII, 20, p. 216.

Roman, Constantine, in his pagan days cast captive Teutonic kings to the lions? Even the Franks reproached the Romans with cruelty, and the prologue to the Salic Law declared that the Franks were decorating with gold and precious stones the reliquaries of the martyrs, whom "the Romans had burned with fire, bored through with iron, and cast to the beasts."[6]

As to religion, the barbarians were in the position of Rome herself at the advent of Christianity, when all the different peoples were blending their faiths. Thus, the Teutons could feel that Wodin, to whom they assigned the fourth day of the week, Wodin's day, that is Wednesday, was the same as Mercury to whom the Latins allocated that day as *mercredi*. Similarly, the next day of the week among the northern peoples was Thor's day (Thursday), and for the Latins it was Jove's day—*jeudi* and *giovedì*. The Germanic peoples were similarly receptive to combinations of their religion with Christianity, but this was, of course, precisely what Christian leaders could never tolerate, as far as essentials were concerned. Yet, among the populace, the saints became the successors to the gods.

Conversions

The task of converting these northern peoples was formidable. To bring them to a nominal adherence to Christianity was not so difficult, because they desired to enter into the grandeur that was Rome, and Christianity was now the Roman religion. But to Christianize, to civilize, to tame, refine, and educate, to transmit to these peoples the best in the culture of antiquity, to disabuse them of the notion that Christianity was to be esteemed on the ground that it had made Rome an empire, above all to induce the practice of even a modicum of Christian deportment—confronted

[6] Albert Hauck, *Kirchengeschichte Deutschlands*, I, p. 171 (Cf. Bibliography).

with such a task the Church might well have wished that God had terminated history in 410 with the sack of Rome.

The barbarians to be converted were of two sorts. Some were pagans: the Franks and the Anglo-Saxons; others were already Christians, but they were Arians who had embraced Christianity at the time when Arianism was dominant in the Empire. The missionary to whom the colossal achievement of converting these peoples to the Arian faith is attributed is Ulfilas, himself of barbarian extraction.

This Arianism was more ecclesiatical than theological, because the Germans were not interested in all the niceties of the consubstantiality of the Father and the Son, though theology did enter to a degree, inasmuch as the Arian Christ was a creature, albeit the first-born of all creation. This view made it possible to think of him as a glorified Viking chieftain. But the main difference between the Arians and the orthodox in the West lay in the structure of the Church. The Arians had no ecclesiastical center. They did not recognize orthodox Rome, and they had no counterpart of their own. The Arian churches were decentralized. The Christian priests had taken the place of the pagan priests as chaplains to kings. The Arian churches belonged to the clan. We are not aware even of any Arian synods. After the conversion of these barbarian Arians to orthodoxy, they were still loath to accept centralization through Rome. The system of local proprietary churches dependent on the king or patron was so well entrenched that the conflict between the centralizing and decentralizing tendencies within the Church is one of the persistent themes of medieval Church history.

For a time, however, the setting up of Arian kingdoms aided the centralization of orthodox Christianity under Rome, because the Arian kings tolerated the orthodox Church and did not intervene in its internal affairs. The connection, which this Church had had with the Empire was severed, nor was she attached to the ruling power in any one of the new kingdoms. For this reason, she was able to maintain her independence and universality throughout all these kingdoms. The orthodox old Romans, now living under the various barbarians, looked to Christian Rome as to the focus of their faith—as *Roma aeterna*.

Western Monasticism

In the conversion of Europe, three Christian institutions were at work: monasticism, the papacy, and the civil state. Of the three, monasticism was the most important, because monks were missionaries, whereas popes and kings were not. Eastern monasticism was transferred to the West by St. Martin who established a monastery near Poitiers in 362. Distinctive shape was given to Western monasticism by St. Benedict, a contemporary of Justinian, in the middle of the sixth century. After a period as a hermit, he established a community at Monte Cassino, looking down on the valley of the Garigliano. For his spiritual sons he devised a rule, temperate, sensible, and livable. He encouraged no contests in austerity, no spectacular macerations of the flesh. He would not allow monks to be hermits or holy vagabonds. They should live in a community, subject to strict discipline. To the vows of poverty, chastity, and obedience, he added that of stability. Only on urgent business should the monk leave the monastic enclosure, and then only with a companion. On their return, the brothers should not relate what they had seen. The monastery, of course, had to be self-sustaining and was provided with its own tillable soil, a well, buildings and, later on, a fishpond, rabbitry, and poultry yard. The monks provided all the labor. The food was frugal; bread, wine, and vegetables, but no meat, save for the sick. One must remember that few people in that day could afford much meat. The farmers could not feed cattle to be eaten, and slaughtered only what would not survive the winter.[7] No such restrictions applied

[7] Robert L. Reynolds, *Europe Emerges* (Madison, Wisc., 1961), p. 66.

to fish, and monasteries were commonly located beside a stream, which was dammed for a fishpond. Bathing, being a luxury, was discouraged. The life was austere but scarcely ascetic.

The Rule of St.Benedict does not go into great detail. We have fuller pictures of monastic life at a later period in some of the English monasteries, where we learn that baths were allowed three or four times a year. Foot washing was practiced once a week. Tonsures were renewed every three weeks, the old monks receiving first service, while the water was hot and the towels were dry. Straw for mattresses was changed once a year. Linen was washed every two weeks in summer and every three in winter.[8]

The purpose of the monastery, however, was not to ensure comfort, but to honor God by praise and to benefit the community by prayer. The Benedictine rule called for the chanting of the entire Psalter every week. The monks rose at two in the morning and engaged alternately in community worship and private meditation until five, and studied then for four hours, until nine. The next three hours were spent in the fields. The one meal came at noon—the ninth hour, *nona*, whence, noon. Since the day began at six a.m., the ninth was three in the afternoon but, because the monks could not hold out so long for their meal, they simply applied the word noon to the middle of the day. After the meal came a rest period of an hour. Then work again in the fields until compline in the late afternoon and bed at six-thirty, with the older monks sandwiched between the younger to prevent scuffles, and no knives allowed to be kept under pillows. Each monk was allotted a knife, a needle, and a stylus for writing, apart from clothes, of course, but nothing at all was to be privately owned. Property was vested in the monastery. Sunday differed little from other days, because every day was filled with devotions. The daily schedule varied somewhat in accord with the seasons. Benedictine monasticism was not devised either as a tool for missions or for scholarly pursuits but gave, eventually, eminent service to both.

[8] F. H. Crossley, *The English Abbey* (New York, 1936), p. 20.

The first monasteries were located on mountain tops, like Monte Cassino, or on an island, like St.Lérins, removed from barbarian encroachments. The inmates were recruited at first from the older Roman population. The only Goth in Benedict's Monte Cassino was a phenomenon, and not the least because this barbarian was so meek. Just when the barbarians began to enter the monasteries in appreciable numbers we do not know. At first, these lusty warriors viewed monks with incredulity and contempt. One may conjecture that only after monasticism became an active force in society did it appeal to the Germans; and, monasticism did become active. The monks came down from the mountains, or back from the islands, and became the Church's militia in the winning of the West. Their organization suited them admirably for the enterprise, since missionaries had to be self-sustaining. Neither the papacy nor the Church in any Christianized area could deploy their wealth to finance missions in heathen territory because of the breakdown in universal currency, and especially the lack of small coins. In any case, how could a missionary be in close enough touch with his base to replenish his coffers? He was on his own and could survive only out of the largesse of a converted prince or by his own labor, and labor was more productive when carried on by a group. A band of monks would break in a plot of uncultivated soil and establish a community radiating out to those who dwelt nearby.

The role of the monastery as a center for scholarship came gradually. Benedict thought it desirable that his monks should be literate, but only to the extent that they might peruse the Scriptures and the Holy Fathers. That they should become renowned as copiers of manuscripts and as transmitters of ancient culture would have seemed to him a perversion of his purpose. The new development came by stages. Cassiodorus (490–583) envisaged the monastery much more nearly as a school. The Carolingian Renaissance was to give an added impetus and, by relieving the monks of manual labor, provide the time for scholarly pursuits. The ancient distrust of pagan authors was retained in a symbolic gesture, for the sign used by a brother who wished to borrow a copy of a pagan author was to scratch himself behind the ear like a dog. Yet plainly the monks loved the classics; else they would never have copied Seneca, Cicero, Ovid, and Virgil, at a time when the transcription of a single treatise required for parchment the hides of an entire flock of sheep, and for the binding the felling of a deer, a roebuck, or a boar.[9]

The Papacy and the State

The second great institution to foster missions was the papacy. An outsanding figure in this regard was Pope Gregory I (590–604). The title "pope" was not reserved in the West solely for the bishop of Rome until the eleventh century and it was never recognized as his exclusive prerogative in the East. But, in common parlance today, it is applied to all bishops of Rome, beginning with the first. Gregory I occupied the See of Peter in the period just after Justinian, when the sway of the Eastern Empire over the West had again receded and when the Lombards had replaced the Ostrogoths in the north and in other scattered portions of Italy. The Byzantine emperors had not renounced suzerainty, however, and committed the rule of the portions of the peninsula unoccupied by the barbarians to an official called an exarch, with his capital at Ravenna. The Saracen invasion had not yet taken place and the sea lanes were open to the east.

Gregory is important for missions partly because of his direct initiative in instituting the conversion of the Anglo-Saxons in the British Isles, but even more so because he enhanced the prestige of the papacy and increased its allurement among the barbarians. He is often called the first medieval pope because in point of fact he exercised functions that belonged to temporal sovereignty. The papacy was on the way to becoming a temporal power in Italy and

[9] Jean Leclercq, *The Love of Learning and the Desire for God* (New York, Mentor Omega Paperback, 1961), pp. 128–29.

a director of kings in the lands beyond. Culturally, Gregory was oriented toward the West and did not acquire a knowledge of Greek.

Conditions in Rome in his day warranted the cry, "Fallen, fallen is Babylon the great!" The sack by Alaric in 410 had been followed by even more drastic pillaging by the Vandals and Goths. Marble statues were smashed, and stone heads, limbs, and torsos were strewed over the weed-clogged cobblestone pavements. More serious was the cutting of aqueducts by the barbarians, so that the higher regions of the city were deprived of water, while the leakage from the breaches in the conduits filled the campagna with malarial swamps. Disease infested the city. Gregory, then a papal deacon, led a penitential procession through the streets to appease the divine displeasure. As the dirgeful suppliants approached the bridge before the mausoleum of Hadrian, Gregory saw above the tomb the Archangel Michael with a flaming sword, which he sheathed in token of an end to the plague. Thereafter, the sepulchre of the Roman emperor was called *Il Castello di Sant'Angelo*, the Castle of the Holy Angel. In the Middle Ages, it became the fortress of the popes. Today, it is a museum, and the statue of the Holy Angel on its summit is overtopped by a radio transmitter.

During the plague, the pope died and Gregory was chosen to succeed him, quite against his inclination, for he would have vastly preferred instead to be a monk of St.Benedict. Well might he tremble, because at that moment the pope was called upon to assume an appalling burden. The Lombards to the north were continually extending their sway, and refugees poured into Rome. Gregory records that the Church in the capital was supporting three thousand nuns, the majority of whom could scarcely have been permanent residents of the city. And then, there was the problem of the normal residents. For centuries the government had supplied them with "bread and circuses," but now the government at Byzantium, with its exarch at Ravenna, was unable to land grain ships from Africa or the islands. Moreover, the Lombards frequently captured members of the Roman populace and held them for ransom. The emperor had not the funds to redeem them.

At this point, the Church stepped in. Her resources were astounding and available for use in areas where transport was not impeded by enemies or by natural barriers like the Alps, and where currency was viable. The Church had grainlands in Sicily and Sardinia, forests in Brutium and Calabria, and possessions even in Istria. She was able to charter vessels to bring grain to Rome from the islands, ship lumber to churches in Egypt, or blankets to the monks at Mount Sinai, but it was even more to the point that she had the money to ransom prisoners from the Lombards. How did the Church come to have such enormous possessions? We cannot answer in detail, but the obvious explanation, which covers everything, is donations. Philanthropy had come to be regarded as a good work, contributory to salvation. In the administration of this wealth, the papacy became as extensive an organization as that of the imperial officials in Italy, but considerably more efficient. Gregory's letters crackle with commands and reprimands. Here are examples of questions submitted by subordinates to the pope, and his answers: A man has bequeathed to the Church an amber cup and a boy slave to cover his funeral expenses. But the cup was not his. What then? Answer: In civil law a bequest is inalienable. If it was not owned by the deceased, his legal heir must recompense the owner. But, since the Church does not operate according to civil law, the cup must be returned; in any case, no charge should be made for funerals. A second case: Inasmuch as a Christian slave cannot be held by a non-Christian, what shall be done in the case of a Christian slave freed because his master was a Samaritan, who thereupon became a Christian and demanded him back. Answer: By no means may he claim his return. A third case: Money has been borrowed to redeem captives and cannot be repaid. May the sacred vessels of the Church be sold to meet the debt? Answer: They may.[10]

Some of the activities of Gregory belonged normally to the

[10] Gregory I, *Epistulae* vii, 13; viii, 6 and 21.

state, but the exarch at Ravenna was not able either to feed Rome or to ransom prisoners. The assumption of these burdens by the Church led further to political negotiations and treaties with the Lombards. The emperor at Constantinople fulminated against usurpation of power, but the pope paid the bills. The rise of the temporal power of papacy is commonly assigned to the middle of the eighth century, but what happened was only a formal recognition of what had existed already in fact and to a degree for a century and a half.

Gregory was at the same time equally concerned for the internal administration and spiritual life of the Church. "Walls," said he, "are dried before the roof is put on, and for the roof the wood must be seasoned. Shall we exercise less care in the choice of the clergy?"[11] As a theologian, Gregory is reckoned as one of the great doctors of the Church. He first formulated the doctrine of purgatory, which played so large a part in the religion of the Middle Ages. He was interested in the liturgy and is credited with the chants called Gregorian. His pontificate was a notable example of the role played by the Church in disordered times when government by the empire had so nearly collapsed.

The third institution that supported Christian missions was the civil state. Sometimes the king of a barbarian people would adopt simply a policy of non-interference, leaving the missionary to operate unimpeded in his territory. Sometimes the king himself would embrace the faith without coercing his subjects. On occasion, however, kings did force their people. In the case of lands beyond his own, the king might furnish a missionary with credentials such as to make him almost an envoy. Once, and once only, constraint was applied to convert a conquered people. Examples will be given as we proceed.

In the process of the conversion of barbarian kingdoms, the role of queens is not to be ignored. Not infrequently a Teutonic king would choose as his queen a daughter of old Roman stock

[11] *Ibid.*, v, 53.

and she would press upon her husband the claims of the Roman faith. Such a union on the part of a sovereign was a phase of the marriage of cultures.

Ireland

The first of the northern lands to be evangelized was not one invaded by barbarians, but one that itself had hitherto always been barbarian, namely, Ireland. The conversion of this land is attributed to Patrick, early in the fifth century. In nearly every country one single figure, like Ulfilas, garnered all the credit for what must have been the work of many. For France the accolade is given to Clovis late in the fifth century, for England to Augustine of Canterbury early in the seventh, for Germany to Boniface in the eighth, in the case of Denmark to Ansgar in the ninth, for Bulgaria and Moravia to Cyril and Methodius, also in the ninth, for Norway to the two Olafs in the tenth, and for Russia to Vladimir at the turn of the eleventh. The historian, who cannot recover from the archives of heaven the names of the many who assisted, can do no more than record the traditions as to the few.

We are fortunate, however, to have a brief autobiography from the pen of Patrick, a Briton of the early fifth century. When the Roman legions were withdrawn for the defense of the Continent, the Irish, then called Scots, began swooping on the English coast, sailing up the rivers, raiding the settlements, and carrying off plunder and slaves. Among the captives was Patrick. He had been reared a Christian. His father was a deacon, but Patrick's religion sat lightly until, as a swineherd, he prayed ardently for his release. He managed to escape and found his way to the coast where a ship carrying a cargo of hounds was about to sail for France. Commerce, evidently, had not been entirely disrupted. Patrick was taken aboard to look after the dogs. On the Continent, the company traveled for days without meeting anyone until they ran out of food. The commander suggested that the Christian, Patrick, supplicate his God. This he did, and a drove of pigs appeared. Patrick felt he had earned his passage, slipped away, and soon came upon a monastery. From there he managed somehow to beg or work his way home. The joy of his family turned to dismay when in a dream he was summoned by the unborn children of Ireland to return there with the good news of the Gospel. First, however, he went to the Continent for training and was detained there for fourteen years as unsuited to the task, because of his *rusticitas*. His persistence won, and in the end he did go with papal authorization and the status of a bishop.

At this point his account ends, and from then on we have only legends. From our knowledge of what happened later in Ireland, we can make some inferences as to what must have preceded. Patrick went as a bishop. A century later the entire structure of the Church in Ireland was monastic. Presumably, the monastic community, maintaining itself on the land, better fitted an agrarian culture and tribal economy than the parish-church system. Another point of great significance is that Patrick brought to Ireland the Latin language, thereby making her a participant in the classical heritage. Ireland was made Roman not by the military, but by the missionaries. This expansion of Latinity was a contributing factor to the survival of Latinity. On the Continent, Latin was in the process of being transformed into the Romance tongues and was preserved from complete submergence only because the Church had retained it for liturgical and official documents and the state followed suit. Yet the danger was always at hand that even this Latin would be corrupted by the emergent vernaculars. There was no such danger in Ireland where the native speech was Gaelic. Here, Latin continued separate and undefiled, to be brought back to the Continent, after subsequent invasions, by Irish monks.

Gaul

At the time when in the East the non-Greek elements were splintering from the orthodox Empire, in the West a barbarian kingdom embraced the orthodox faith. The key figures were King Clovis and Queen Clothilda. The story of their conversion, as narrated in the next generation by Gregory of Tours, ascribes the initiative to the queen. Clothilda had long reasoned with her husband, telling him that his gods were mere idols, and the stories about them most indecent. Curiously, as Gregory reports her arguments, she was inveighing against the unnatural amours of the Roman gods rather than against those of the Teutonic deities to which her husband adhered. Clothilda spoke to him of the one God, who, out of nothing had created heaven and earth, who adorned the firmament with stars, who caused the air, the earth, and the waters to teem with life, who bedecked the land with verdure, who created man and sustains him as his own. Clovis replied, "Nonsense!" yet allowed their first son to be baptized. The babe died in his baptismal robes. Clovis blamed the baptism, but Clothilda rejoiced that God had taken a soul directly from her womb to enjoy eternal bliss. Another son was born, baptized and fell sick. Clovis claimed that baptism would kill him, too, but the mother prayed and he recovered. Then, Clovis was engaged in a battle with the Alamanni and in danger of being wiped out. He cried, "Jesus Christ, Clothilda says thou art the son of the living God, and thou canst give victory to those who hope in thee. Give me victory and I will be baptized. I have tried my gods and they have deserted me. I call on thee. Only save me." The king of the Alamanni fell and his army fled. Clovis returned and told Clothilda.

She then summoned Bishop Remigius (St.Remi) of Rheims, who exhorted the king to renounce his gods. "Yes, holy father," said Clovis, "but my people will not consent. However, I will speak to them." He did so, and with one accord they renounced the mortal gods. The baptistry was hung with tapestries, fragrant candles flared, the aroma of incense filled the shrine with divine fragrance so that many thought they were amid the odors of paradise. Clovis advanced like another Constantine to the baptismal font and the bishop said, "Bend your neck. Worship what you burned and burn what you worshiped." Then the king was baptized in the name of the Father and of the Son and of the Holy Ghost and anointed with the holy oil, the oil of Clovis, the sacred oil which gave divine sanction to the monarchy of France. And with Clovis were baptized three thousand of his army, presumably by sprinkling.[12]

What lay behind this unsophisticated account? Some think that Clovis made an astute political move. He was not yet master of Gaul. The other kingdoms, such as those of the Alamanni and Burgundians, and in the south those of the Visigoths, were Arian. Clovis had passed directly from paganism to Nicene orthodoxy. Was this, or was this not, politically astute? It eliminated the possibility of an Arian confederation, but Clovis did not want a confederation. He wanted a conquest. If divergence in faith provoked hostility, so much the better. In this conflict he would have the support of the old Romans in his own territory, and they constituted presumably about eighty per cent of the population, and in the territories he aspired to conquer he would have the sympathy of those of the Nicene faith. On the whole, it would appear that for the conquest of Gaul the move was strategic and it did succeed.

The conversion of Clovis had far-reaching consequences. Gaul became thereby the highway to the north for the militia of the Church. If the king of the Franks had been hostile, missionaries from Rome would have had great difficulty in passing to Britain, Germany, and Scandinavia. These points in the conversion of the Franks may all be assigned to the credit side in the conversion of Europe, but there were also debits.

[12] Gregory of Tours, *History of the Franks* (New York, 1927), II, pp. 30–31.

The mass conversion entailed the paganizing of Christianity. There are two ways in which missions can proceed, one of which is the way of individual conversion with a goodly period of instruction prior to baptism. This has been in general the technique of Protestant missions under the great revivalist movements of the eighteenth century, with their emphasis upon individual change of heart. The disadvantage of this method is that the Christian converts in a pagan culture become, by reason of their change in faith, deracinated from their own culture and compelled to move into an alien enclave. The other method is mass conversion and it was this method which converted Europe. Kings like Clovis embraced the faith. Their people followed suit by acclamation. This meant that individuals were not deracinated, but it also meant that the converts brought with them into the Church their old beliefs and mores.

Mores

This is evident in many instances, starting with Clovis himself. Jesus was for him a tribal war god, a new Yahweh of hosts. The Franks martialized St.Peter, whose noblest exploit in their eyes was that to protect the Lord Jesus he had wielded his broadsword and sliced off the ear of the high priest's servant.[13] The Archangel Michael of the flaming sword became a heavenly champion and his name was given to the Norman citadel, Mont St.Michel. St.Denis took charge of France's particular fortunes, with some help from St.Martin, who had once been a soldier himself. Similarly, St.George, a military saint, became the patron of England, and St.James the patron saint of Christian Spain in the struggle against Islam.

After the nominal conversion, the mores of the Frankish aristocracy, lay and clerical, fell appallingly short of Christian stand-

[13] *Heliand*, German translation K. L. Kannegiesser (Berlin, 1847), pp. 145-46.

ards. The behavior of kings and queens, of bishops and their wives (the bishop was called *episcopus,* his wife, *episcopissa*), would have shamed the gods of Olympus, not only for sexual irregularities but for stark brutality. A queen requested the execution of two physicians if they failed to cure her disease. She died and the king fulfilled her request. A duke buried alive his servant and a maid because they had married without his consent. A priest who obdurately refused to surrender some property to the bishop of Clermont was buried alive, together with a corpse. Despite the frightful stench, he managed to breathe through a crack which let in light and also disclosed a broken tool with which he pried off the lid and escaped. The bishop of Le Mans thought it ridiculous that because he was a cleric he should not avenge himself. The laity did not regard the clergy as sacrosanct, and some of the parishioners of the bishop of Rouen murdered him at the altar. Gregory of Tours, the narrator of these events, was once standing before the palace of King Chilperic with the bishop of Albi, who asked him what he saw on top of the palace. Gregory, who had grown inured to atrocities, answered placidly, "A roof." The other replied, "I see the naked sword of the wrath of God."[14]

The people in general were perhaps not as bad as their leaders. They were certainly pious. Churches and monasteries were built in great numbers. Unhappily, few survive because of later invasions. More is left of Visigothic Spain than of Merovingian Gaul. Every Sunday the bells summoned the populace to Matins and to Mass. The throngs in the churches were such that King Guntram feared to attend without a guard, lest an assassin lurk amid the mob. The laity received daily the bread and wine from the altar.

Vast possessions came into the hands of the Church. In the Merovingian period, the churches and monasteries held from one-quarter to one-third of all the land in the kingdom. The same causes were operative here as earlier in Italy. Rulers made use of churchmen in administration because they constituted the only

[14] These details are from Gregory of Tours, *History of the Franks,* abundantly assembled in Hauck, *op. cit.,* Vol. I.

learned class. The bishops and abbots resembled the counts and dukes in their status, function, and behavior, the more so because ecclesiastical property was no longer vested in the Church as a corporation, but personally in the hands of bishops or abbots. In extremities, kings, notably Charles Martel, confiscated the lands of the Church to finance the repulse of the Saracens, but new donations replenished her holdings and the total tended to be constant. The king used the despoiled lands of the Church to reward services by the nobles, while the nobles, in turn, gave to the Church.

The faith of the populace centered on Christ the heavenly ruler, rather than the suffering redeemer. These lusty barbarians were not oppressed by any deep sense of sin and the consequent need of redemption. They required rather to be ruled and defended. The saints, with their particular assignments, may well have meant more to the people than Christ, the universal redeemer. St.Anthony took care of pigs, St.Saturninus of sheep, St.Gall looked after hens, and St.Medardus protected vines from frost. St.Apollonia, whose jaw had been broken in the persecution, cured the toothache, St.Hubert was responsible for hydrophobia, St.Geneviève cured fever, and St.Blaise was responsible for sore throats. A ribbon inscribed with the name of St.Aimable, if wrapped around the wrist of a child, prevented nightmare.[15]

Many were the tales circulating about the miraculous powers of the saints. The story was told of two beggars, one lame, the other blind. They happened to be caught in a procession carrying the relics of St.Martin and were fearful lest they be cured and so deprived of their alms. The one who could see but not walk mounted the shoulders of the one who could walk but not see, and they hurried to get beyond the range of the saint's miraculous powers, but, poor fellows, they failed to make it. The saints were often more potent dead than alive. Hence the great concern to possess their relics, be it even the wisp of a beard or the parings of fingernails. Holy men exercised extraordinary powers before they died. Witness the case of a bishop whose church was in a blaze.

[15] Émile Mâle, *The Gothic Image* (New York, 1958), p. 228.

He went to the altar and wept so copiously that the fire was extinguished.

The conversion of the Franks, however superficial, by a direct course from paganism to Nicene orthodoxy led, in the fifth century, to a very close rapport between this people and the papacy, eventuating in the eighth century in a religio-political alliance. The development was quite different in the case of the Lombards in northern Italy, the Visigoths in Spain, and the Vandals in Africa. The Arian Lombards accepted Nicene orthodoxy nearly a century after the conversion of the Franks, when Queen Theodolinda, prompted by Pope Gregory I, induced her husband Agilulf to make this change. But unity in the faith, in this instance, did not lead to friendly neighborly relations, for the Lombards continued to harass papal lands until their kingdom was absorbed by the Franks in the eighth century.

The Visigoths survived in Spain until the Mohammedan invasion. After their conversion from Arianism to orthodoxy under King Reccared in 598, a century after Clovis, they exhibited speedily a pattern, intermittently recurrent in Spanish history, of fanatical orthodoxy, close association of Church and state, and great independence from Rome. All three of these aspects were connected with the preceding Arianism, even though they were in part opposed to it. The fanatical orthodoxy was a reaction against the previous heresy. One may suspect that the Visigoths, in order to vindicate their own theological rectitude, were much harsher toward the Jews than were the Merovingians. But the other two points showed a continuance of the Arian pattern. Among the Arian tribes, the priest had been attached to the ruler, the Church to the crown, with no dependence upon a universal ecclesiastical authority. Adherence to orthodoxy on the part of the Visigoths did not alter the alliance of the Church with the state, nor did it induce a disposition to take directives from Rome.

The Vandals did not enter the picture as possible allies of the papacy. They adhered to their Arianism, as we have noted, until submerged by the Moslem invasion. Reasons have already been advanced as to why they were absorbed by Islam. A further explanation sometimes adduced is that the Arian Christ, being only a glorified Viking, could not withstand Allah and his Prophet.

The Irish Monks Columbanus and Columba

Returning now to the Continent, Ireland repaid her debt in the sixth century, when some of her monks came to arrest the anemia of a semi-pagan Christianity by a new transfusion. They came not as missionaries, for the land was already ostensibly Christian. They came because as monks they desired to make the supreme sacrifice of living and dying away from home. But men of such dedication, by their very deportment, were a rebuke to bishops who committed murder in the cathedral. The most notable among these monks was Columbanus, who founded a monastery at Luxeuil in 590. He speedily infuriated the Gallic clergy who took more seriously a divergence in liturgy than a lapse in morals. The quarrel had to do with the celebration of Easter and was called, in memory of the earlier dispute, the Quartodeciman Controversy, though the point now in question was not the date but merely the calculation of the date for the celebration. Ireland still followed the old reckoning in vogue in Patrick's day, whereas on the Continent, in the intervening period, Rome had made progress in devising a more accurate reckoning. The difference was the mark of Ireland's long severance from the Continent by reason of the invasions. The result was that the monks of Luxeuil might be fasting during Lent while the Gallic clergy were feasting after Easter. Columbanus was anachronistic when he insisted on the Irish practice, but not so when he scathingly denounced the conduct of the son of Queen Brunehild. Columbanus, in consequence, was driven out of the Frankish kingdom and went to Italy where he founded the monastery of Bobbio. His disciple, St.Gall, established a monastery, known by his name, in Switzerland.

The British Isles

Coincidentally, missionary activity was being directed to the British Isles. Before Columbanus went to the Continent, Columba had gone from Ireland to Scotland in 563, where he established a monastery at Iona. After the conversion of the king, the saint and his disciples won the Gaelic Scots, who were then called the Picts. One contribution of these Irish monks was the innovation of rhyme in Latin poetry which, hitherto, had been based on vowel quantity.

The Gaelic Irish were ready to convert the Gaelic Scots, but there was at first no disposition on the part of any of the Celts to convert the Anglo-Saxons, who, unlike other barbarians, had not suffered the conquered to stay in the land but, in England, had pushed them into Wales, Cornwall, and Lancashire. The first move for conversion came from the Celts in Scotland who had not been displaced. The missionary was Aidan, who worked down from the north into Northumbria.

In the meantime, the Church of Rome initiated a movement working up from the south. Gregory the Great, already encountered, sent forth St.Augustine, called Augustine of Canterbury, to distinguish him from Augustine of Hippo. He commenced in Kent under the favor of Queen Bertha, another of those Christian queens eager to convert a pagan husband. King Ethelbert was willing to grant an audience but only out of doors, where Augustine would be less able to exercise his magical powers, for he was reputed to be able to make tails grow on the backs of those with whom he was displeased. The king was so far persuaded that he granted land for the foundation of a monastery at Canterbury, ever after to be the seat of the English primate. Successors of Augustine worked further north, in particular Paulinus in Northumbria. By the time of King Oswy, in the late seventh century, the two missionary thrusts converged, the followers of Aidan working toward the south and those of Augustine toward the north. Oswy's queen was from the south and followed the Roman practice as to Easter, but Oswy had received his Christian impetus from the north and observed the Celtic practice. The discord between feasting and fasting had reached even unto the king's very household. There were also other points in dispute. The monks of the Roman observance shaved their heads on top, leaving a rim of hair above the ears in token of the crown of thorns, whereas the Irish, perhaps in imitation of the Druids, shaved up to a tuft on the crown. Such trivial practices symbolized the independence of Celtic Christianity from Rome. Oswy brought the matter to a decision at the Synod of Whitby in 664. The Celtic advocate appealed to the authority of Columba, the Romans to that of Peter, to whom Christ gave the keys. "Is that really so?" Oswy asked of the Celtic defender. He, of course, acquiesced. Oswy promptly resolved to take no chances of alienating the doorkeeper of heaven. One is not to suppose that all differences automatically ceased, but the trend was toward unification. The British Isles moved back into the orbit of Rome.

The Mohammedans

But in the meantime Spain was lost. In 711, Taric led the hosts of Allah across the Straits of Gibraltar, and before him fell Roderick, the last of the Visigothic kings. In accord with the general Muslim practice already observed, the natives were not forced to give up their religion. Jews and Christians might worship as they would, but they must pay heavier taxes. The Jews found such pressure less onerous than the persecution they had endured under the fanatical Visigoths. For the Christians, of course, there was a complete reversal in status. In consequence, some renounced their faith and then entered into all the privileges of the Muslim. Such Christians were known as *renegados*. Those who remained faithful were known as Mozarabs. The Arabic government underwent a change in the eighth century, when the Omayyad dynasty in

Bagdad was supplanted by the Abbasids. A prince of the Omayyads, escaping, went to Spain and there overthrew the native government. Under the new dynasty, the culture of the Saracens reached a pinnacle far loftier than any in contemporary Christian Europe. The relations of Mohammedans, Christians, and Jews were intermittently hostile or friendly. There were wars in plenty, but sometimes Christian and Muslim fought on the same side against Muslim and Christian on the other. The Christians, however, were never entirely subjugated, and in the northernmost provinces of Galicia, Navarre, Aragon, and Castile they maintained themselves at first in mountain fastnesses and then began to push south for the *Reconquista*. Not even in the period when the crusading spirit was driving the unbelievers either to Africa or to the faith were the cultural relations altogether severed. The great Arab philosopher Averroes (1126–1198) was to have far-reaching influence on Christian thought, even beyond the confines of Spain.[16]

---

[16] Pius Bonifacius Gams, *Die Kirchengeschichte von Spanien* (Regensburg, 1862–79).

36. ST. AMBROSE

36

This mosaic of St. Ambrose from the church named after him, S. Ambrogio, in his own city of Milan, dates from the first half of the fifth century. Since he lived to A.D. 397, it may very well embody some sketches or reminiscences of his actual appearance. Pure imagination would hardly have made so formidable a figure look so innocuous. On the other hand, churchmen were often portrayed by stereotypes, and one cannot be certain that this is a true likeness.

37. THE WISE MEN AMONG THE OSTROGOTHS

37

This mosaic from the church of S. Appolinare Nuovo at Ravenna, mounted by order of Theodoric the Ostrogoth, and dedicated in A.D. 549, affords a striking example of the fusion of cultures in the barbarian kingdom. The style is Byzantine, the inscription is Latin (notice the abbreviation for Sanctus), the names Balthazar, Melchior, and Gaspar (at the time only recently introduced) are of diverse origin. Melchior, meaning "king of light," is Hebrew; Balthazar is Babylonian and is mentioned in the book of Daniel; Gaspar is presumably Persian. The most striking feature is that the Wise Men wear Germanic trousers. (Cf. Hugo Kehrer, *Die heiligen drei Könige in Literatur und Kunst* [Leipzig, 1908].)

38. ST. MARTIN

St. Martin, who always appears in Christian art dividing his cloak with a beggar, was born in Pannonia in A.D. 316. His father, displeased by his conversion to Christianity, put him in the army. He served in northern Gaul for five years. At the age of eighteen, when he was stationed at Amiens, he saw a naked beggar in the snow and, to the jeers of his barracks' companions, divided with him his cloak. That night he is alleged to have had a vision of Christ wearing the portion of the cloak with which he had parted. St. Martin later secured his release from the army and began his career in the Church. (Cf. Herbert B. Workman, *The Evolution of the Monastic Ideal* [London, 1913], p. 105.)

39a

Ulfilas or Wulfilas (ca. A.D. 311–383, the name is of Germanic origin) translated the Scriptures into the Gothic language, the ancestor of the Germanic tongues. A number of copies of his translation are extant. The most complete dates from about A.D. 500, and is preserved at Uppsala, Sweden. It is called the *Codex Argenteus* because it was written with silver letters on a purple background.

ᚢᛁᚺᚾᚨᛁ	ᚾᚨᛗᛟ ᚦᛖᛁᚾ·	ᛩᛁᛗᚨᛁᚢᛁᛏᚨᛁ
veihnai	namo thein	quimai thivdi
HALLOWED	NAME THINE	COME KING-

nassus / theins· / vairthai vilja
DOM / THINE / BE DONE WILL.

theins· / sve in himina jah ana
THINE / AS IN HEAVEN SO ON

airthai· / hlaif vnsarana thanasin
EARTH / BREAD OURS THIS DAI-

teinan gif uns himma daga·
LY GIVE US THIS DAY.

39b

Ulfilas devised an alphabet by using the letters common to Greek and Latin. Where they differ, he followed the Greek for g, d, and l, but the Latin for f. Some of the characters are runic; for example, the sign for th. One may observe in the brief example here from the Lord's Prayer (Matt. 6:10-11) cognates to words in German, Scandinavian, and English (e.g.: *namo* = name, *thein* = thine, *vilja* = will, *himina* = heaven, *ana* = on, *airthai* = earth, *hlaif* = loaf, *gif* = give, *uns* = us, *daga* = day).

40. ST. BENEDICT

40

St. Benedict's Monte Cassino, though withdrawn from the lowlands ravaged by Totila the Goth, did not escape the notice of this barbarian chieftain, who had heard that the saint was endowed with the gift of prophecy. Wishing to test him, Totila dressed his captain Reggio in his own royal apparel, and sent him to St. Benedict, pretending he was the king. But as soon as Reggio came within earshot, St. Benedict called out, "Take off those clothes. They are not yours." Reggio fell to the ground, but his companions returned to report to Totila, who then came himself and likewise prostrated himself before the saint. Benedict, raising him, took him to task for his cruelty; Totila is said to have been more humane thereafter. The drawing is from the painting by Aretino Spinello in the sacristy of San Miniato in Florence, painted ca. 1360. (Cf. Henry B. Washburn, *Men of Conviction* [New York, 1931].)

41. FOUNDING OF MONASTIC ORDERS

St. Benedict gives to Abbot John a copy of the Rule, which was to remain normative, with a few variations, for about a thousand years. The illustration is a miniature in *Codex 278* at Monte Cassino. The date is not given.

42. ST. GREGORY THE GREAT

Pope Gregory I is always represented in Christian art with the dove of the Holy Spirit on his shoulder communicating divine truth.

43. OCCUPATIONS OF THE MONKS

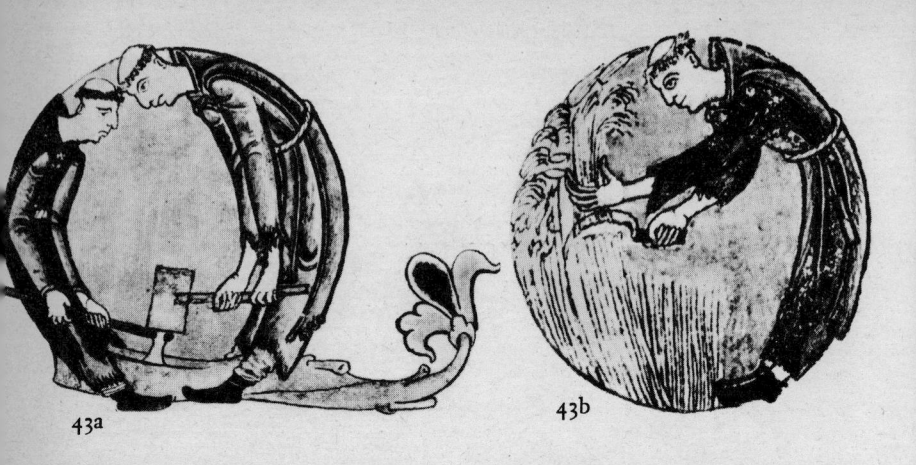

Fig. 43a: Splitting wood. Fig. 43b: Reaping. Fig. 43c: Copying. Fig. 43d: Illuminating.

44. THE ALBA BIBLE

44

Cultural and religious interchange between Christians and Jews continued intermittently into the first half of the fifteenth century. Witness the Bible of the house of Alba, a translation of the Old Testament made by Rabbi Moses Arragel between 1422 and 1430 at the request of Don Luis Guzman, Lord of Algaba and Grand Master of the military order of Calatrava. The Vulgate was taken as the base and errors were corrected. The comments of the rabbi show him versed not only in Hebrew but also in classical and Christian writings. This Bible passed into the possession of the house of Alba in the seventeenth century. It was published in 1920 under the title *Biblia (antiguo testamento) traducida del Hebreo al Castellano por Rabi Mose Arragel de Guadalajara (1422–33?). Y publicada por el Duque de Berwick y de Alba*, 2 vols., 1920.

This illustration from it shows in the lower panel its presentation by Rabbi Moses to the duke, who is surrounded by knights of the order of Calatrava wearing crosses. The rabbi wears on his shoulder what appears to be the badge distinguishing the Jews, which was no more distinctive than the cross, except that the latter was voluntary, the former imposed. In the upper panel are displayed works of mercy performed by the Christian knights for the Jews. St. Francis and St. Dominic are depicted standing as witnesses on the sidelines. Note that the Christians are all shaven, the Jews bearded.

45

Frank's casket, a little box carved in whalebone, takes its name from the donor of the relic to the British Museum about one hundred years ago. A missing side was later found at Florence. The language of the inscriptions is in part Latin, in part the Anglian dialect of Anglo-Saxon carved in runic characters. The casket was formerly assigned to Northumbria and dated ca. A.D. 700, but the most recent study contends that by its form the language points to about the middle of the sixth century; since at that time England was not capable of producing such work, the casket must have originated in Merovingian Gaul, where a colony of refugee Angles was then settled on the left bank of the Loire. King Theudebert had sent one

CASKET

of them as an ambassador to the court of Justinian, where it is assumed he learned the art of bone carving. The subjects depicted are for the most part clear: Romulus and Remus, Titus' capture of Jerusalem, an adventure of Achilles, and, according to a recent investigator, the story of Balder, the Nordic god of the dying and arising vegetation.

The side shown here consists of two panels. On the right are the Wise Men in pantaloons, the one in front carrying a vessel topped with three coins, indicating the gold, the next carrying a pot of burning incense, and the third, by elimination, must be offering myrrh. They are led by a bird much like a goose. The word MEXI inscribed above them is a form of Magi. Mary and Jesus are enthroned, faces forward, eyes turned to the right, in a combination of the Syrian frontal and the Hellenistic profile styles. The star is a large rosette.

The left panel relates the Nordic myth of Wayland the smith, who was forced to work solely for the king by having his tendons cut at the knees. He revenged himself by luring the king's sons to pluck birds and bring him the feathers, from which he made wings for his escape. Then he killed the boys and made goblets out of their skulls. He induced the king's daughter to bring him a beaker of beer, which he drugged and gave her to drink. He then assaulted her and fled. In the panel he stands over his forge holding tongs, a decapitated prince at his feet. The daughter appears twice, bringing the beaker and reaching for the drink. To the right are the plucked birds. Did the artist mean to contrast this gory tale of vengeance with the advent of the Prince of Peace? Was he a pagan who added a bit of Christian lore to his mythology or a Christian who thought all history led up to Christ? (Cf. Karl Schneider, "Zu den Inschriften und Bildern des Franks Casket," *Festschrift für Walther Fischer* [Heidelberg, 1959], pp. 4–21. See also Philip Webster Souers, "The Magi on the Frank's Casket," *Harvard Studies and Notes in Philology*, XIX [1937], pp. 249–54; and "The Wayland Scene on Frank's Casket," *Speculum*, XVIII [1943], pp. 104–11.)

VI

The Quest for Order

SARACEN advances had been arrested by the middle of the eighth century and the invasion of the continental Germanic tribes was spent. During an interlude of relative freedom from external pressures, prior to the Viking invasions, there began in Europe a process of consolidation marked by the strengthening of the kingdom of the Franks, the conversion of Germanic tribes, the linking of the northern churches with Rome, the centralizing of papal power, and the cementing of an alliance between the kingdom of the Franks and the papacy.

Consolidation of Power

In the first phase of the consolidation of a new order, the central figures were the Frankish King Pepin and an Anglo-Saxon missionary called Winfrith, lover of peace, in his native tongue, and in Latin, Boniface, the doer of good. In his person the newly converted Saxons in England were undertaking, without any prompting from Rome, to convert their northern neighbors. Boniface is called the apostle of Germany, though actually he was not the first missionary in the area and might better be called an organizer rather than an originator. He traveled far, beginning in Frisia and reaching as far as Hesse, Bavaria, and Saxony. What is most amazing is that his Anglo-Saxon speech should have been intelligible over so vast an expanse. We read of his addressing thousands, but never is there any mention of an interpreter. These

Teutons, despite political division, had a more integrated culture than that of the Roman Empire, where Greek had never supplanted Armenian, Syriac, and Coptic in the East, and Latin had not expelled Punic, Basque, and Gaelic in the West. All these Germans had one basic tongue, and the Bible of Ulfilas could serve them all. The fact that it was the work of an Arian did not disqualify it as a translation.

Boniface was a great integrator. He brought together England and the Continent. He brought together France and Germany, for the Merovingian kings gladly gave him all the benefit of their prestige. He brought together the churches of the north and Rome. Whereas the proprietary churches in the north were inclined to look rather to their patrons than to the pope, Boniface took an oath of allegiance to Rome and called upon the churches of Gaul to profess likewise their fidelity. Boniface combined in his own person the secular and the regular forms of the ministry. The term "secular" was applied to those of the clergy who served in the world (*saeculum*), whether as priests, bishops, archbishops, or popes. The "regular" referred to those who observed the monastic rule (*regula*). Boniface was a secular as the archbishop of Mainz, a regular as the founder of the monastery of Fulda.

Finally, Boniface had a great influence on the relations of Church and state. It was he who cemented the alliance of the papacy with the kingdom of the Franks. The popes needed some strong defender. They were still menaced by the Lombards, but their most persistent threat came from the populace of Rome itself. Now that the papacy had come to represent wealth and prestige, the great Roman families desired to have their own members elected to the office. Papal elections were often attended by riots resulting from family feuds. The pope had no armies of his own with which to suppress them. Where could he turn for a defender of St.Peter, if not to some political power? The Lombard king obviously could not assume the role, for he himself was threatening to seize Rome. Africa and Spain had both succumbed to Islam. The emperor at Constantinople was not only busy fighting the Avars and the Turks, but was also quarreling with the popes, who resisted iconoclasm and were infuriated by the threat that imperial troops would come and smash the image of St.Peter. Help might be expected only from Gaul, the land of Clovis, the oldest of the orthodox kingdoms, and the only important Christian power in western Europe. The popes looked to Gaul in times of molestation.

Gaul had troubles of its own. Although the decadent Merovingian kings had been anointed with the oil of Clovis, the actual administration of the kingdom was assumed by the mayors of the King's palace. Charles Martel, who had repulsed the Saracens near Tours in 732, was one of this able line of palace administrators. Nineteen years after the battle, Charles's son, Pepin the Short, considered the time to be both propitious and imperative to bring the actual power and the title into conjunction through divine sanction. But how? How indeed, if not through the papacy, the institution which administered the sanction of the divine in the name of that saint to whom had been given the power to bind and to loose? But Peter's successor was at some distance removed However, an emissary happened to be at hand in the person of Boniface, by whom the crown was conferred on Pepin with papal approval in 752. The rite was later repeated by Pope Stephen II. In all this, there was no claim that the pope conferred authority. He was really only recognizing authority. But he did convey something that was evidently worth having, and the inference was that without such sanction the monarchy would be invalid.

Pepin repaid his debt. Journeying to Rome, he disciplined the Lombards and brought order to the capital. Then he conferred upon the pope political authority over a strip of Italy that ran from Rome over the Apennines to Ravenna, a territory called Pentapolis because it embraced five cities whose keys the king laid upon the tomb of St.Peter. One of those cities was Ravenna, the seat of the exarch of the Eastern emperor. To confer this city upon the pope was tantamount to a declaration of independence from the Second Rome. Pepin's act, in 754, is called the Donation of Pepin, and is commonly regarded as the beginning of the temporal power of the papacy. But, as we have noted, this can be regarded as correct only in the formal sense, inasmuch as the popes had long been exercising essentially political functions.

The theory underlying the behavior of the pope and the king was not made explicit. Centuries earlier, in 494, Pope Gelasius, concerned to ward off any interference in the affairs of the Church by the Byzantine emperors, had made a pronouncement regarding the relation of spiritual and civil powers. Gelasius insisted upon their mutual independence. At the same time, however, he stressed the superiority of the spiritual power, to the degree that the things of the spirit and the life to come are superior to the things of the body and the life terrestrial. Yet, however little Stephen and Pepin were disposed to theorize, an anonymous forger at this time produced a document, the so-called Donation of Constantine, destined to buttress the Church's authority for centuries. According to this spurious treatise, Constantine, in his heathen days, suffering from leprosy, was advised by his priests to bathe in the blood of babies. The humane sovereign shrank from the cruelty. In consequence, Peter and Paul appeared to him in a vision and instructed him to seek out Sylvester, the bishop of Rome, who was in hiding. Sylvester baptized the emperor, who was thereby completely cured and who then withdrew to Constantinople, saying that the imperial dignity should not detract by its presence from the papal. He conferred upon the pope primacy over Antioch, Constantinople, Alexandria, and Jerusalem, and temporal jurisdiction over the whole of the West.

Not until the Renaissance was it shown that Constantine had done nothing of the kind. The document was a forgery. In considering the ethical standards of this forger and of others like him in the next century, we should realize that in antiquity men sought to gain authority for their convictions by attaching them to a great name, rather than prestige for themselves by avowing their authorship. Thus the Jews attributed their laws to Moses and their psalms to David, and the earlier Christians sometimes ascribed to the apostles books that modern scholarship considers of uncertain authorship.

Charlemagne

A more dramatic encounter between the kingdom of the Franks and the papacy occurred under Pepin's son and successor, Charles, known as Charlemagne. The need for aid in this instance was more obvious on the side of the Church than on that of the state. The Lombard menace continued until Charlemagne put an end to the Lombard kingdom. The emperors at Constantinople frequently tried to dominate the popes as they had dominated the patriarchs. Pope Martin had been killed and Pope Vigilius expelled. Then, in 799, the Roman populace became intractable again and, having first besmirched the reputation of Pope Leo III, beat and imprisoned his person.

Charlemagne swept into Italy again, imposed order on Rome and restored Leo to the papacy. Unsolicited, the pope repaid his debt by placing on the head of the monarch, kneeling on Christmas Day in the Basilica of St.Peter, the imperial crown, whereupon the people with apparent spontaneity broke into the well rehearsed formula: "To Charles, the most pious Augustus, crowned of God, to the great and pacific Emperor, life and victory, to him who by all is constituted the Emperor of the Romans."[1]

Charlemagne's biographer, Einhard, said that had the Emperor known this was going to happen he would never have gone into the church that day. Why should he have objected? Probably because the assumption of the title "Emperor of the Romans" would have been an affront to the Eastern emperor, whose subjects called

[1] Walter Ullmann, *The Growth of Papal Government in the Middle Ages* (London, 1955), p. 97, and the Bibliography to this Chapter.

themselves Romans. Apparently, what Charlemagne desired was a system like that formerly instituted by Diocletian, of two Augusti, one for the East and one for the West. Such an arrangement might conceivably have been achieved by negotiation with Constantinople. The claim that Charles was displeased is borne out by his acceptance of the title only with the modification that he was not the "Emperor of the Romans" including the Byzantines, but the "Emperor of the Roman Domain," by which he meant not simply the city of Rome, nor the lands once forming the old Roman Empire, but the entire territory under his sway, including the Germanic lands, which by adherence to the Christian faith had come to be Roman. The city of Rome, the spiritual center of this emergent Christendom, was on the periphery of Charlemagne's empire, with the Alps, in between, forming a more formidable barrier than any that had ever separated Rome from Constantinople. The very distance may have eased the friction of alliance.

The Carolingian Empire was a royal theocracy. In his relations with the Church, Charlemagne was devout, concerned, and commanding. Every morning he went to Mass and every evening to Vespers. He took an active share in the life of the Church, summoning councils and interfering with their decisions. He instructed priests how to baptize and he was concerned with the liturgy. In his administration he used churchmen who, by reason of their numerous holdings of land in a society based upon land, were not only prelates, but also magnates. Bishops and abbots were appointed and controlled by patrons. The emperor, himself a patron, saw to it that the patrons did not arouse his displeasure. The Church was virtually a department of state, though Charlemagne never made of himself a caliph, and preferred the role of a David, who with his sword defended the Ark of the Lord.

Charlemagne promoted the revival of the classical Christian culture. He could understand Latin, even though he could not train his clumsy fingers to write. To his court he invited learned men of many extractions, Goth and Frank, Saxon and Celt. Einhard, his biographer, was a Swabian. Warnefrid, known as

Paul the Deacon, was a Lombard, and Alcuin an Anglo-Saxon. His career shows that England was now entering into the former role of Ireland, partly because she had as the Archbishop of Canterbury a Greek named Theodore, who had brought with him a competence in the ancient tongues. Like Ireland, England was in no danger of debasing Latin through approximation to the vernacular. Alcuin, who had earlier headed the famous cathedral school at York, became Charlemagne's adviser in educational and religious matters and the principal intellect of the Carolingian Renaissance. It was his hope, he told Charlemagne, that in the land of the Franks might be reared "a new Athens enriched by the sevenfold fullness of the Holy Spirit." Alcuin revived the ancient disciplines of grammar, rhetoric, and dialectic as tools of the teacher, whom he regarded as a better propagator of Christianity than the warrior. In protest against Charlemagne's imposition of baptism by force on the Saxons, Alcuin asked of what avail baptism had been to these wretched folk: "A man can be driven to baptism, but not to belief," he observed. It was he who first used the figure of the two swords with reference to the roles of Church and state, and Charlemagne was informed that he was not to use his sword—the political power of the state—to impose religion. Charlemagne admired his great adviser, but did not always heed his counsel. When the emperor listened with relish to the reading of Augustine's *City of God*, he was attracted more by the denunciations of paganism than by the excoriation of empire.

The attachment of the Frankish Empire to Rome was evidenced by the standardization of ecclesiastical practices in conformity with Roman and Italian models. With the encouragement of the emperor, the Rule of St. Benedict supplanted other rules, notably those of Irish provenance, in Frankish monasteries. The canon law, compiled in Italy in the age of Justinian by Dionysius Exiguus, enshrining the principle of papal centralization, was accepted by the Frankish Church in 802. Since the liturgy was of inestimable importance in the formation of a Christian culture, Charlemagne desired uniform practice throughout his domains and commissioned Alcuin to prepare a standardized version based on the Roman rather than the Gallican form. However, Alcuin enriched the Roman version by introducing certain prayers from the Gallican recension, and his revision was then adopted by Rome. Similarly, the Apostles' Creed, emanating from Rome, received its present form among the Franks in the Carolingian era and then became standard at Rome. There was thus, at times, a two-way process toward conformity between Rome and the Frankish world.

So-called Dark Ages

The unity and order that Charlemagne had imposed on the Western world did not long survive the emperor's death in 814. The three following centuries, roughly from 800 to 1100, were marked by a recession in political power and cultural attainment, by a struggle to recover order, and by a conflict between the two great powers for whom order was a goal, the Church and the state. This period, especially the tenth century, is commonly designated by modern historians as "The Dark Ages." No informed person, however, would apply that term today to the whole of the Middle Ages, and there are some historians who would not use it at all, for, to call the tenth century dark, they say, is to assume that literature outranks agriculture in significance. But, all agree that during these years men were occupied with the elemental business of keeping alive. The reason was a new wave of invasions.

The Vikings came swooping down along the northern watercourses. Those who dwelt by the rivers feared almost less the fires of hell than the cold light of a clear moon. There is a revealing prayer in the Gallican liturgy: "Let not our own malice within us, but the sense of thy long-suffering be ever before us, that it may ceaselessly keep us from evil delights and graciously guard us from the disasters of this night."[2] By 835, a Scandinavian kingdom

[2] Gregory Dix, *The Shape of the Liturgy* (London, 1952), p. 581.

had been established in Ireland. In 845, the Danes sacked Hamburg and Paris. Again in 850, there were raids along the Loire and the Seine. In 865, the east coast of England was occupied by the Danes, and they almost succeeded in seizing control of the whole country. In February, 880, an entire Saxon army was routed by these same Danes. Two bishops and eleven counts were slain among others. By 900, the Viking raids were subsiding, only to be succeeded by Magyar pressures from the east. Meanwhile, the raids in the west had wiped out monastic culture in the east of England. Many churches and monasteries in France were wrecked. The Carolingian Empire was a shambles.

The attempt to restore order after this debacle occupied both Church and state. For two centuries, while the pressures were unremitting, their relations were marked in the main by collaboration, with now the one and now the other taking the lead. When the menace from without receded and each gained strength, clashes commenced as to priority. But, for two hundred years the question was not, which institution should direct the social order, but whether there would be a social order to direct. Initially, the state continued to decline and the Church became the prime force for integration.

The structural unity of the empire was lost when the Germanic principle of divided inheritance triumphed over the Roman principle of single succession. In 843, the empire of Charlemagne's son and successor, Louis the Pious, was divided among his three sons: Charles the Bald received western Francia, the future France; Louis the German, eastern Francia, the future Germany; and Lothair, a middle strip that included what later became the Netherlands, Belgium, Luxembourg, Alsace, Lorraine, Switzerland, Burgundy, and northern Italy—much of which area has remained a buffer zone ever since.

But, one may doubt whether even Charlemagne and his undivided empire would have been able to cope with the invaders. No government had the strength. When the raiders glided up the watercourses, struck, burned, pillaged, captured, and fled, the inhabitants of the assaulted areas had no recourse but self-help. Bridges had to be fortified, fords protected. Small forces of militia had to be constantly ready. Arms were necessary, but arms were costly. How could a peasant afford an exchange of six oxen or twelve cows for a breastplate, seven cows for a sword, and three for a sword belt? Nor was he in a position to construct a stockade. He was forced to request protection from a richer, stronger man and pay for this with service.[3]

Thus grew up a complex series of interrelationships, with everyone, except a slave, over someone else, and everyone, except the emperor, under someone else. The one below swore fealty and service, the one above swore to provide protection. The whole structure rested on good faith. This, in essence, was feudalism, which was to be the basis of the medieval world and which carried within it the seeds of constitutional government, since it involved contractual relationships with mutual obligations. Such localized social organization, however necessary, led to further disorder within the land, because the small feudal lords warred with each other. "Every man does what seems good in his own eyes," it was reported in 909, "despising laws human and divine and the commands of the Church. The strong oppress the weak, the world is full of violence against the poor and of the plunder of ecclesiastical goods."

The degree to which centralized government had collapsed is illustrated by the fate of Augustine's doctrine of the just war. He had said that war should be conducted only under the auspices of the state, because private war is anarchy. But where now was the state? He had said that justice must be on one side only and that the prince should determine the justice. He had been thinking in terms of the Christian Roman Empire over against the hordes of barbarians, but now that multitudinous Christian princes were feuding with each other, one prince had as much right as another to call his cause just, and no superior power was in a position to adjudicate. Consequently, theory was thrown to the winds, and

[3] Sartell Prentice, *Voices of the Cathedral* (New York, 1938), p. 96.

those attacked took care of themselves, including bishops, priests, monks, and nuns, though the clergy often scrupled to use swords and, instead, bashed the enemy with clubs, because "the Church abhors the shedding of blood." The code had utterly collapsed.

Amid these disorders, men looked to the papacy as to a symbol of universality and the force making for order. Significantly, a document was promulgated in this period seeking to enhance papal authority, and the source from which it emanated was not Rome but Gaul. It was in part a forgery called the False or Pseudo-Isidorian Decretals, because attributed to Isidore, the bishop of Seville under the Visigoths and the author of an encyclopedic work of learning. This collection included both forged and genuine letters of earlier popes interspersed with spurious documents making pretentious claims, such as that the Roman Church in the second century had exercised authority over all other churches. The forger introduced a provision for the creation of a body of churchmen beneath the pope but above the metropolitans—in other words, the college of cardinals, which actually did not come into being until the eleventh century. The purpose of this provision was to establish the supremacy of the pope and to downgrade the metropolitans. The Decretals strongly supported the right of appeal to Rome and further required that civil rulers should not interfere with the internal life and property of the Church.

Likewise in the ninth century, a theoretical justification was given to the centralization of authority within the Church under the pope, and within society under the Church, by the introduction into the West of writings attributed to Dionysius the Areopagite, mentioned in the Book of Acts as a hearer of the Apostle Paul at Athens. He had been equated with the patron saint of France, the martyr St.Denis (French for Dionysius). His name was also attached to Christian Neoplatonic writings, composed in the East in the sixth century. A copy of this work had been sent by the Byzantine emperor to Louis the Pious, who presented it to Hilduin, the abbot of St.Denis (814–840). He promptly attributed these writings to his patron saint and thereby invested them with an enormous prestige in France, which was the more enhanced in 860 when the Greek was translated into Latin by John Scotus Erigena (the Erin-born).

In these writings, the structure of the heavenly and the earthly societies is viewed as hierarchical. From the ultimate intelligence the hierarchies descend. The divine afflatus is transmitted from the heavenly to the earthly society, and within the earthly from the sacraments to the clergy and from the clergy to the laity. Within the Church, the heavenly hierarchy descends from the pope to the acolyte, and within the state the terrestrial hierarchy descends from the emperor or king to the serf. The hierarchies themselves are hierarchically structured, with the ecclesiastical above the civil. The Pseudo-Dionysian treatises thus provided theological grounds for the papal theocracy.

Actual practice was moving in that direction at the time, notably during the pontificate of Nicholas I (858–867). One of the controversies in which he was involved illustrates the development of papal supremacy over local autonomy. Hincmar, the archbishop of Reims and metropolitan of France, claimed complete jurisdiction over his own clergy and inflicted discipline upon a bishop, who thereupon appealed to Rome. Nicholas responded to this appeal, claiming for himself jurisdiction, and took the case out of the hands of Hincmar. This was a reassertion of the principle of centralization that had been enshrined in the canon law.

Another controversy, between Nicholas and Lothair II, ruler of the middle region of Charlemagne's empire, illustrates the power that the Church had come to exercise through the sacraments. Lothair had repudiated his wife, whom he accused of incest, and had made his concubine queen. The pope commanded him to restore his proper spouse or suffer excommunication. Although Lothair's brother, Emperor Louis II, marched on Rome, Nicholas refused to be intimidated. Lothair was excommunicated. After some tergiversation he capitulated. In such instances, even if the king were not cowed by the belief that hell awaited one excluded from the sacraments, this conviction had such a hold upon his subjects that their allegiance would waver were he not reconciled to the Church. Hence, excommunication was for centuries a dread weapon in the hands of the popes.

Although the sacraments do not lose their efficacy when administered by the unworthy, the prestige of the Church is undermined by the scandalous deportment of prelates. This happened in the case of the papacy in the middle of the tenth century. The reason was that the papacy fell again into the hands of Italian factions, and this time there was no Charlemagne to intervene. Roman nobles controlled the papacy and two women of ill repute, Theodora and her daughter Marozia, controlled the nobles. Hence, this era in papal history has been called the Pornocracy.

But the vitality of the Church was not confined to Rome. The work of Christian missions went on independently. A great reformatory movement had its inception in a monastery, and civil rulers took a hand in the purging of the papacy. As for missions, newly converted lands passed on the Gospel to their neighbors. As the Vikings continued their raids on the islands and the mainland, the Church started the Christian offensive. In the ninth century, Harold of Denmark, having been expelled from his kingdom, sought restoration through the help of France and was informed that assistance would be more readily forthcoming if he were a Christian. He accepted baptism and encouraged the missionary activity of the Frankish monk Ansgar, who is remembered as the apostle of the North for his work in Denmark, Norway, and Sweden. Early in the eleventh century, there was a real possibility that England might be brought into the Scandinavian confederation by Canute, who then ruled over Denmark, England and, for a short time, Norway. This was prevented by the Normans, the residue of an earlier Viking invasion that had been assimilated into northern France, who realigned England once more with the Continent as a result of the Norman conquest. The populace in Norway had become nominally Christianized late in the tenth and early in the eleventh century under her kings Olaf I and Olaf II, the rival of Canute. Together, they brought their land into the orbit of Christendom, unhappily not without coercing their subjects. The pagans in Sweden were not fully converted until about 1100. Contemporary with Ansgar's endeavors in the West, the Church in the East, as we have noted, was Christianizing the peoples of the Balkans through the labors of Cyril and Methodius.

Cluny

Again, at the very time when the papacy was a scandal, a great movement of reform was initiated in a monastery. In 910, William, by the grace of God Duke of Aquitaine, and his wife, Ingelborga, in honor of the blessed Mother of God and of St. Peter, made over to the said apostle the town and manor of Cluny for the erection of a Benedictine monastery. The monks should "ardently pursue celestial converse and sedulously offer prayers and petitions,"[4] alike for the donors and for all mankind. Along with the lands, waters, and revenues went also the workers on the lands, serfs, male and female. The monks, declared the grant, should be free in perpetuity, to retain their possessions without alienation, and to elect their own abbot without any interference from the patron, or his successors, or the king, or the pope, under penalty of the wrath of Peter and Paul. These provisions were of high significance. Since the tillers of the soil went with the land, the monks were relieved from a great deal of that manual labor which had been part of the Rule of St. Benedict. The time thus released was to be spent in unremitting prayers of intercession. The independence of the monastery from bishops and popes—save that popes were to protect the Cluniacs from other interference—meant decentralization with reference to the papacy, but there was a compensatory centralization in the structure of monasticism, because when daughter houses were established, whether in

[4] Full translation in R. H. Bainton, *The Medieval Church* (Princeton, 1962), pp. 115–17.

France, England, Germany, Italy, or even Spain, all new foundations were subject to the mother house. The erection of such a chain integrated the movement of reform.

The program of Cluny differed from that of other Benedictine monasteries because it envisaged a Christian reordering of the whole social fabric, monastic, civil, and ecclesiastical. The role of the monastery in the world was no longer directed to conversions, often nominal, but to the permeation of society by Christian ideals. Therefore, the monks, now largely free from manual labor, were expected to dedicate themselves to prayer, to the transmission of even pagan learning, to prayers for the world, and to hospitality toward the world. Whereas St.Benedict had sought to segregate his monks from society, the Cluniacs tried to integrate monasticism and society.

The monasteries thus served as the inns of the Middle Ages. Cluny had a guest house to accommodate forty men and thirty women, and a guest-master to look after the visitors. In the course of centuries, the Benedictines also became integrated into society, largely because they, too, began to offer hospitality to visitors. The Benedictine monastery of St.Albans, for example, had stabling for three hundred horses, and Abingdon even shod the steeds of the guests. The duties of the hosteler were to provide clean towels, uncracked cups, spoons of silver, blankets, and sheets of full width, of pleasing color, and untorn. In winter, he should supply candles and candlesticks, a fire that did not smoke, and writing materials. The guest house should be free from spiders' webs and strewn with rushes underfoot. On departure, the guests should be checked to see that no one left a sword and that no one carried off the linen or the silver of the house, either inadvertently or otherwise. Guests were expected to make some contribution, but the cost of their entertainment was often greater than the cost of maintaining the monastery. The abbot was burdened with many cares. Abbot Samson at Bury St.Edmunds, in the course of twelve years, pulled his house out of monstrous debts, the while his hair was blanched.

These examples of the monastery's growing involvement with society are, to be sure, centuries apart, but they indicate a continuous process which brought the world to the monastery and helped to spread monastic ideals throughout the community, though reintroducing the danger that worldly values would infiltrate and corrupt the monastery.

The Cluny reform made a particular point of seeking to eliminate feudal warfare. It wished the nobles to be at peace among themselves and use their arms only to vindicate the weak and protect the Church. Cluny supported the Truce of God and the Peace of God, to be described later. Cluny envisaged also the reform of the Church, demanding among other things that the clergy be celibate. It also forbade the clergy to buy benefices from their ecclesiastical superiors, from lay patrons, or from civil rulers —a practice called simony, from Simon Magus, who, in the Book of Acts, sought to buy the gift of the Holy Spirit from the apostles. But, for the implementation of these reforms, Cluny did not object to assistance from civil rulers, nor even to initiative on their part. They, too, were ordained of God. They constituted the temporal arm of a Christian society and had the responsibility for the purity of the spiritual arm. There was no valid reason why good emperors should not depose bad popes.

This the emperors did, but obviously they could never have done so had there not been emperors. While the papacy in the tenth century reached a nadir, the empire was reconstituted not in France, as in the days of Charlemagne, but in Germany. The chief reason was presumably an economic upsurge more marked in the north. France made gains by the development of the manorial system in which communal farming was applied to extensive tracts, but farther north the more abundant rainfall made possible the discontinuance of two-field farming, with one always in fallow, in favor of three fields, with two always under cultivation. The increase in yield enabled the farmer to keep a horse, more costly to maintain than the ox because it was not used for food, yet was much more agile in plowing, and the horse was rendered more efficient, besides, by a new style of harness which shifted the weight from the neck to the chest. The introduction of the stirrup and the bit made the horse more manageable in peace and war alike,[5] for the horse is the only mount as senseless as man in plunging into battle. Mules will not, which is why churchmen were supposed to ride only mules. A further aid to economic recovery was a mitigation in climate due to glacial recession. An additional factor favoring the north resulted from a discovery made by a horse. During a hunt, while the dogs were slow in flushing out the quarry, an impatient steed pawed the ground and disclosed a vein of silver. The mines of the Hartz helped the economy of the new emperors.[6]

Finally, it must be borne in mind that even Viking and Magyar raids were never as all-inclusive as modern warfare and that many areas remained untouched, where men could still enjoy the sunshine. In the ninth century, Walafrid Strabo, a monk later to become the abbot of St.Gall, a very learned man whose glosses on the Scripture, called the *Glossa Ordinaria*, were still in standard use in Luther's day, wrote a little poem on horticulture, dedicated to his abbot, in these lines:

> *Think of me, Grimwald, as you sit*
> *Beneath the mantle of your apple leaves,*
> *Or where the peach from sun and shade*
> *A variegated pattern weaves.*
> *There, sporting scholars garner fruit*
> *To aproned folds of tender wool*
> *And others scramble to grasp more*
> *In hands already overfull.*[7]

Technology, climate, and islands of peace account for an upward trend in Europe's population, commencing presumably in the ninth century and plainly demonstrable in the tenth.

[5] Lynn White, *Medieval Technology and Social Change* (Oxford, 1962).
[6] Sartell Prentice, *op. cit.*, p. 91.
[7] J.-P. Migne, ed., *Patrologiae Cursus Completus*, Series Latina (Paris, 1844–65), CXIV, 1130, tr. R. H. Bainton.

Since these developments were more marked in the north, one can understand why, when the empire of Charlemagne was reconstructed in 962, its center was in Germany. The emperor was Otto I. His domain included Germany and that middle area once assigned to Lothair, including Italy but not France. Otto and his successors looked upon themselves as the temporal arm of a Christian society with authority directly conferred by God to administer justice, protect religion, and even to discipline the Church. If popes were scandalous, let them be removed by the civil authority and replaced by candidates worthy of their calling. Otto I deposed John XII and instituted a line of German appointees to the papacy. One of these was Gerbert, the most learned churchman of his day, who had studied even in Spain. As pope he took the name Sylvester II (999–1003), in honor of that Sylvester who had baptized Constantine. The very choice of the name witnessed to his intent to restore the glories of the more primitive Church. This reform was, however, short-lived and the papacy came again under the domination of the Italian nobility and once more became disreputable. For a second time the reform emanated from the empire when Henry III, a passionate reformer, intervened to expel the traffickers from the temple and install men of good repute. He deposed three popes, but when his son Henry IV continued this policy, he met with determined resistance on the part of a new type of reforming churchmen.

The Investiture Controversy

These churchmen are called the Gregorians, from Pope Gregory VII. They differed from the Cluniacs in their concept of a Christian society and in how it should be achieved. The Cluniacs chose the way of permeation and believed that kings, having been permeated, could further assist even to the point of placing worthy candidates in the papacy. The Gregorians were imbued with the spirit of a new wave of monastic austerity manifest in the rise of the Cistertians, Premonstratensians, and Carthusians, who felt that the program of Cluny had resulted in a lowering of the standards of the Church. These must be held aloft without compromise and could be thus maintained only if the Church were independent of the control of kings who often enough were not reformers but sons of Belial. This was the case more in the area of Lorraine from which the Gregorian reformers emanated, than in Germany under the emperors, or in Normandy under the dukes. The Church must be free from lay dictation and, being free, must then impose her ideals upon society. This program looks in the direction of papal theocracy. But, if the ideal were not attained, then the strategy could easily shift to a withdrawal from society at large in order to realize the pattern of the gospel in small communities of committed individuals. This is the way of sectarianism. Both, the papacy and the sects of the high Middle Ages, owed their inception to the spirit of the Gregorian reform.

Its program called for an end to the system of lay investiture whereby a civil ruler invested his own appointee as a bishop, abbot, or even a pope. The latter possibility was forestalled by the reformers in 1059, when they secured a decree that, henceforth, popes should be elected only by a body of churchmen with sees around Rome and known as cardinals. Hildebrand was thus elected and took the name of Gregory VII. The demand for the cessation of lay investiture met with stout resistance on the part of the rulers in Germany, because abbots and bishops had a dual role; as princes they were lords of more than one-third of all land in Germany where financial and military levies were assessed on land. The emperor, to insure the loyalty of these princely clerics, controlled their appointments and himself as patron would bestow churches on the appointees with the formula *accipe ecclesiam*, "accept the church." Then, if popes interfered, they might be replaced. This was another reason for imperial intervention.

The Church had reason to complain that emperors were generally not reformers but that they utilized ecclesiastical appointments simply as plums with which to reward retainers devoid of spiritual qualifications. Nobles were permitted to provide for younger sons in ecclesiastical posts, and families built up their power by obtaining several sees in the name of one incumbent. A certain bishop flippantly justified such pluralism on the ground that if one man held several bishoprics fewer men would be damned.

A further and worse evil was that bishops of this type had sons who succeeded to their posts. The cure for all these ills, according to the Gregorian reformers, was that no ecclesiastical appointment should be made by laymen, not even by an emperor, be it for a fee or without a fee. The term "simony" was extended to mean all lay appointments, even if no payments were involved. The Gregorian reformers demanded further the institution of obligatory and universal clerical celibacy, partly so that there would be no male heirs to the bishoprics and partly in accord with the spirit of the new wave of ascetic monasticism.

The question at issue was more than administrative. The theory of the source of power was involved. Were Church and state instituted independently and directly by God, or was the civil power derived from the spiritual? The Gregorians appealed to the hierarchical theories of Dionysius the Areopagite, the imperialists to the word of the Apostle Paul that rulers were ordained of God, with not a word said about any delegation of power through the Church or St. Peter. Such were the arguments in a body of tracts.

The conflict became overt in a disagreement between Emperor Henry IV and Pope Gregory VII, shortly after the latter was elevated to the papacy. The struggle illustrates how in the rivalry between Church and state each attempted to reduce the centralized authority of the other. The papal offensive began about 1074 by the prohibition of clerical marriage, simony, and any lay investiture of ecclesiastical posts. The laity was exhorted to refuse to receive the sacraments at the hands of married priests. This was a most dangerous provision, for the inference was very easy that at the hands of the unworthy the sacraments would be invalid, precisely the view of the ancient Donatist heretics. The German clergy in Henry's entourage declared that they would rather give up their lives than their wives. The emperor retaliated against Gregory's decree by making an appointment to the archbishopric of Milan. Milan was the chief see of Lombardy, where the populace was strongly opposed to clerical celibacy; in focusing his defiance of the pope first on a city in that region, Henry sought to undermine papal authority at its weak spot.

On the other hand, during the course of the struggle the pope abetted the Saxons in their rebellion against Henry, who was a member of the Franconian ruling house. Furthermore, Gregory could lean on two important allies. The Countess Matilda in Tuscany was a warm adherent of his policies; and the Normans, who had recently broken into the Mediterranean world, had been enlisted as allies. A previous pope had, by force of arms, resisted their encroachment on papal lands in southern Italy, but before he became pope, Gregory had had the discretion to help one of his predecessors win their allegiance.

To the pope, Henry sent a defiance, accusing him of innovation in regard to papal powers. Had not Henry's father, the Emperor Henry III, deposed and appointed popes with the full consent of a pope and a council? To this, Gregory replied that his own program was indeed an innovation with reference to the immediate past; but the immediate past was a corruption of a more primitive past, to which he was seeking to return. The emperor made a further charge that the pope was stepping out of bounds by fomenting war, in that he incited the Saxons to take up arms against the emperor. Henry therefore summoned Gregory to come down from the throne of St. Peter, which he had usurped by the sword, that it might be filled by another more worthy of the holy apostle.

The pope replied with an apostrophe to the blessed Peter, the Mother of God, the blessed Paul, and all the saints, calling upon them to witness that he had not seized his holy office for the glory of the world. He declared Henry to be deposed from the governance of Germany and Italy and to be bound in the bonds of anathema, so that all people might know that on Peter, the Rock, the Church was founded and that no man would prevail against it. Like Lothair before him, Henry found himself completely undone. His political enemies of the Saxon house could, of course, be expected to exploit the anathema. But even his own party withdrew support, and the German bishops, so opposed to clerical celibacy, interpreted the sudden death of their leader, William of Utrecht, as God's corroboration of the pope's curse. A diet of princes, meeting in October, 1076, in Tribur on the Rhine, decreed that Henry must resign all royal insignia and that only if he made his peace with the pope would his status as emperor be reviewed at a council to be held the following February in Augsburg.

Henry had no recourse save to stoop to conquer. With his wife, infant son, and a few retainers he set out for Rome. Christmas was approaching and even the swift Rhine was frozen. Yet with guides he made his way over the Alps. In the meantime, the pope had started north to attend a council called by Henry's German enemies. Fearing violence, Gregory took refuge at Canossa, a fortress of the Countess Matilda, the emperor's cousin but the pope's supporter. It was now January, 1077. The emperor, learning of the pope's location, sought him out there. Clad as a suppliant in white wool, Henry stood barefoot in the snow in the castle enclosure, seeking admission. For a day he stood, and the gate did not open; for a second day likewise, and for a third. Then the emperor requested the mediation of the countess, and the obdurate pope was softened by the entreaty of a woman. Abbot Hugh of Cluny supported Matilda in her plea. But what could the pope do? Would St. Peter ever reject a penitent? The emperor was admitted, but was received to communion only after accepting strict conditions of obedience to the Church. This appeared to be a papal victory.

Immediately, Henry's subjects returned to obedience. However, his opponents in Germany, supported by Saxony, elected an antiking. Rallying his forces, Henry bore down on the Saxons without waiting for any diet to decide whether or not he should be emperor. The Saxons appealed to the pope, who at length excommunicated Henry again, this time for impeding the meeting of the diet. But the second excommunication did not work; the pope had overstepped his limits. Henry marched on Rome, imprisoned the pope in the Castel Sant'Angelo, and set up another pope, who crowned him emperor. Gregory was liberated by the Normans. With them, he withdrew from Rome to die, saying, "I have loved justice and hated iniquity. Therefore I die in exile." Some years later, Henry was forced to abdicate by civil wars and died soon after.

After long negotiations between new principals, the dispute between emperor and pope resulted in a compromise. The Concordat of Worms in 1122 stated that bishops were to be appointed solely by the Church. After having been installed, they should swear fealty to the emperor. The system of lay investiture was at an end, but lay control did not cease because the emperor could interpose a veto if he were not satisfied with the oath of allegiance.

The clash had been between the papacy and the German Empire. The great conflict between France and the papacy was postponed until the beginning of the fourteenth century. In Normandy, there was no rupture, despite the lack of any concessions on the part of the kings. The concept of sacral kingship had always prevailed among the Normans, and their kings had completely controlled the Church. When William the Conqueror took England, he continued this practice without opposition from Archbishop Lanfranc of Canterbury. The reason for Gregory's toleration of the Normans in Normandy and England may have been that he did not wish to alienate his Norman allies in Italy. Conflict ensued in England under William Rufus and later under the first two Henrys, with the Church increasing her leadership of Christian society.

The First Crusade

Another step in that direction was taken by the launching of the crusades, a compound of Viking lust for conquest and of zeal for the faith. They were also the culmination of a great effort to eradicate war between Christians in Europe. We have noted that the Cluny movement had sought to arrest feudal warfare by the imposition of restraints through the Peace of God and the Truce of God. The Truce restricted the times for fighting, allowing no hostilities from sunset Wednesday to Monday morning or on holy days, of which there were so many that warfare would have been reduced to a summer sport were the restrictions enforced. The Peace of God restricted the range of the combatants. There should be no attacks upon priests, nuns, or pilgrims, or upon merchants or farmers, their animals, tools, or properties. Princes were called upon to vow to observe the rules, which were not too rigorously phrased. Robert the Pious, for example, swore that he would not attack women traveling without their husbands, unless they were to blame. Such concession, however, meant little. Princes took the vows and broke the vows. Then bishops organized armies to punish the oathbreakers, and the armies of the Church got out of hand and ravaged the country, so that kings raised armies to suppress the Church's armies.

Then, in 1095, Pope Urban II, a former monk of Cluny, convoked the Council of Clermont. The Eastern Emperor, Alexius Comnenus, had appealed to the pope for help against the Seljuk Turks, who had recently irrupted into the Levant. It was a period of unrest and strife within Europe itself. The investiture struggle was still dragging on, but Urban was on strong ground when he addressed the council in terms reminiscent of the great peace speeches in the councils of the preceding fifty years. Let Christians allay their feuds, he urged. Let them unite. Let them take to heart the atrocities practiced by the accursed Turks. Let them deliver the holy places from these infidels, and all the assembly cried, *"Dieu le veult"* (God wills it).

A new concept of war was involved here. Augustine had required that war should be conducted under the auspices of the state. Now it was done under the auspices of the Church. Kings, to be sure, took the cross, but at the behest of the pope. According to

Augustine, the common soldier simply obeyed his prince. Now he volunteered by taking the cross, though, of course, a prince might summon his retainers. The object of the just war, according to Augustine, had been the vindication of justice, meaning primarily the defense of life and property. Now, war was for the defense of the faith, or at any rate for the right of the faithful to exercise their faith. The code of the just war called for good faith with the enemy, regard for non-combatants, respect for hostages and prisoners. But all such restraints were abandoned in dealing with the infidel. The warrant for this view of warfare was found in the biblical account of the conquest of Canaan by Joshua.

The first crusade was primarily French. The Council of Clermont had been attended only by the French, among whom there were four groups of participants: the northern French, under Godfrey and Baldwin of Bouillon; the Provençals, under Raymond of Toulouse and Bishop Adhemar of Puy; the Normans of the north, under Robert of Normandy—the son of the Conqueror—and Robert of Flanders; and the Normans of Sicily, under Bohemund and Tancred. The Provençal group, which included a bishop, chosen as papal representative, was the most loyal to the pope.

Urban's hope would seem to have been that the holy places should be delivered from the Turks and then turned over to the Eastern Empire, but the crusaders were not so disinterested and were soon at odds with the Eastern emperor and with each other. The emperor distrusted them at the outset; this was partly because the Greek and Latin Churches had broken decisively in 1054, when the Orthodox Church sharply rebuffed the demand of the Gregorian reformers that it recognize their claims for the papacy. A deeper reason may have been that these reformers, as we have observed, were northerners from Lorraine who had no sense of belonging to the Mediterranean world and no feeling for the Byzantine heritage. Another difference between the Eastern emperors and the Franks lay in their attitudes toward the Moslems. The Byzantines, of course, considered themselves to be the guardians of the true faith. But they had relaxed sufficiently to permit a mosque in Constantinople, and they received emissaries from Moslem courts with ceremonial deference. To the Easterners, the crude zeal of these Franks was obnoxious and the participation of their clergy in fighting was shocking. Their motives also were suspect, for had not the Normans in 1082 tried to capture Durazzo from the Byzantines for no better reason than plunder?

But the emperor could not well turn back the crusaders when they arrived at Constantinople, and they could not go on without him. His solution was to demand oaths of fealty, after the manner of Western feudalism. The resistance to taking the oath was most persistent on the part of the Provençals, who thought of themselves as the pope's men. But all, in the end, had to swear in order to secure support. After the host had crossed the Bosporus, an initial victory over the Turks at Nicaea opened the way through Asia Minor, where the native Christian population regarded the crusaders as liberators. The struggle with the Moslems was resumed when the Christian forces reached Syria.

Then, the divergence in aims among the crusaders became apparent. Baldwin, who was supposed to protect the flank, withdrew and ensconced himself in Edessa with every intention of setting up there an independent, feudal kingdom. Bohemund and Raymond of Toulouse quarreled as to who should have a kingdom in Antioch. The city resisted siege. Bohemund secured from the allies the promise that if he took Antioch he might keep it. Through a traitor he succeeded, but once inside the city the crusaders in turn were besieged by a newly arrived Turkish force. Famine threatened. Peter Bartholomew, one of Raymond's men, received a revelation that the holy lance, which had pierced the side of Christ, was buried in Antioch. Excavation produced a lance. The crusaders then, in joyous confidence, marched out of the city. The Turks were surprised and routed. Once more the question arose: who should have Antioch? Bohemund claimed it because he had taken the city; Raymond claimed it because his man Peter had found a way out of it. The solution was to give Bohemund Antioch and Raymond Tripoli. The leaders appeared more inter-

46. THE DONATION OF CONSTANTINE

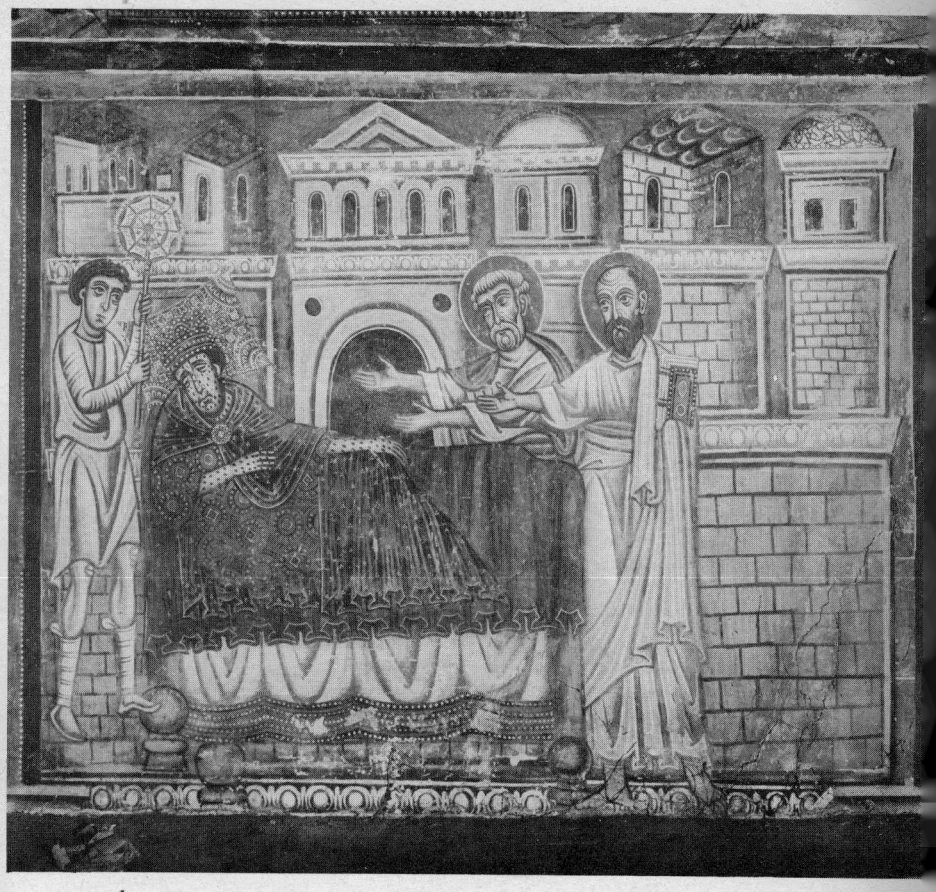

46

The legend that Constantine, afflicted with leprosy, was cured by Sylvester I, the bishop of Rome, and in gratitude conferred upon him sovereignty over the West, is depicted in a series of twelfth-century murals in the church of the SS. Quattro Coronati, in Rome. The mural, above, shows Constantine suffering from leprosy.

47. ST. BONIFACE: MISSION AND MARTYRDOM

In the above miniature, on the left, is depicted the baptism of a pagan convert at the hands of St. Boniface and his companions. The font is symbolic rather than proportionate in size. The bare spots on the heads of some of the saint's assistants are the tonsures. On the extreme left, a helper carries a baptismal robe for the neophyte. On the right is the scene of martyrdom. St. Boniface holds what may be a book, or possibly a box filled with relics of the saints. This miniature is from *Sakramentar Cod. Theol.* 235 in the library of the University of Göttingen.

48. CHARLEMAGNE AS LAWGIVER

The words at the top read: ANNO UNDECIMO FELICITER ("in the eleventh year happily"). The drawing is from the capitulary of Mainz of the year 779, in a transcript made in the eleventh or twelfth century.

49. CHARLEMAGNE

49a

These two versions of a contemporary mosaic in the triclinium of the Lateran at Rome show St. Peter conferring the pallium on the pope and giving a banner to the emperor. On the left we see the mosaic in its present state, following reconstruction in the eighteenth

49b

century. On the right is a drawing made prior to the reconstruction by Ciacconio in the sixteenth century. The essential point is the same in both: that the pope and the emperor derived their authority directly from St. Peter and independently of each other.

50. THE WISE MEN AS KINGS

50

Depictions of the Wise Men over the centuries reveal changes in culture. Their prestige was enhanced in the middle of the fourth century when the celebration of the birth of Christ (Christmas) was transferred from January 6 to December 25, leaving the older date entirely to the Magi, whose journey was assumed to have filled the interval between the appearance of the star and their arrival on the twelfth night. Quite early, they came to be regarded as kings, because verses 10 and 11 of Psalm 72 were incorporated into the liturgy: "The kings of Tarshish and of the isles shall bring presents; the kings of Sheba and Seba shall offer gifts. . . ." When the locale of the celebrations moved from Palestine, the camels gave way to horses, both in the East and the West and, after the introduction of stirrups, the Three Kings were also thus equipped. European monarchs enhanced their own prestige by making a great holiday of the Feast of the Three Kings. The French kings rode in processions carrying gold, incense, and myrrh for the King of Kings. From France the custom passed to England. In Germany, the *Dreikönigsfest* was likewise a day for pageantry.

The above illustration is from the *Luttrell Psalter* of 1325, much later than the tenth century to which we are referring, but traditions once set continued for centuries. (See Hugo Kehrer, *Die heiligen drei Könige in Literatur und Kunst* [Leipzig, 1908].)

51. THE CONFLICT OF HENRY IV AND GREGORY VII

51a

51b

This illustration from the *Chronicle of Otto of Freising* (now at the university library at Jena) shows in the upper panel three main figures, their names inscribed above their heads: to our left, Henry IV; in the middle, Guibert, the anti-pope he set up; and, on the right, Gregory VII being driven out by the sword. His name appears in the upper right corner. In the lower panel on the left Gregory VII is shown amid his bishops; on the right is depicted his burial.

52. THE EMPEROR HENRY IV IMPLORES THE INTERCESSION OF THE COUNTESS MATILDA AND OF THE ABBOT HUGH OF CLUNY

Vatican Library; Ms. Vat. Lat. 4922

The inscription says: "The king entreats the abbot! He beseeches also Matilda." The king is not wearing a crown, but a cap adorned with what may be three lilies. The significance of the abbot here is that the Cluniacs did not support the Gregorians in their campaign to exclude civil rulers from any share in the appointment of ecclesiastics. This miniature is from the life of Matilda, done at her request by Donizo, a monk of the cloister of Canossa, and completed in 1114.

53. THE CRUSADES

53a

53b

53c

The crusaders believed not only that God willed their enterprise, but that Christ himself was the leader of their hosts. In Fig. 53a he is depicted with a sword in his mouth, as described in Rev. 19:15. God the Father appears in the upper left. (From a fourteenth-century manuscript now in the British Museum [19 B XV fol. 37a].)

Fig. 53b shows the capture of Jerusalem in 1099 in a miniature of the thirteenth century. Frankish soldiers with the fleurs-de-lis on their shields are on the left and, in the center, a soldier operates a catapult. On the right, soldiers boost a comrade onto the battlement. Sappers crawl through a hole under the tower. The defenders are shown striking down with a sword, emptying a jar of boiling oil, and hurling a stone.

The crusaders established a Latin kingdom in Jerusalem which lasted until 1244. Almost one hundred years earlier, in 1143, Baldwin III had become king at the age of thirteen; he reigned until his death in 1162. He had the good sense to cultivate friendly relations with the Byzantine emperor. Although he acquired considerable military renown, he was unable to restore to his kingdom the prestige it had lost at the fall of Edessa in 1144. He is shown in Fig. 53c accompanied by his knights. (From *De Passagiis in Terram Sanctam*.)

53d

In July 1270, St. Louis of France set sail from Aigues-Mortes on his second crusade (Fig. 53d). He died of the plague in Tunis less than two months later. This fiasco of a crusade led many people to conclude that *Deus non vult*, "God does not will it." (From *Les Grandes Chroniques de France*, a fourteenth-century manuscript.)

ested in carving kingdoms than in reaching the Holy City. Only the pressures from the papal party and the common soldiers held the crusaders together until they reached the walls of Jerusalem. The city succumbed in 1099. The crusaders waded to the fetlocks of their horses in the blood of the infidel, then proceeded to the Church of the Holy Sepulcher, singing in jubilation that Christ had conquered.

The first crusade did aid in the fashioning of France because it held the four groups together until their objective was achieved and the crusades undoubtedly instilled a consciousness of Christendom in the West, be it only in the negative sense of something opposed to Islam.

VII

Medieval Christendom

THE élan, which had launched the crusades, initiated in Europe at the same time other and much more salutary endeavors. The twelfth and the thirteenth century witnessed an intellectual revival with the rise of the universities and of Scholasticism, a greater refinement of life by way of chivalry and romantic love, an increased ethical sensitivity, resulting in a sense of guilt with a craving for redemption through the passion of the Redeemer, and an efflorescence of religious art known to us as Gothic. Especially in the thirteenth century, the papacy, more than any other institution, directed even the political life of Europe, and the ideals of the Church had an impact on every aspect of culture, politics, economics, and jurisprudence. A new type of monasticism resisted commercialism while ministering to an urban society. Thomism constructed a full-orbed theology, integrating the revelation given by God and the truths ascertainable by man. At the end of the period, Dante unfolded in the Italian vernacular the drama of human destiny with a dimension too deep to be contained by traditional forms.

These changes were facilitated by and themselves aided in the revival of urban life. The empire of Charlemagne had been a web of villages. If the old Roman centers of population had not been entirely deserted, it was because they remained the seats of bishops, who administered both the spiritual and temporal affairs of the dioceses. The late tenth century saw the beginning of the resumption of urban life, together with the renewal of commerce and a monied economy; even the Vikings had come to prefer trading to raiding. The cities in the West, to be sure, were never large during the Middle Ages, in comparison, for example, with Constantinople, which in medieval times had about one million inhabitants. Even at the beginning of the fourteenth century, the largest European cities rarely exceeded a population of between fifty and one hundred thousand people. Most had probably a population of less than ten thousand.[1]

The Rise of the Universities

Yet even such smaller gatherings suffice to produce encounters of minds. The cities became the seats of universities. During the Middle Ages, some eighty universities were founded, many of which have had an unbroken, distinguished history to our own day: for example, Paris, Montpellier, Bologna, Padua, Oxford, Cambridge, Vienna, Prague, Leipzig, Heidelberg, Basel, Coimbra, Salamanca, Cracow, and Louvain. The oldest of these schools were in operation before 1200, although they were not chartered until about that year or slightly later. Salerno, in southern Italy, whose medical school dates back at least to the eleventh century, early achieved distinction, although it did not become a true university until the thirteenth. It was a great medical center for two centuries, but then declined, probably because other universities had instituted medical faculties. Paris, for example, had four faculties: arts (which included philosophy), canon law, theology, and medicine; the outstanding faculties were philosophy and theology. Bologna was pre-eminent in law, both canon and civil. (The degree of LL.D. stands for Doctor of Laws, with "laws" in the plural, signifying the two varieties.) In the twelfth century a new compilation of the canon law was made by Gratian, a monk of Bologna. For centuries to come his work had a vast influence on the administration of the Church and on the rendering of jus-

[1] Ernst Maurer, *Zunft und Handwerker der alten Zeit* (Nuremberg, 1940), p. 145.

tice throughout the Christian world. The civil law was the old Roman law, which in the centuries of disorder had been partially supplanted by Germanic codes but which, following the rediscovery of the Justinian Code, was now revived. Other centers of legal studies were the universities at Padua and Orleans.

The interest in theology at the universities was the more pronounced since in many instances they had developed from church schools. With the rise of the cities, monastic schools were first supplanted by educational centers attached to cathedral chapters, some of which in turn developed into universities; as, for example, the cathedral school of Notre Dame at Paris. Everywhere throughout the Middle Ages, theology was considered the queen of the sciences, with philosophy and other disciplines as her handmaidens. The intense preoccupation with the problems of theology and philosophy marked the revival of a spirit of enquiry and of confidence in the power of human reason such as the world had not known since the great age of Greece. The later Middle Ages might well be called the age of Logic.

Scholasticism

The problem that agitated philosophers and theologians concerned the ultimate nature of reality: does reality cohere—that is, is it a unity of immaterial and material things bound by an essential universal relationship—or does it consist simply in the sum of independent and unrelated individual elements?

The advocates of coherence were called realists, because they believed in the reality of universals: that universals were the only reality and that individual things had no reality except as they partook of the nature of universals. Thus, the concept of humanity is a reality, a universal in which all individuals cohere.

Those with opposing views were called nominalists, because they held that humanity, for instance, has no reality but is just a name (in Latin, *nomen*) for a set of common characteristics shared by all human beings. In other words, mankind has no reality, only individual men.

The realists were divided into extremists and moderates. The first maintained that universals exist as entities conceived in the mind of God before becoming concrete, so that there is humanity apart from human beings. The moderate realists said that universals do exist but only in particulars. Humanity is a reality, but it does not exist apart from individual men.

Such views had far-reaching implications for theology, ethics, science, and all social institutions. In theology, the doctrine of the Trinity was supported by the view called realism, for if deity is a universal, then the Father, the Son, and the Spirit are held in unity by deity; in the extreme nominalist view, on the other hand, reality consists only of individuals, the three persons become three individual gods, and the concept of the Trinity becomes tritheism—in short, heresy. In ethics, the concept of natural law was affected. In the one case, law is the expression of universal principles grounded in the very structure of the universe; in the other, it is simply the common element in the ways in which people actually behave. In science, the realistic view led to a quest for universal law; the nominalists centered attention upon the examination of individual phenomena, collecting data, and constructing categories, mainly for purposes of convenience, without claiming for them any objective reality.

On the realist basis, the Church, the state, and the family cohere within themselves, because they are the concretions of transcendent reality, whereas on the nominalist assumption the Church is an assemblage brought into being by a covenant between individuals; the state is an association created by contract, and, similarly, marriage is a contractual union. In the Middle Ages, the great conflicting tendencies of centralization and decentralization received from these divergent views a philosophical undergirding. The realist view subordinates the individual and can rationalize even a totalitarian degree of centralization, but the nominalist view, with its individualism, encourages decentralization, conceivably even to the point of anarchy.

A more vexing problem for the theologians was whether God's existence can be proved. One may marvel that the question should have been raised in the age of faith, but there has never been an age of faith so unquestioning that men would have experienced no difficulty in believing the claims of the Christian religion. From the Middle Ages we have the confessions of the monk Othlo, who was driven to desperation by his inability to believe in God. To assuage the torment of such a spirit, St. Anselm, the archbishop of Canterbury from 1093 to 1109, sought to discover an irrefragable proof for God's existence. Rumination on the subject so disturbed his devotions that he was about to abandon the attempt as presumptuous when, in the night watches, a flash of illumination presented the solution.

Anselm argued that the existence of the idea of God necessarily implies the very existence of God. Thus, by the notion of God we mean something so great that nothing greater can be conceived. Something so great must exist, because that which does not exist, but which in other respects is greater than anything else which can be conceived, can never be as great as something than which nothing greater can be conceived and which does exist. Therefore, something than which nothing greater can be conceived, exists. God, being that something, must consequently exist. This is called the ontological argument for God's existence. It did not satisfy all theologians even in the Middle Ages but in variant form it has never ceased to attract religious thinkers.

The attempt to find solutions for theological problems of this sort is called Scholasticism. Strictly speaking, the term means that which is taught in the schools, but in a more restricted sense it means a form of Christian theology which commences with an affirmation, a thesis, sets over against it a critical doubt, an antithesis, and then by logical ratiocination seeks to achieve a resolution, a synthesis. Scholasticism operated within certain first principles.

It rejected any pantheistic tendencies, some of which infiltrated from Arabic thought in Spain, it rejected any sharp dualism between matter and spirit, or between God and the Devil. Within Scholasticism there were varieties: Augustinianism, Thomism, Occamism, and so on, which will engage later attention. Scholasticism, while recognizing a realm of truths transcending human reason, yet sought to demonstrate and elucidate these truths to the limit of human capacity.

Chivalry

Another concomitant of the growing prosperity and the resumption of urban culture was the refinement of life. One aspect of this tendency was chivalry. It applied to the knightly class and well has it been said that one could not be chivalrous without a horse. The obligation of the knight to promote justice and vindicate the weak grew out of the feudal obligation of the man with the horse, the mail, and the lance to succor him who had none. Such a method of vindicating justice was itself anarchic because each knight was on his own. But, when more stable institutions of government took over the administration of justice, knighthood found its outlet in the tournaments, which served to resolve feuds and sometimes to allay wars. The object of a tournament was not to kill but to worst the opponent and hold him for ransom. The tournament became also a sport. The object was personal honor and the cult of fame, which arose centuries before the period called the Renaissance. But he who would win honor must be honorable. The game had rules, and better were it to be defeated than to tarnish one's escutcheon. This entire development could meet with a qualified endorsement on the part of the Church. Although the glorification of the martial evoked qualms, the concept of *noblesse oblige* could be sanctioned.

Among those whom the knight undertook to protect were ladies, especially those in distress. His interest was often more than a concern for their distress. In courtly circles in the south of France arose the cult of romantic love, celebrated in the poems of the troubadours. The romantic view of love was something new in history. Not, of course, that man and maid had never loved before but in this respect that love was invested with an aura akin to religion. Woman was idealized and nobility was believed to be transmitted from her to the worshipful lover, who owed to his lady an undeviating devotion.

But, courtly love was not associated with marriage. Commonly the lover addressed himself to a woman already married. The languishing in the poetry of the troubadours reflected his constant frustration. Romantic love was held to be incompatible with marriage because such love must be free, a gift of grace, not something to be claimed as due. Eleanor of Aquitaine declared that ideal love and marriage are incompatible. She had had experience enough of loveless marriage, having been wed for political reasons first to Louis VII, king of France, and then to Henry II, king of England.

Romantic love was a rebellion against the prevalent medieval view of marriage, in accordance with which unions were arranged by landowners with an eye to consolidating properties, and by royalty in order to enlarge kingdoms. Property married property. Children were betrothed in infancy. Henry II of England, for example, arranged to marry his six-year-old son John to the heiress of Maurienne, a territory that commanded the passes of the Alps. In all this, there was almost no regard for personal feeling. However, the system made for stability in the institution of marriage; infidelities were tolerated and did not disrupt marriages. And in some instances, to be sure, a tender mutual affection developed out of such arrangements.

The romantic view of love and marriage contrasted also with the attitude of the Church, for whom marriage was numbered among the seven sacraments, which were first formulated by Peter Lombard about the middle of the twelfth century. Yet the campaign for clerical celibacy had been waged with a general disparagement of marriage and of woman, who was portrayed as the gateway to hell. In any case, the sacrament was not contingent on love between the partners, and the union might in certain circumstances be dissolved, without regard for personal attachments. For example, the Church was strict in applying the rules of consanguinity: these forbade the marriage of cousins to the seventh degree of relationship, corresponding to the number of days in the week. (The degree was reduced to the fourth by the thirteenth century.) If after marriage even a remote blood relationship was discovered, the couple, no matter how devoted, had to be separated. The godparent also was considered to be related to the godchild, and his children to the godchildren, and they were subject to the same marriage restrictions as were those related by actual blood ties.

Romantic love was a passionate rebellion against loveless marriage and an affirmation of the dignity of the relation between the sexes. So long as it was extramarital, the Church looked upon it as heresy, but in time marriage was considered proper only if it was the consummation of a romantic attachment.

Abelard and Heloise

The nature of romantic love and the intellectual ferment of scholasticism were both exemplified in the life of Peter Abelard (1079–1142), one of the outstanding figures of the age. When he was twenty he became a student at the cathedral school of Notre Dame in Paris, where he was later to teach. His generation was dazzled by the brilliance of his dialectic and the acumen of his conclusions. On the great problem of universals he took the position of moderate realism, a view called conceptualism. The universals conceived by man, he said, are not intangible realities, as the extreme realists believed, nor are they mere names, as the nominalists claimed; but they are clues to reality. His view became the common scholastic assumption in the thirteenth century.

Abelard did much to develop the scholastic method of reasoning by his book *Sic et Non* (*Yes and No*), in which he compiled real or apparent contradictions in the writings of the Scriptures and of the Church Fathers. His purpose was not to discredit the faith but to resolve the problems. When challenged, Abelard accepted the authority of the Church, but sought always to understand, so that he might believe. In this respect, also, he was an architect of the scholastic method.

When he was about forty and she about eighteen, Abelard was attracted by the intellectual precocity and by the comeliness of Heloise, niece of Fulbert, a canon of the cathedral of Notre Dame. Abelard became her tutor, with the consent of her uncle, who lodged him in his own dwelling, where Heloise also lived. Abelard faithfully discharged his assignment in instruction, but, as he later recalled, soon there were more kisses than theses and he was singing to her the songs of the troubadours. When she informed him that she was pregnant, he took her to his sister's home in Brittany, where they were together until the birth of their son, whom they named after a newly discovered astronomical instrument, Astrolabe.

Then Abelard proposed that they marry, but she demurred. Her objections reveal the various crosscurrents of the age. First of all, she told him that he should continue in a churchly career calling for celibacy. He might have pursued an academic career as a married layman, but a teacher's fees would not support a family. She pointed out that he would have to take on extra employ to the detriment of his studies. She was not willing to ruin his career in Church and school. But, if they were to continue their relationship she preferred to remain unwed, because marriage had been so demeaned by subordination to the interests of property; "I desire," she said, "not yours, but you." The tragic sequel has often been related with sensitivity in modern times and need not be recounted here, save to note that they did marry and yet ended their lives in monasticism, she as an abbess, he as a monk of Cluny.

Cistercians and Bernard of Clairvaux

The age that conceived the ideal of courtly love witnessed also a resurgence of ascetic monasticism, as we observed in connection with the Gregorian reform. Among the new orders to arise in the twelfth century, one of the most influential was the Cistercian. Like the others, it arose out of discontent with the Cluniacs, who were criticized for having accomodated their way of life too greatly to worldly practices. They were reproached because of their wealth, because they left manual labor to servants, and because as hosts they fraternized too much with the world. The Cluniacs, it was claimed, were not spiritual even in their prayers, for they rattled off interminable petitions for the souls of others while making no provision for solitude to cultivate their own. The Cluniac churches were regarded as vast monuments to the pride of man, decorated with grotesque hybrid forms, as in the sculptured capitals of their cloisters and chapter houses, serving to distract rather than aid devotion. The Cistercians returned to unadorned simplicity and would not tolerate stained glass windows, even without portraiture.

The Cistercians called for a withdrawal from the world with its wealth, complexity, clutter, and bustle, and a return to a literal observance of Benedict's rule, especially in its emphasis on manual labor in the fields. They were resolved to accept no gift of rich, cultivated land with retainers to do the manual labor. Instead, they took wasteland and broke it in. They reduced forests to fields and turned swamps into "golden meadows." They had experimental greenhouses and devoted themselves to animal husbandry, intensive agriculture, milling, and weaving. Such activities had a marked effect upon the economic advance of Europe, especially of the northern lands.

Much of the ground that the Cistercians took over, however, was untillable, and they used it to pasture sheep. In time they produced more wool than the monks could wear and took the surplus to the market; the wool of the Cistercians became famous. They then became involved in the world they had eschewed. Moreover, although they would have no serfs, they did accept lay brothers called *conversi*, who, having taken vows, would not tend to secularize the monastery, but who nevertheless did relieve the monks of manual labor. Within two centuries, in matters of discipline and austerity the Cistercians were scarcely to be distinguished from other orders. For a century or more after their founding, however, the Cistercians had a profound effect upon the culture of Europe, partly inadvertently through the impact of their improved and highly successful husbandry, partly because they constituted the most important monastic order and the chief religious influence in the West.

The degree and nature of this influence is well illustrated in the career of the great Cistercian abbot, Bernard of Clairvaux, who was more powerful than any pope of the twelfth century. Bernard was born of a noble family in southern France in 1090. He was deeply religious from an early age and devoted to the Virgin Mary. With irresistible zeal he gathered a band of thirty companions, including his brothers, relations, and friends, who with him joined the Cistercians at Cîteaux. In 1115, Bernard was appointed abbot of a daughter monastery in a desolate and forbidding valley he named Clairvaux, the beautiful valley. He remained the abbot of Clairvaux until his death. Subjecting himself to hard labor and great privation, he was so abstracted from the things of sense that when he drank he did not distinguish oil from water. But he was also a marvelous preacher and a person of such great moral force that the world would not leave him alone. He was constantly called away from his cell to adjudicate disputes in the Church, rebuke the mighty, and vindicate the Church and God.

Following the death of Pope Honorius II in 1130, for instance, a disputed election left two contenders for the papacy, Anacletus II and Innocent II. Bernard considered the latter the better man and decided in his favor, without concern about which of the two elections conformed more to canonical rules. The next and greater task was to persuade those sovereigns of Europe who supported Anacletus II to transfer their allegiance to Innocent II. A further complication was that in every diocese, when the bishop declared for one pope, a rival, in the name of the other pope, would lay claim to the see, and the king might be willing to accept the right pope without being willing to renounce the wrong bishop.

Bernard ensured the allegiance of all the rulers of Europe but two: William of Aquitaine and Roger, the Norman, of Sicily. William would not repudiate the wrong local bishop. Bernard placed him under excommunication, then proceeded to celebrate the Mass. William, being excluded, stood outside the door. After consecrating the elements Bernard strode down the aisle, and with the host in his hands addressed him: "We have besought you and you have spurned us. The company of God's servants has implored you and these also you have spurned. See before you now the Virgin's Son; the head and master of the Church which you persecute, comes to you. Before you is your judge, the judge of heaven, earth, and hell in whose presence every knee shall bow. Before you is the judge into whose hands your soul will fall. Dare you spurn and disdain him as you have done his servants?"[2] At these words the duke became rigid with terror and fell as if dead. His knights lifted him, but he fell again, salivating over his beard like an epileptic. Bernard pushed him with his foot, told him to get up and kiss the right bishop of Poitiers, and William complied.

Roger of Sicily remained. His lawyer adduced all the canonical arguments. Bernard brushed them aside. "There was," said he, "only one Ark in the days of Noah, in which eight souls were saved and all others perished. Now we have two arks. If Anacletus has the true ark, then all the churches of France, Germany, Spain, England, and the barbarian kingdoms are lost. The religious orders of the Camaldolese, Chartreuse, the brethren of Cluny, Gramont, Cîteaux, and Prémontré, all will fall into the abyss. Can it be that all these will perish, and only Roger and that dastardly

---

[2] "Vita Prima" II, 6, 38, J.-P. Migne, ed., *op. cit.*, CLXXXV, 290, tr. R. H. Bainton.

Anacletus will alone be saved?"[3] Roger could not long withstand such eloquence plus political pressures and, after some squirming, transferred to Bernard's ark. When later one of Bernard's own monks was elected pope as Eugenius III, Bernard continued to advise and chide as if he were still his abbot.

Bernard looked upon his withdrawal from the world as vocational and did not expect or wish all men to take the cowl. Some should be monks, some should be soldiers, and soldiers should devote their swords to the vindication of justice and the service of the Church. Obeying Eugenius' command, one year after the pope's consecration, Bernard preached the ill-fated second crusade with such extraordinary eloquence that, as he wrote the pope, "villages and towns are now deserted." Writing to the crusading Knights Templars, Bernard said: "The soldier may securely kill, kill for Christ and more securely die. He benefits himself if he dies and Christ if he kills. To kill a malefactor is not homicide but 'malicide' [the killing of the bad]. In the death of the pagan the Christian is glorified because Christ is glorified."[4] The Knights of the Temple were so named because in Jerusalem they were lodged in quarters adjacent to what was assumed to be Solomon's temple. They adopted a form of the Cistercian rule, said to have been drafted by Bernard. In any case, the order combined monasticism and militarism to a degree which would have shocked an earlier age. Unable to eradicate militarism, the Church sought to direct it to Christian ends.

The great impact of Bernard on the centuries to come lay in his mysticism and particularly in his spiritualizing of romantic love. Famous were his sermons on the Song of Solomon, for instance the passage from his commentary on the verse "Let him kiss me with the kiss of his mouth." Bernard asks,

> Who is speaking? The bride. And who, then, is she? The soul thirsting for God. Among the various affections, that which per-

---
[3] *Ibid.*, II, 7, 45, p. 294, tr. R. H. Bainton.
[4] "Liber ad Milites Templi" III, J.-P. Migne, ed., *op. cit.*, CLXXXII, 924, tr. R. H. Bainton.

tains to the bride has a peculiar splendor. A slave fears the face of his master, a hired servant looks for reward, a pupil awaits instruction, a son honors his father, but she who asks for a kiss loves utterly. This affection of love exceeds all the gifts of nature, especially when directed to its source, which is God. No names can be found so sweet as those which express the love of the bridegroom to the bride, for they have all in common. Nothing is owned by one alone. Nothing is divided. There is one inheritance, one home, one table, one bed, and one flesh. If then there is an especial love of the bridegroom and the bride, the name may fittingly be used of the soul which loves. She who loves asks for a kiss. She asks not for freedom or reward, inheritance or instruction, but for a kiss. The most chaste bride, breathing a sacred love, does not dissimulate the flame. She is neither shy nor coy, but from the abundance of the heart bursts abruptly the cry, "Let him kiss me with the kiss of his mouth!"[5]

Gothic

The crowning glory of the twelfth century was the development of the Gothic style. There was a veritable fever of church building in that century and the next. France carted several million tons of stone to construct eighty cathedrals, five hundred large churches, and thousands of smaller edifices. The Gothic style had also a great vogue in England, Germany, and Scandinavia, and penetrated Christian Spain but not Italy, save in the late period just below the Alps, at Milan. The Gothic style was basically an expression of northern piety. The line of transition from the Romanesque to the Gothic is difficult to draw with exactitude, but the first example of Gothic is usually taken to be the reconstruction of the abbey church of St. Denis near Paris by the Abbot Suger in the year 1037.

The Gothic style is an expression of the new piety in which the tension of religion had grown more acute. This century revived

[5] "Sermones in Canticas" I, 1, *ibid.*, CLXXXIII, 807, tr. R. H. Bainton.

the sense of sin. St. Augustine had known it acutely, but the early barbarian converts were lusty sinners, uninhibited, and surely not tormented by any pangs of remorse. The penitential system, with its graded scheme of compensations for particular acts, did not increase the penitential mood. The weekly recital by the monks of the penitential psalms was no guarantee of their contrition. Men have to get better in order to feel worse. Only with the increase in sensitivity does the sense of unworthiness revive. One finds it late in the eleventh century in an unexpected quarter. Peter Damian, a supporter of Gregory VII, was so passionate a denouncer of the sins of others that he might be thought to have considered himself an impeccable saint, until among his works one happens upon these lines:

> Seek I to weep, my heart is stone,
> Seek I to pray, thoughts wander far,
> Seek I the light, phantasies blur.
> Seek I to fight and arm for war
> The spirit fails, the flesh will score.[6]

Perhaps to excuse himself, man in this period magnified his foe. Satan, the lord of Hell, was portrayed as combining all that is repulsive in the beast with all that is sinister in man: the snout of a hog, the paunched chin of a toad, the bristles of a porcupine, the tail of a serpent, the jaw of a bulldog, the brow of an ape, cavernous eyes, and a sardonic leer, unknown among beasts, befitting a fallen angel, carrying from his one-time glory only vestigial wings. The devil was the more seductive because he could assume any form he would. He was claimed to have survived the flood by changing himself into a flea and hiding under the tail of the donkey. He could appear as an angel of light, or even disguise himself as the Redeemer. He had to be very clever to play so many roles and, if he appeared as a monk, he must know all Scripture and all theology and must be more plausible even than God. But the deceiver usually overlooked something. The devil

---

[6] *Ibid.*, CXLV, 971, tr. R. H. Bainton.

once stood in the guise of Christ, resplendent before St. Martin. The saint scanned him critically, then inquired, "Where are the nail prints?"

To the nail prints men now turned for their protection. For Constantine and for Clovis, Christ had been the victor over death rather than the suffering Redeemer. But with a deeper sense of sin came an emphasis upon the passion of Christ and the expiation of sin. This may explain why St. Anselm in the last years of the eleventh century wrote his *Cur Deus Homo* (*Why God Became Man*). His answer was not that of the Greek Fathers of the Church, that God became man in order that man might become God, but rather in order that man might be forgiven. Anselm's views were based on the feudal view of sin, which rated its magnitude in terms of the rank of the person against whom it was committed. Since God is infinite in his greatness, a sin against him is infinite. Such a sin requires infinite satisfaction, or atonement; and since it is man who commits such a sin, it must also be man who suffers in atonement for it. But man, a finite being, is not capable of infinite suffering. Only a being who is both human and divine, and thus infinite, can offer adequate satisfaction as expiation; that being is Christ, in whom God became incarnate and who offered himself in death as atonement for the sins of man. That same Anselm who had devised the ontological argument for the existence of God wrestled here with the excruciating question of the redemption of man, the infinite sinner.

A poignant expression of this view of atonement is found in a letter of Abelard to Heloise, written after the calamity that terminated their carnal relations, when he was seeking to divert her passion from himself to the heavenly Bridegroom. He wrote:

> Dearest sister, are you not moved to compunction by the sight of the only begotten of God who, although he was innocent, yet for you and for all men was taken by the impious, was scourged, mocked, spat upon, crowned with thorns, and executed between thieves by so frightful and shameful a death? Look upon him, your bridegroom and the bridegroom of the Church. See him on

the way, staggering beneath his cross. Take your place with the throng and the women who wept as he passed by. He bought you not with his own but with himself. With his own blood he bought you and redeemed you. What, I ask, did he, who lacked nothing, see in you that he should do battle for you in the agonies of so ignominious a death? What did he seek in you except yourself? He is the true lover who seeks not yours but you.[7]

Gothic architecture enshrines the torment and the tension, the sense of guilt and the joy of redemption, the struggle of man to scale the battlements of heaven and the outstretched arm of God reaching down to assist his ascent.

The dominant note in Gothic is the upward reach, in contrast to the Romanesque style prevalent in the great monastic establishments, a bold architecture with round arches and thick walls supporting barrel vaults, reminiscent of the structures of ancient Rome as the name implies. Gothic differs also from the Byzantine in which the dome seems to be suspended in the firmament as that which comes down from above. Gothic reaches for the stars. The first effort on the part of the Gothic builders was to attain to the utmost height of which the materials were capable, and the heights achieved were astonishing. The cathedral of Chartres equals the elevation of a skyscraper of thirty stories, and that of Strasbourg rises to forty stories. But, there were limits to physical height and they were discovered in the course of repeated failures. An historian of cathedrals has remarked that the question to put to a guide is, "When did the tower fall down?" That of Mont St. Michel collapsed twice. But, when the greatest height consonant with stability had been reached, then the architect sought to create the illusion of elevation. The employment of the flying buttresses eliminated the massive walls of the Romanesque and made possible slender pillars which, in turn, were carved in the form of a cluster of still more slender shafts reaching into infinity. The sculptured forms standing in their niches were elongated: the neck, the arms, the legs seemed not to be in repose but leaping upwards. Stone

---

[7] *Ep.* 5, *ibid.*, CLXXVIII, 2030, tr. R. H. Bainton.

was made to belie its very nature, so that it seemed to soar.

There was a two-way movement. While man ascended, God descended. All such language is, of course, figurative, for God is not more above than below. But, because fiery eruptions belch from the bowels of the earth, whereas sun and rain stream down from above, man has always described spiritual aspiration in terms of ascent, and the response of God as descent. Among all that comes down from above, nothing is so impressive as light. The language of religion is replete with the imagery of light. In the forty-third Psalm light and truth are associated, "Send forth Thy light, send forth Thy truth." In the Gospel of John, Jesus proclaims himself as "the light of the world." The elements of the solar cult came into Christianity with Constantine, who named the first day of the week "the Sun's Day." The Neoplatonists, who thought of light as an intermediary between God and the world, left their imprint on the Christian theologians of the Middle Ages, who, noting that according to Genesis God had created light prior to the sun and the moon, made a distinction between created and uncreated light. Since, then, this light emanated from God immediately and was communicated as well through the heavenly bodies, light was regarded as a direct medium of God's self-impartation, culminating in the incarnation of Christ, the light of the world. Such ideas were adumbrated in the writings attributed to St.Denis, the reconstruction of whose abbey church was the first example of the Gothic style. The Abbot Suger built a cloister of windows about its apse to let in the light. The walls became diaphanous as soon as the areas between the buttressed columns were filled with glass, not clear cold glass, but ruby, crimson, azure and indigo, as golden as the sun, opalescent, sparkling like jewels, twinkling like stars, and changing hourly its manifold hues from the dazzle of dawn to the glow of dusk.

The stained glass and the sculptures portrayed the whole drama of the Redemption, from the Creation to the Last Judgment. Here were the patriarchs and the prophets, the apostles and the evangelists, the doctors and the saints, and above all the blessed Redeemer, especially in his Birth and Passion. The Passion received a prominent place as the focus of the piety of the age. The separate episodes of the Passion were depicted on the walls of the church in the stations of the cross, among which were the trial before Pilate; Christ, with the crown of thorns, receiving the cross; the several scenes of the *via dolorosa*, with Christ stumbling and Simon of Cyrene being given the cross to carry; the Crucifixion; the descent from the cross; and the entombment of Christ. Whether in stone or glass, there were also portrayals of the Resurrection and Ascension, of the Last Judgment, the enthronement of Christ, the coronation of the Virgin and, presiding over all, God the Almighty and Beneficent Father surrounded by the company of the heavenly host singing the praises of the Lamb that was slain. And here, too, were scenes from the lives of the saints depicted in anecdotal detail in some cases not otherwise recorded, as well as themes from the apocryphal gospels and other popular religious literature.

The cathedral was more than a church. It was a community house and the seat of municipal government. The cities with cathedrals did not at first build *hôtels de ville*, because business was conducted in the church, whose sacred portion was only the chancel, whereas the nave would not be desecrated if put to mundane uses. The cathedral was often large enough to accomodate the entire populace of the bishopric. The cathedral of Amiens could hold nearly ten thousand persons, the total population of the city at the time of its completion.

The building of a cathedral did much to unite the community. During the construction of the cathedral at Chartres, for example, the town's inhabitants, from nobles to children, harnessed themselves to carts like beasts to haul the stones, and, it is said, tugged in silence, save for penitential prayers in a pause for rest. Even mortal foes competed in the common purpose of beautifying the house of God. At Chartres, the rose window of the south transept was given by Pierre de Dreux, and the rose window of the north transept bears the fleurs-de-lis of France and the castles of Castile, showing that it was given by King Louis and the queen mother Blanche. Although Pierre, with other French barons, had at one point conspired to kidnap Louis and incarcerate Blanche, the rose windows face each other across the transepts, and from each the ruby light is blended in the roseate glow upon the stones beneath.[8]

Unlike the Byzantine church, the Gothic cathedral did not convey a sense of composure but rather one of precarious balance. Thrust was met by counterthrust, as in scholastic theology thesis was confronted by antithesis. The capitals of the columns and the borders of the windows set forth the glory of creation with accurate delineations of the flowers and the foliage of the burgeoning spring; the water spouts take the form of leering gargoyles, sardonic minions of the Prince of Darkness, who could insinuate himself into the very house of God. The cathedral expresses all those forces battling for the soul of man, to whom tranquility is not granted on his earthly pilgrimage. He can but walk in hope and faith that he who was slain has conquered and "the Lord God Omnipotent reigneth."

That the Gothic style spread as rapidly as it did, first within France and then to neighboring countries, reflects not only the predominance of French culture but an essential unity within the supranational church organization, while at the same time the thrust and counterthrust reflect tensions within the body of Christendom. The Gregorian reform that envisioned a Christian theocracy governing the world through the Roman pontiff underwent further developments in the late twelfth and the thirteenth century, with struggles increasing between Church and state over the source of authority and the hegemony of power.

Law and Justice

One aspect of this persistent controversy was the dispute over the administration of justice. Both Church and king had their

[8] Sartell Prentice, *The Heritage of the Cathedral* (New York, 1936), p. 119.

separate courts and systems of law. The canon law of the Church applied to a wide variety of circumstances, which often brought it into direct conflict with the claims of the secular law under civil authorities. The Church defended the right of women to inherit property; she first introduced the making of wills; she denied that possession is nine-tenths of the law and prohibited usury. The Church claimed jurisdiction over all cases involving clerics, and this meant a vast number of property disputes, because the Church held so much property vested in the names of abbots and bishops. Since she claimed jurisdiction over all cases involving the sacraments, and since marriage was a sacrament, all matrimonial cases were referred to Church courts. Usury and perjury were sins in her eyes, rather than simply civil crimes, and where the state did not act in such matters the Church presumed to judge and sentence.

The greatest clash came over the application of penalties. The Church was scarcely more humanitarian than the state, although when the punishment involved the shedding of blood, the execution of the sentence was delegated to the secular power. For example, St. Dunstan, the abbot of Glastonbury in the tenth century, refused on one occasion to say Mass until justice had been executed on some counterfeiters. The justice consisted in chopping off their hands. In the twelfth century, St. Bernard sent a letter of reproof to Theobald, the count of Champagne, on whose orders a man defeated in a duel had had his eyes put out and his goods confiscated. Bernard protested against the confiscation of his goods because this impinged upon the rights of his innocent family, but had no word of remonstrance over his being blinded.

But the Church would not suffer capital punishment or bodily mutilation to be inflicted on clerics, although clerics were quite as capable as laymen of any crime. In England, the crown maintained that a criminal should not be treated more leniently because of clerical status. This was part of the conflict between King Henry II of England and Thomas à Becket, the archbishop of Canterbury. Henry was struggling valiantly to organize the judicial administration in his realm. He did not demand that the courts of the Church be disbanded. He was quite willing that clerics be tried by the Church, but if they were pronounced guilty, Henry wished that they then be committed to the secular arm for the same punishment accorded to laymen. Becket had been made archbishop by the king because he had been His Majesty's chancellor and the king wanted strong support in his reforms; but, after his consecration, Becket transferred his homage from the king to the Church, and he would not suffer the rights of the Church to be abrogated. The outcome of the subsequent conflict between the two is well known. Henry, being at the time in France, muttered in the presence of some knights, "Is there no one to rid me of this priest?" The knights made off for England. Henry surmised their intent too late to intervene. Becket fell in 1170; Henry in his contrition did penance at his tomb, and the elimination of clerical immunities in England was postponed to a later age.

At the same time, on the Continent, Pope Alexander III came into conflict with Frederick Barbarossa, the first to be called Holy Roman Emperor. The emperor was seeking to regain control of the Italian territories held by his predecessors. In the attempt, the liberties of the newly risen Italian towns of Lombardy were threatened, as was the independence of the papacy itself. After a struggle of many years, the emperor was defeated in 1176 by the towns united in the Lombard League; he was forced to submit to the pope, and some years thereafter he was drowned while on the third crusade. The papacy had been victorious and was ready to enter upon its most dazzling century of power.

Innocent III

In terms of papal supremacy, the thirteenth is the greatest of centuries, and the greatest pope in that century was Innocent III, who served as pontiff at the dawn of the century, from 1198 to 1216. Innocent was a trained canon lawyer; a marvelous administrator; an indefatigable champion of justice; a drastic foe of corruption; a mystic to whom could be attributed the authorship of the *Stabat Mater Dolorosa*, a hymn describing the sorrows of the Virgin at the cross; and, the author of the treatise *De Contemptu Mundi (On Contempt of the World)*. Innocent has been called the greatest of medieval popes, and in his pontificate the Gregorian ideal of Church leadership was most nearly approximated.

Innocent's most spectacular achievements appear in his dealings with Europe's crowned heads. He asserted his authority in the elections and investiture of the Holy Roman emperor by dint of adroit and continual manipulation, seeking always to keep in power the party most favorable to the papacy. There were two parties striving for the imperial dignity, the Guelphs and Ghibellines. These parties had adherents in Italian cities as well as in Germany, and their names were Italian corruptions of German words: *Guelph* was derived from the German family named Welf; *Ghibelline* from Waiblingen, the name of a fortress belonging to the House of Hohenstaufen, the family of Frederick Barbarossa. The Guelphs became identified as supporters of the papacy, the Ghibellines as the imperial, anti-papal party. By playing off the one against the other in a series of maneuvers, Innocent succeeded, in 1212, in placing his candidate on the throne in the person of Frederick II. In the struggle for authority, the papal victory was assured.

In France, Innocent had trouble with Philip Augustus, who had set aside his Danish wife, Ingeborg, and married the daughter of a Bavarian duke. The pope laid France under an interdict, an excommunication that applied not merely to the king but to all those within his realm. Within the interdicted area, the rites of the Church were forbidden. No incense was burned, Mass was not said, and the dead were denied Christian burial. Whether marriage was invalidated is not altogether clear, but the prudent went beyond the interdicted territory to cement their vows. When Philip yielded and the ban was lifted, in 1200, so great was the rejoicing that three hundred persons were killed in the celebrations.

On the Iberian Peninsula, Innocent annulled the marriage of Alfonso IX of Leon and Berengaria of Castile on grounds of consanguinity. They resisted for five years, but then Berengaria went into a convent. The king of Navarre was deposed for making a treaty with the Moors. The king of Aragon was crowned in Rome and gave his kingdom as a fief to St.Peter, with the promise of a yearly tribute. In 1212, by his approval of a crusade against the Moors, Innocent encouraged the kingdoms of Aragon, Navarre, and Castile in a common action that culminated in a victory for the Christians in the battle of Las Navas de Tolosa, a major step in their long-drawn-out reconquest of Spain.

The liveliest conflict of Innocent was that with King John of England. The monks at Canterbury elected an archbishop who went to Rome for confirmation. King John and the bishops, getting wind of this, chose another candidate and sent their delegation to Pope Innocent III. He decided that the right of election belonged to the monks but then took the choice out of their hands by instructing them to elect Stephen Langton, actually the ablest and noblest churchman in England. John was furious and threatened to burn the cloister of Canterbury, monks and all. The pope put England under an interdict (1208). John swore "by the teeth of God"—it was customary to call Christ God and to swear by various parts of his anatomy: eyes, liver, shins, wounds—that he would cut off the noses and put out the eyes of all the Romanists in England. If the clergy would not perform their functions, he would confiscate their revenues. The pope then called upon Philip Augustus of France, no longer under interdict, to lead a crusade against John. At this, the barons in England took advantage of the crown's predicament to assert their own claims. When John perceived that he could not resist the barons, the king of France, and the pope at the same time, he decided to come to terms with the most powerful of the three. He submitted to Pope Innocent and made England a fief of the papacy. When the barons presented John with the Magna Carta, he had papal support in offering them resistance, since the pope claimed that the king was in no position to make an agreement without the approval of his new feudal overlord, the pope.

Innocent also had dealings with all the outlying regions of Europe and with the kingdoms of the East. He aided Sweden in the establishment of a legitimate line of sovereigns. In Norway, he protected the clergy from being brought before lay tribunals. In Denmark, he resisted an ambitious bastard aspiring to the crown. In Hungary, he supported the king against his brother and the bishop against the king. In Ireland, the king of Connaught was made to respect the right of asylum. In Poland, the bishops were incited to reform. The churches of Bulgaria, Serbia, and Armenia were induced to join the Roman fold, though these unions were only temporary. The Jews were protected against violence and intimidation.

In 1215, Innocent summoned the great Fourth Lateran Council, which was attended by the patriarchs of Jerusalem and Constantinople, close to a thousand ecclesiastics, plus the envoys of the major rulers of Europe and the Levant, including the Holy Roman emperor, the emperor of the Eastern Empire, and the kings of England, France, Aragon, Hungary, and Jerusalem. Among other enactments of far-reaching importance, this council officially formulated the doctrine of transubstantiation, which teaches that when the priest at the altar pronounces the words *"hoc est corpus meum"* (this is my body), the substance of bread and wine is changed into the substance of the body and blood of Christ.

St. Francis and St. Dominic

During the pontificate of Innocent III, the introduction of a new type of monasticism strengthened the Church's leadership and influence in the changing medieval society. The members of the new orders were called not monks but brothers—in Italian *fratello*, or simply *fra*, in French *frère*, in English friar. The leaders of the new movement, St.Francis and St.Dominic, were partly opposed to and partly in accord with the spirit of their age. Both men, particularly Francis, rejected the rising commercialism. But, at the same time, they did not withdraw from society but accommodated monasticism to urban culture by giving up the Benedictine rule of residence in the monastery and allowing their members to circulate wherever men were to be found.

Francis was the son of a merchant of Assisi and of a French woman from the land of the troubadours in the *midi*. Francis loathed the acquisitiveness of his father and adored the blithe insouciance of his mother. He was a gay blade who preferred larks to ledgers. Yet, revelry soon palled and disquiet invaded his spirit. One night, when he had been masquerading as the king of fools, his companions discovered him sitting in dejection on a curb, and they inquired, "What's the matter, Francis? Did you get married?" "Yes," he replied, "to the fairest of all brides, to *La Donna Povertà*, the Lady Poverty." Here was the cult of romantic love applied to a personification. She was more exacting than any mistress, for she imposed an absolute poverty. Francis might live by work, he might live by begging, but he might accept alms only for the needs of the day and only the worst, the cast-off garment of an Umbrian peasant, and if food were tasty he should make it unpalatable by a sprinkling of ashes. Franciscan poverty was not Cynic poverty. The object was not to secure peace of mind by divesting oneself in advance of all that might be taken away. It was not the poverty of the early Church Fathers who steeled themselves thereby for martyrdom. The poverty of Francis was indeed an emancipation from care, but basically it was a device for social regeneration. From what do wars arise, he asked, if not from quarrels over property? The renunciation of any claim to "mine and thine" is a more effective path to peace than the Peace of God, the Truce of God, and even the building of a cathedral.

The poverty of Francis bears no trace of despising the created world. Possessing nothing, he possessed everything, and rejoiced in wonder at God's creations. The saint composed the first recorded poem in the Italian language, "The Canticle of the Sun," in which the Most High is praised for the sun, who is called a brother, for the moon and stars, "precious, bright, and fair", for wind and fire, for water, flower, and fruit; and, for the love of those who meekly suffer woe.

This very song expresses the thrust and counterthrust of joy in salvation and pain at the thought of Christ's Passion, as does more markedly a legend from *The Mirror of Perfection:*

> Inebriated with the love and compassion of Christ, the blessed Francis would betimes voice in the French tongue the most sweet melodies that welled up within him. . . . He would pick up a stick from the ground and lay it across his left arm and then in his right hand would draw another across it like a bow, as if he were playing on a viol or some other stringed instrument, and making appropriate gestures, he would sing in French of the Lord Jesus. But all this pantomime ended in tears, and his exuberance was dissolved in passion for Christ.[9]

Francis' followers grew in numbers. Their mission was to bathe the lepers, work with the peasants, preach to the people. They were different from the older monastic orders in that their poverty was more drastic; further, Francis sought to guard it against any mitigation, either through the accumulated fruits of the friars' labor or the acceptance of large donations, lest his order go the way of the older Cluniac and Cistercian orders. The Franciscan friars might work or beg, but only for the needs of the day. The other difference was, as we noted, that for the Franciscans *stabilitas* was to be replaced by *mobilitas*. The brothers might have some rude shelters as a base, but their mission was to go to the people wherever they were congregated and where the need of physical help and spiritual guidance was greatest, and that meant primarily in the cities.

The mission on which Francis and his followers had embarked

---

[9] *Speculum Perfectionis,* ed. P. Sabatier (Paris, 1898), tr. R. H. Bainton.

would not for long be tolerated by the local churchmen, with whom they competed wherever they traveled, unless authorized by the pope. In 1210, Francis sought and obtained approval of his group as a separate order from Innocent III, who, however, laid upon them a restriction in view of their lack of learning. They were not to discuss theology, but were to preach penitence. This meant that they must center on sin, remorse, and forgiveness through the merits of the Passion of the Redeemer. The sins against which they most commonly inveighed were sodomy, usury, luxury, vanity, and vengeance. The Franciscans were renowned for the reconciliation of feuds. Into town and hamlet, village and farm, market or leper house went these troubadours of God, preaching and singing.

The order grew and that made for trouble. Society can manage a dozen unpredictable, improvident poets, but five hundred is another matter. How could they survive by begging only for the day? Some days were bound to be lean. When one of the brothers was seen sorting filthy lucre with a stick, he was reproached by another, but he replied, What was to be done with so many bellies to feed? Cardinal Ugolino, the protector of the order, came forward with a happy suggestion. Let the Church assume the burden of ownership (*dominium*), and let the brothers have the use (*usus*). Some of the brothers agreed to this, and they became the Conventuals. Some did not; they became the Spirituals.

Francis was very unhappy over the trend away from the stark simplicity of his original program. After his death, the rift among the Franciscans became overt. Brother Elias, who had fallen in love rather with Francis than with Lady Poverty, started to build a church in the saint's honor at Assisi. But great churches cannot be built by unskilled troubadours of God. Masons must be engaged and paid. Elias set up a money box which Brother Leo smashed. Sister Clare—an early convert who became the head of a branch order for women—sympathized with Leo. The unity of the order was seriously imperiled and the Spirituals were subjected to persecution. In time, the order went the way, by and large, of the earlier monastic orders, although radical groups repeatedly split off from the parent organization.

The Dominicans, named for St.Dominic, a Spaniard of noble birth, were in many ways similar to the Franciscans. Late in the twelfth century, heretical sects—notably the Albigenses around Albi and the Waldenses around Lyons in southern France—had risen to challenge the papacy. While accompanying his bishop through the *midi*, Dominic observed the devoutness of these heretics, who outdid the monks themselves in their extreme asceticism. He perceived that they would never be reclaimed by bishops riding on luxurious palfreys. The upholders of the true faith would have to commend it by imitation of the Master, "who had nowhere to lay his head." With Dominic, poverty was not so much an ideal as a technique, and poverty of itself, he realized, would not suffice. To overcome false teaching, there must be true teaching. Dominic founded his order to combat the ignorance of both clergy and laity. Hence, the Dominicans became primarily a teaching order, even though they were called the Order of Preachers.

Economy of the Middle Ages

The new orders assisted in the permeation of every aspect of medieval life with the ideals of the Church. The reality of this permeation is more evident in the political sphere, because dramatized by conflicts, than in the economic, but in both, though practice often fell short, the ideals were acknowledged.

The Church distrusted the merchants as tainted with the lust of lucre, yet encouraged them to expiate their avarice by contributions to the Church. Bad consciences helped to build cathedrals. The Church, in the main, put the contributions to good use. She was a great loan association, succoring the victims of famine and like disasters by lending without interest, though on security. Since the loans were for consumption, interest appeared to be robbery.

Interest, which in any form had been called usury, had been condemned in the Book of Leviticus, and Aristotle had taught that money is not capable of generating money. Rent was distinguished from interest because the land that is rented is plainly productive.

The organization of economic groups arose out of self-interest, but not without regard to the ethical restraints imposed by the Church. First there arose merchant guilds and later craft guilds. In their relations to each other, these associations were competitive and monopolistic. Trade secrets were rigorously guarded. The guilds in a given town did not permit competing goods to enter from another city. Quarrels were frequent between guilds in related crafts; between harness makers and saddlers, between cooks and mustard makers, between the sellers of old clothes and the makers of new.

But, within the guild, there was a spirit of fraternity. The three ranks, the apprentices, the journeymen, and the masters, were often a small family and one such family was to help another. A master with more than three helpers was not to refuse the loan of a man to another master in an emergency. The guild assured its members of fair wages, of assistance in poverty, sickness, and death. Women workers, like weavers and seamstresses, were admitted. In dealing with the consumer, the guild guaranteed sound wares and honest weights. Fishmongers used scales with holes, to drain off the water. There was an obligation to observe the just price in terms of the cost of production and not to take advantage of scarcity.

The guilds were also charitable organizations. Because the Church objected to usury, charities could not be supported by endowments bearing interest. Instead, special societies called "confraternities" assumed responsibility for particular charities out of current income. Guilds were often also confraternities, building and maintaining hospitals, canals, seaports, town halls, monasteries, and cathedrals, including stained glass windows in which, as at Chartres, the crafts are depicted. The guilds were very prominent in the religious life of the communities, and heretics were excluded. Each guild had its patron saint, for, as there were saints to ward off particular diseases, so there were others to protect particular crafts. St.Eloi was the patron of the goldsmiths, St.Vincent of the wine growers, St.Fiacre of the gardeners, St. Blaise of the masons, St.Crespin of the shoemakers, and St.Julien of the village fiddlers. The Christian year had about thirty holy days, observed as holidays. At such times, the guilds put on gorgeous pageants in honor of their respective patron saints.

The guilds assumed responsibility for the performance of mystery plays, often produced on an enormous scale. We read that in the early sixteenth century a presentation of the Acts of the Apostles at Bourges required forty days and called for four hundred and ninety-four actors. Early in the fifteenth century, the guild of masons at York asked the mayor and aldermen to relieve them of staging the Fergus play. Fergus is a Scotch name which a malicious English playwright bestowed upon a Jew who tried to prevent the burial of the Virgin Mary. The masons objected to the production because the incident of Fergus is not in the Bible and because the play always came at dusk. They were permitted to offer the pageant of Herod, instead.

The total picture of guild life reveals a combination of economic self-interest and public philanthropy, as well as efforts to practice the ethical injunctions of the Church and to discharge with splendor the offices of religion.

Heresies

Strangely, the period when the Church exercised her greatest control over European society also saw the revival of schisms and heresies. Why, when the ecclesiastical structure was most completely integrated, should these fissures have appeared? The early Church had known many splits, and the period from the twelfth century to the twentieth has been notoriously divisive. But, from the barbarian invasions until about 1100, the Church in the West was able to maintain a fairly united structure, perhaps because the low level of general culture during that period militated against theological concern. But men can quarrel without theology, and the divisions of the twelfth and thirteenth century were not solely theological. The Church in the early Middle Ages was held together by the struggle against paganism and anarchy, while monasticism provided a sufficient outlet for individualism and diversity. When the Church grew more rigid, the cracks began to appear.

Such troubles were apparent before the pontificate of Innocent. The Albigenses, the Waldenses, and other sects originating in the twelfth century maintained that moral reform was too imperative to wait for ecclesiastical permission. The spirit of the sects, as already observed, was the same as that of the eleventh-century Gregorian reformers and of the monastic reform orders like the Cistercians, but disillusionment with the achievements of previous reformers gave the sects an added impetus. The great "peace" movement had resulted in a crusade against the infidels, but the crusaders, increasingly recruited from the dregs of society, were falling into disrepute; the second and third crusades had been failures. The fourth, which was launched by Innocent III, was a disaster. The crusaders were excommunicated for having destroyed a Christian town to pay off their debt to their Venetian carriers; but, heedless of the pope's curse, they went on to Constantinople, and there, quarreling with the Greeks, captured and looted the city, doing more damage to its sacred shrines than the Turks ever did in the years that followed.

In addition to these failures, the requirement of clerical celibacy had resulted in widespread concubinage. The efforts of the Church to administer the world had involved her even more in the affairs of the world. The monastic orders, as noted, were forever being undone by their virtues, which created wealth that in turn corrupted virtue. The conclusion to be deduced from the relative failure of such vast endeavors was that if reform could not be achieved on a large scale, it should be undertaken on a small one, and if not by institutions then by convinced individuals who should not wait for the assistance or even the permission of the authorities.

One such individual was Peter Waldo, a twelfth-century merchant of Lyons and the founder of a sect called the Waldenses. Waldo was induced to embrace a life of poverty by hearing the song of a wandering minstrel celebrating not the deeds of a knight but those of a saint, Alexius, who on his wedding day forsook his bride and went on a pilgrimage. Returning too emaciated to be recognized, he lived for years as a beggar in a shed beside his parents' house and was identified only after his death. Impelled by this ideal of renunciation, Waldo gave a portion of his goods to his wife and distributed the rest to the poor, thereby reducing himself to mendicancy. Thus far, there was nothing to which the Church could object. His next step was to engage a priest to translate large portions of the Gospel into the vernacular. These he learned by heart and began passing them on to others. He and his followers were thus entering upon the role of teachers and preachers, and here his archbishop intervened and forbade them to continue. Waldo appealed to Pope Alexander III. An examiner reported that the sectaries were utterly unlearned. Nevertheless, the pope granted them permission to preach if they had the consent of their bishop, but they refused to accept such a condition and were eventually excommunicated.

The Waldenses were widespread in southern France and were soon joined by followers in northern Italy. At first they were not heretical but merely anti-clerical. But, eventually they went so far as to maintain that sacraments administered by unworthy priests were invalid, recalling the ancient heresy of the Donatists. From literal obedience to the command to sell all, they passed to an equally literal observance of the injunction against swearing and resisting evil. Popular piety was affronted by their unwillingness to do reverence to a crucifix. The rejection of oaths in a society where all agreements were so sealed and the refusal to participate in war caused them to be regarded as a menace to society. Rejected by the community at large, they could no longer live by begging and were forced to develop two classes within their own society, one of which supported the other. Under persecution, they survived by withdrawing to the fastnesses of the Italian Alps, and there they continued to live until the nineteenth-century *Risorgimento*, when they were permitted to expand into Italy and the New World.

The Albigenses, so called because they were numerous in and about the town of Albi in southern France, were another heretical sect that challenged the Church in the twelfth and thirteenth century. Commonly known as the Cathari, or the "Pure," these sectaries probably infiltrated into Europe from Bulgaria, where one of their chief branches bore the name of Bogomiles. In line with the Gnostics and Manichaeans of the East, the Albigenses shared the dualistic view of two basic world principles, of good and of evil: spirit was the creation of the good principle, matter of the evil one.

Like the Gnostics before them, the Albigenses rejected the Old Testament, because it testified to the goodness of the created world. Since in their eyes matter was evil, nothing material could be used in the service of religion. Also, since they believed that Christ did not have a physical body, they rejected the idea that the bread and wine of the Eucharist were transubstantiated into his body and blood. Their Lord's Supper was merely a commemoration. They would tolerate no images, not even the crucifix, and they derided music.

Plainly, the Albigenses were more drastic than the iconoclasts in their effort to spiritualize Christianity. They branded sex as utterly evil and would eat nothing they knew to be a product of sexual reproduction. Fortunately they were ignorant of sex in fish. They held that birth is an imprisonment of the spirit in the flesh, inflicted as punishment for sins committed in a pre-existent state. Sins committed in this life had to be expiated by the transmigration of the soul through further births. Should one attain perfection in this life, the Albigenses believed, it would be better to commit suicide than run the risk of a subsequent lapse. If universally adopted, their ideas would have led to the termination of the human race; but not all their members practiced the full rigors, and a division was made between the *perfecti* (the "perfect") and the *credentes* (the "believers"), of whom less was required. Since, for them, expiation had to be made in successive reincarnations, the Catholic doctrine of purgation in purgatory was naturally rejected.

In the eyes of the Albigenses, the popes who had introduced so many corruptions into the Church were not the successors of Peter but of Constantine. Innocent III attributed the popular spread of the Albigensian heresy to the dissoluteness of some of the clergy in the Provence. No sectary ever denounced the clergy more mercilessly than did the pope. He sent Peter Castelnau as a legate to exhort Count Raymond of Toulouse (a successor of that Count Raymond who had gone on the first crusade) to suppress heresy in his domain; but the count was extremely dilatory, since the sectaries had a great many adherents among the nobility. Then Castelnau was murdered, and the count was suspected of complicity in the crime. Like Thomas à Becket, Castelnau achieved more by dying than by living. In 1179, the pope declared a crusade, offering the northern French the salvation of their souls as well as property in the south in return for forty days of sacking cities and burning heretics. The northern French were eager to reduce the power of the south, but the Albigensian crusade was not actually undertaken until 1209. After twenty years of warfare, the heretics were crushed and the Provence was wrecked. Eventually, the territory was annexed to the crown of France.

Several concepts played a role in the ideology of the medieval sects. One was the effort to recover the past. All Christian groups, of course, appealed to the authority of the past, since for them all the Golden Age was the period of the New Testament. The papal Church appealed to the mandate given by Christ to Peter, as the empire appealed to the Apostle Paul's endorsement of the state. But, these mandates were not construed as constricting the Church and the empire to the pattern of the past, whereas the sects were more disposed to attempt to follow New Testament precepts, including that of poverty, as closely as they could. Whereas the Church based its authority on the unbroken continuity of Church history and tradition, the sects repudiated the authority of the centuries since the Golden Age.

Other extremely important ideas in the sectarian movements had to do with the beginning and the end of history. The idea of predestination did not take hold until the fourteenth century and will be considered later. In the late twelfth and thirteenth century, the primitive Christian expectation of the imminent end of the age was revived and did much to diminish the importance of the Church dominant in the present age. This view had been promulgated at the end of the twelfth century by a Calabrian abbot, Joachim of Flora, who divided history into three ages: one of the Father, one of the Son, and one of the Holy Spirit. Each was subdivided into seven others. His own generation, he claimed, fell in the second age and the sixth period, so that very shortly the advent of the age of the Spirit could be expected. Then the visible Church would be dissolved into the Church invisible and "the eternal Gospel" would be ushered in. The date would be the year 1260, a number taken from an account in the Book of Revelation, which tells how a woman clothed with the sun fled from a dragon with seven heads and hid in the wilderness for 1260 days. Not too far in advance of his own time, then, the mighty papacy would have served its historical purpose and would give way to a nobler successor.

The heretics, who put such ideas to their own use, menaced the supremacy of the Church, which held that salvation lay only within her fold.

Inquisition

To deal with them and with the remnants of the Albigenses and Waldenses, the Holy Office of the Inquisition was instituted under papal control. In 1233, under Pope Gregory IX, the bishops who had previously dealt with heresy were replaced by papal inquisitors selected largely from the friars.

The inquisition sought its justification in Augustine's theory that constraint may be exercised on heretics for their salvation, out of love for their souls. As earlier explained, he had in mind only fines and imprisonment, but now the penalty was death by burning. Beheading was avoided because "the Church abhors the shedding of blood." Augustine had also used the analogy of saving the body by amputating the rotten limb. The body was now interpreted as the Church, and the rotten limb, the heretic. Heresy was considered the greatest of all sins because it was an affront to the greatest of all persons, God; worse than treason against a king because it was directed against the heavenly sovereign; worse than counterfeiting money because it counterfeited the truth of salvation; worse than parricide and matricide, which destroy only the body. Whatever penalties were appropriate for these crimes were all the more fitting for the greatest crime. To burn the heretic was an act of love toward the community, by fear deterring others inclined to the same sin, and an act of love toward the heretic, who might be recalled by terror of the fire and save his soul.

The inquisitors tried to secure a confession of guilt from the heretic by alternating blandishments and intimidation, solitary confinement and torture. If he recanted, he might be committed to life-long confinement enchained in a dungeon, or he might be granted the mercy of being strangled before being burned at the stake. If after his recantation he relapsed into heresy, he was simply burned. Churchmen themselves did not apply torture, nor did they serve as executioners. The convicted heretic was committed with a plea for mercy to the civil magistrate, who was subject to excommunication if he heeded the plea.

The first emperor to inflict the penalty of death for heresy since the days of the Roman Empire was Frederick II, who was himself suspected of heresy, if not indeed of blasphemy. Both as a man and as a thinker he was one of the most remarkable figures in medieval Christendom. He had been reared in Sicily at a court where Jews and Saracens were welcomed and was reputed to be the author of a work on the three impostors, Moses, Mohammed, and Christ. Frederick may have had nothing to do with any such book; but that one who consorted so freely with infidels should have executed heretics is puzzling. The victims were located in the north Italian cities disaffected by his rule, and perhaps Frederick used accusations of heresy to cow political enemies. That churchmen themselves could have condoned such expedients to crush heretics at the very moment when the papacy was at the pinnacle of power, excites greater wonder than the anomaly of Frederick. Perhaps, after all, these churchmen did not feel so secure, for men are seldom cruel save when they are afraid. The Inquisition was effective in exterminating the Albigenses and dispersing the Waldenses, but in the fourteenth century sectarianism arose again, and in a much more redoubtable form, because joined with nationalism, as we shall see.

Thomas Aquinas

The rise of the universities, the recovery of great areas of ancient learning—particularly the works of Aristotle—and the scholarship of the mendicant orders brought the Middle Ages to their highest intellectual achievements in the thirteenth century. At the peak of this development stood the great system of the Dominican friar St. Thomas Aquinas. Just as scholastic theology avoided extremes, fighting shy of radical monism and drastic dualism, so within the scholastic tradition Aquinas took a middle ground, notably with regard to the possibility of the knowledge of God and the relation of faith and knowledge. Theologians called Augustinians held to the possibility of a vision of God in this life, by which man can have a direct knowledge of God. In that case faith and knowledge do not exclude each other and are but different ways of apprehending Divine Reality. There is really no need, on such an assumption, for any demonstration of the existence of God, but if there is no such vision, then man must seek all the proofs that have cogency. The nominalists said there are no proofs whatever that have cogency, for man experiences only particular objects and cannot deduce from them an all-embracing universal such as God. If one does believe in such an all-embracing universal, it can only be by an act of faith, which is to be distinguished sharply from knowledge and is even at variance with reason, which leads to no such conclusion. The middle ground taken by Aquinas is that faith and knowledge are mutually exclusive, so that one believes precisely at the point where one does not know. But faith and knowledge are not antithetical and reason can make faith plausible.

But reason must have something with which to start and Aquinas felt that Anselm did not have enough to warrant his ontological argument for the existence of God. The arguments that did appeal to Aquinas were those drawn from Aristotle, whose writings had only just come to be more fully known in the West by way of the Arabs in Spain. The distinction of Aquinas is that he effected a new synthesis of the Christian and classical traditions by incorporating into his theology these new elements. Aristotle argued for the existence of God on the ground that causation calls for a first cause and motion requires a prime mover and these are God. Aquinas accepted this argumentation, while recognizing that the roles of the first cause and the prime mover by no means encompass the richness of the Christian picture of God. He agreed with Augustine that human reason can never arrive unaided at the Christian doctrine of the Trinity, but if the doctrine be given by revelation, then it can be rendered intelligible by analogy. The system of Aquinas assumed the shape of a pyramid. At the base is the natural, at the apex the supernatural. Below is reason, above revelation; at the bottom human endeavor, at the summit divine grace. The distinctive point about this hierarchy is that it exhibits no sharp dichotomies at any point. Reason rising from below is met by revelation coming down from above. They meet and mesh. Revelation illumines reason and reason elucidates revelation. Faith and knowledge, though distinguished, support each other.

This system has important implications for politics and ethics, because Church and state, right and wrong, fit into this hierarchical scheme. The state belongs to the order of nature and reason, which lies within the scope of man endowed with reason, and within this area lies the whole realm of natural law. To be sure, man's reason was partly vitiated by the fall of Adam, and that is why natural law has come to endorse property, slavery, and war. Nevertheless, the natural faculties of man are still sufficiently intact to enable him to administer the body politic. Here is a view which undercuts the notion that the political is derived from the spiritual and ecclesiastical. A warrant may be found here for an independence of the state from the Church. Aquinas apparently did not see the full implications of his position, for he did say that every human being must be subject to the Roman pontiff, though this statement is itself ambiguous because it does not make plain whether the word "subject" applies to the political or only to the spiritual authority.

Dante Alighieri

Aquinas provided a certain summation of Christian thought in the high Middle Ages. Dante offered another in his Latin work *On Monarchy*, which vindicates the claims of the empire against the papacy, and in his vernacular poem *The Divine Comedy*, which voices many of the reformatory themes of the age. Dante is Franciscan in portraying Christ upon the cross, abandoned by all save Lady Poverty. But Dante has a feeling for the institutional Church when he places Pope Celestine in hell because he made "the great refusal" and, after a few weeks, resigned from the burdens of the papacy. To place popes and cardinals in hell was no innovation. The Church had never pretended that even her primates were all saints. Romantic love in the *Paradiso* is so etherealized that, though the smile of Beatrice would make a man happy in the fire, she is so unsubstantial that she casts no shadow. The treatment of purgatory and paradise, apart from artistic craftsmanship, is less revolutionary as compared with previous visions of the future life than the portrayal of hell. What Augustine did for sin, Dante did for the punishment of sin. Augustine moved from the outward to the inward. The great sins for him were not apostasy, adultery, and murder, but pride, arrogance, and the lust of domination. Dante rationalized hell. Although he did not disdain the devices of horror, yet for him the ultimate horror was not that man burned, but that sin froze, and man remained for all eternity what once he was. The blasphemer is made to say, "Such as I was when living, that I am now."

All the grotesque demonology of the Middle Ages is dropped. Satan in *The Divine Comedy* does not play a role, as in *Paradise Lost*. Sheer pain is present not only from flames, but also from ice and the nausea from fetid exhalations. Those who on earth in the sweet air made gladsome by the sun, carried a foul and lazy mist within, are now bogged in murky lees, able only to gurgle dolor in their throats. Worse than pain is impotence and confusion. Here are spirits relentlessly whirled like starlings in a gust of wind. Most frightful is the cyclic repetition of creeping horror, climax, and dissolution. Here are naked spirits, hands bound by serpents, with adders darting at the napes of their necks. Fire consumes all, but then the selfsame forms arise like the Arabian phoenix to repeat the cycle of their woes.

But nothing is so terrible as to be forever what one was. Here

54. A CLOISTER CITY

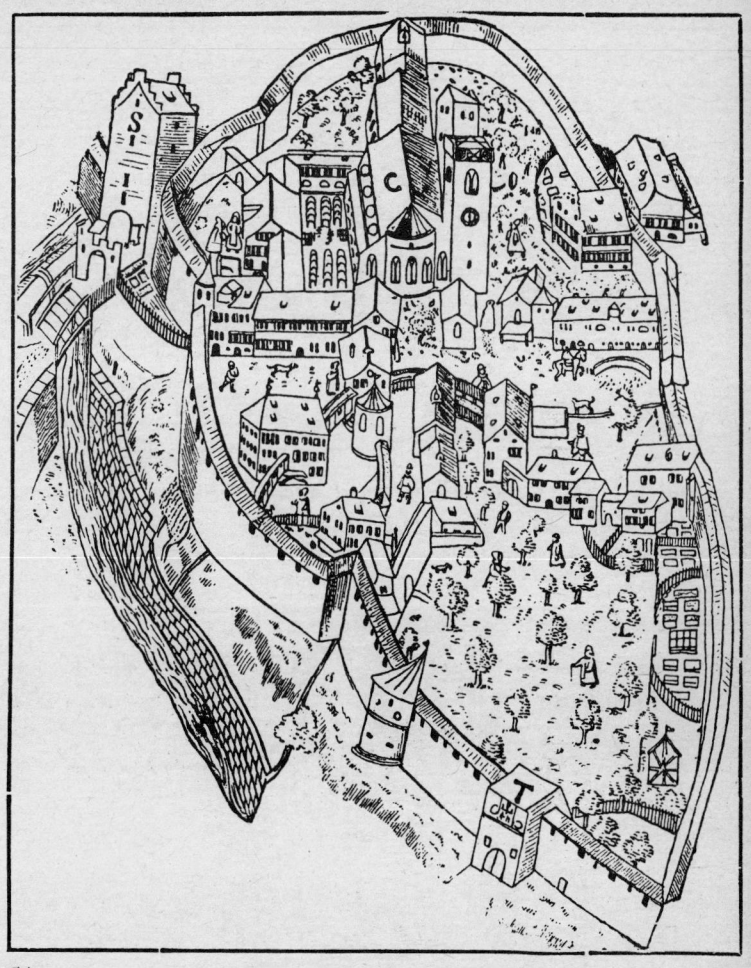

54

A cloister could grow until it became a city with a wall and a moat. Sometimes the townsmen would build their houses all around the cloister's enclosure. Above is the cloister of St. Gallen, from a woodcut of 1596. The letter C on the roof of the chapel and the letters S and T on the gates apparently point to a chart of identification.

55. A UNIVERSITY LECTURE

From the *Romans de Chevalerie Française* (Lyon, Guillaume le Roy, ca. 1480).

56. A TOURNAMENT

A tournament might serve as a military exercise in preparation for war, as a duel between champions in place of war by their retainers, or simply as a game to be conducted in accord with the rules of chivalry. (From *Ogier le Danois* [Paris, Nicolas Bonfours, ca. 1580].)

57. CIVIL LAW AND CANON LAW

58. THE SEVEN SACRAMENTS

58.   Die sieben Sakramente

First formulated as seven in number by Peter Lombard, they were officially declared to be so by Pope Eugenius IV in 1439. Above, top center, is the celebration of the Mass, flanked by Penance on the left and Ordination on the right. On either side of the crucifixion we have Confirmation and Marriage above and, on the bottom row, Baptism and Extreme Unction. This engraving is by Hans Baldung Grien (1484–1545).

59. THE ECCLESIASTICAL HIERARCHY

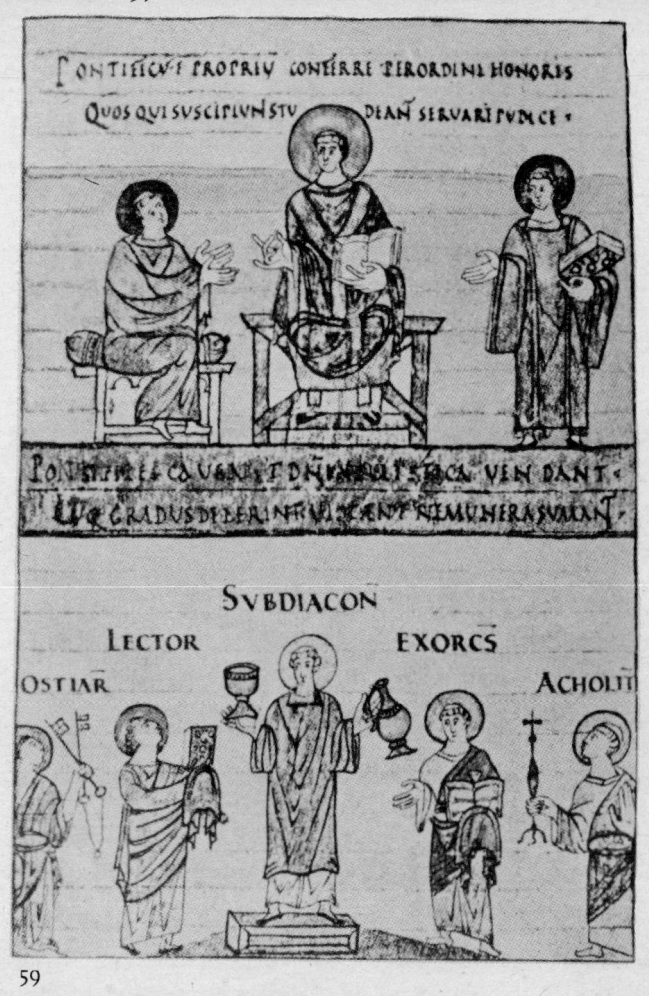

59

The orders of the Church are here shown in their respective robes. At the top center is the bishop, to our left a priest, and to our right a deacon holding a book. On the bottom, from left to right, we have the beadle with his keys, the reader with a book, and subdeacon with the chalice and a flask for pouring wine or water, the exorcist with a book and a bell, and the acolyte with a candlestick. This miniature is from a sacramentary of the ninth century, preserved in the town library of Autun.

60. THE CORONATION OF THE VIRGIN

The cult of the Virgin did not develop as an offset to the image of Christ as the frightful Judge, for it was in the same period when the suffering Redeemer was portrayed in his tenderness, that a greater devotion grew up toward his mother. There may be a connection with the emergence of romantic love in human relationships. The Virgin Mary was the Lady to whom devotion was vowed, and to her were dedicated the Cathedral of Chartres, Notre Dame of Paris, and many other cathedrals. (From a Book of Hours, in Latin and French, of the first quarter of the fifteenth century.)

61. ST. BERNARD AND THE PAPAL SCHISM

In order to ensure the recognition of Innocent II, St. Bernard had to overcome opposition in Rome itself. When the schism occurred, the Roman senate sought to throw off the authority of either pope with the city of Rome and to take over the government for itself. The above illustration from the *Chronicle of Bishop Otto von Freising*, now at the university library at Jena, shows the senators confronting Innocent II.

62a

With St. Bernard there is a shift away from the image of Christ as the terrible Judge to that of the suffering Redeemer, all tenderness and compassion. The tone of St. Bernard's sermons on the Canticles is well illustrated by Fig. 62a (from Anslem of Canterbury, *Explanationes in Cantica*, twelfth century) showing, within the letter O, Christ

ST. BERNARD

62b

the bridegroom embracing the Church, his bride. Fig. 62b (from a manuscript from the one-time Cistercian abbey at Wettingen, founded in the fifteenth century) shows the crucified Christ leaning from the cross to receive the suppliant St. Bernard. This illustration is later than St. Bernard's time, for it was not until the late thirteenth century that the crown of thorns was placed on the head of Christ and his legs were shown crossed and nailed to the cross by only one nail.

63. PENANCE

Men and women seeking absolution from the bishop and his clergy are depicted in this miniature of the eleventh century (from a sacramentary preserved in the library of the University of Göttingen).

64. GOTHIC CATHEDRALS

The cathedral at Lichfield, England, was dedicated to St. Mary and St. Chad (in Saxon, *Ceadda*); the latter became its fourth bishop in A.D. 669. The present building (Fig. 64a), which was preceded by a Norman structure, went through several stages until it was completed in the high Gothic period of the thirteenth and early fourteenth centuries. Its Lady Chapel (Fig. 64b) is the only one in England with a Gothic apse. The windows rise to the curves of the vaulting. The cathedral was subjected to considerable damage at the hands of the early Anglican and, subsequently, of the Puritan reformers. The destroyed glass in the Lady Chapel was replaced in 1802 with panes secured on the dissolution of an abbey of Cistercian nuns in Belgium. The glass itself dates from 1530. The cathedral has suffered its greatest defacements from restorations. (These illustrations are taken from Schuyler van Rensselaer, *English Cathedrals* [New York, 1893]; the drawings are by Joseph Pennell.)

Sainte-Chapelle in Paris (Fig. 64c) was built in the thirteenth century, at the command of St. Louis, to house the crown of thorns.

64a

64b

Lady Chapel

Hidden reinforcement was used: a chain embedded in the walls, and iron bars to strengthen the ribs. The church might be called the crystal chapel because of the expanse of glass. (John Harvey, *The*

64c   Sainte-Chapelle

Gothic World [London, 1950] p. 11. The illustration is from the title page of Louis Gonse, *L'Art Gothique* [Paris, n.d.].)

64d

The cathedral of Beauvais (Fig. 64d) was the supreme attempt of high Gothic in France. Its choir, built between 1247 and 1272, was probably designed by Eudes de Montreuil, the companion and favorite architect of St. Louis. The vaults, which reached a height of 158 feet, collapsed in 1284. The reconstruction was not completed until 1324. Nothing so lofty was ever again attempted in France. (John Harvey, op. cit., p. 67.) The illustration is from the drawing by Auguste Lepère, "Une ruelle au pied de la Cathédrale de Beauvais."

65. LITURGY AND PREACHING

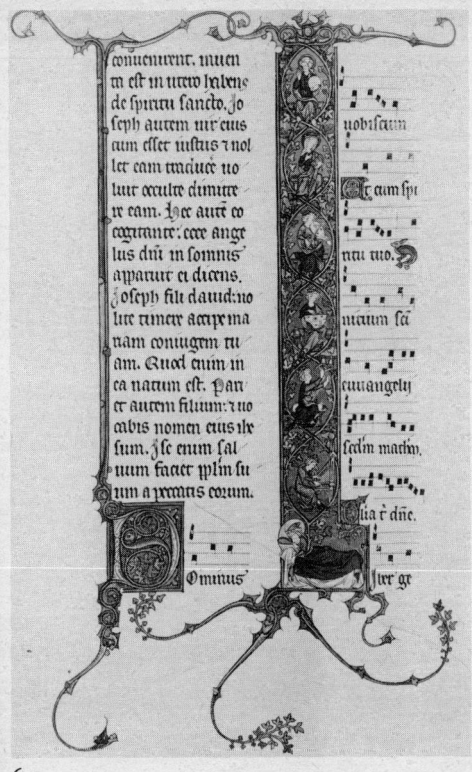

The cathedral itself was a marvelous instrument for the communication of the gospel, yet it was constructed to facilitate the celebration of the sacraments and the preaching of God's Word. The music of the chants became engraved on childhood memories. Here is a page which in a most unusual way sets forth the appeal of music. The form is that of the tree of Jesse, but instead of the ancestors of Jesus springing from his loins we have the players of musical instruments: the organ, bells, a lute, and a violin. On the right, we see the musical notation for the words of the liturgy: DOMINUS VOBISCUM. ET CUM SPIRITU TUO. SANCTI EVANGELII SECUNDUM MATTHAEUM. GLORIA TIBI DOMINE. On the left is the passage from the gospel about the misgivings of Joseph when he discovered Mary's condition. (From a gospel lectionary of the late thirteenth century, British Museum [Add. Ms. 17341, f. 6b].)

66. INNOCENT III

66   *Villa Catena; Leonard Von Matt*

As depicted in a mosaic from the old Basilica of St. Peter.

67. IMPARTIAL JUSTICE: THE IDEAL OF THE CHURCH

This ideal is illustrated by fanciful accounts of a suit against Christ lodged by Satan, complaining he had been robbed of souls rightfully his. Satan is represented by Belial, Christ by Moses. When God is about to act as judge, Satan objects that as the father of Christ He should be disqualified. The objection is sustained and God appoints Solomon instead.

Above we see Solomon as judge. Belial is stating his case; Moses, always depicted with horns because of a mistranslation from the Old Testament, awaits his turn for the rebuttal. A notary takes everything down. When Solomon decides in favor of Christ, Satan objects that as Christ's ancestor Solomon should be disqualified; God then appoints Joseph. Lengthy arguments end inconclusively. Belial seeks the counsel of David who proposes a court of arbitration. Belial chooses Caesar Augustus and Jeremiah. Moses selects Aristotle and Isaiah. Again Belial loses. But what meticulous care to observe the strictest form and spirit of justice! (There are several versions of this story. The one from which the above illustration is taken was reproduced by Dittmar Heubach, "Der Belial. Kolorierte Federzeichnungen aus einer Handschrift des XV. Jahrhunderts," *Studien zur deutschen Kunstgeschichte*, Heft 251 [Strassburg, 1927], Fig. 8.)

68. THE MARTYRDOM OF THOMAS À BECKET

Harleian MSS. 5102, fol. 32, British Museum

69. THE ALBIGENSIAN CRUSADE (1208–1229)

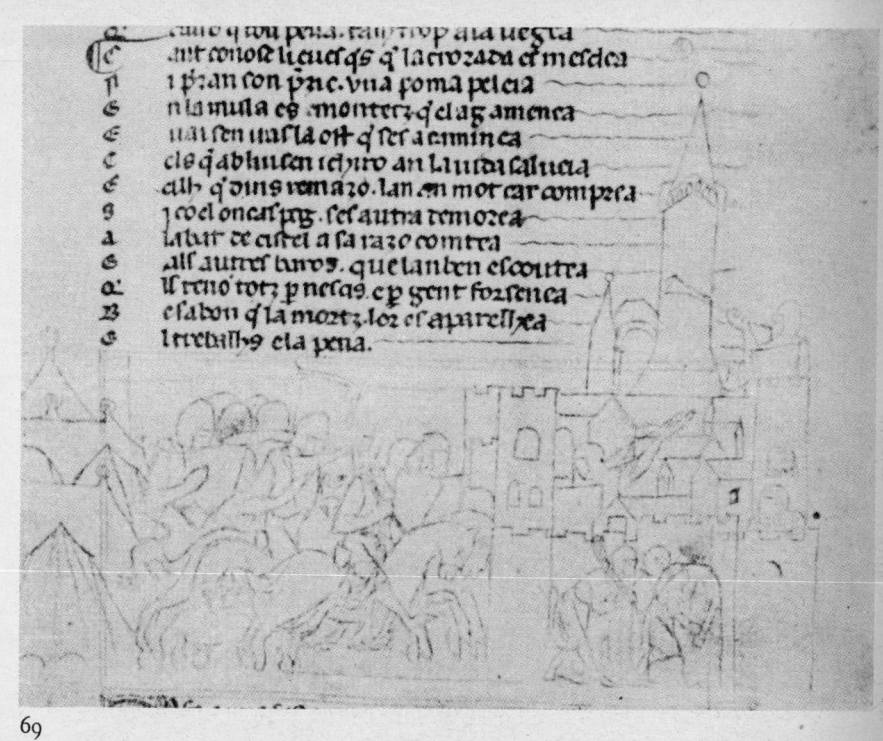

The goriest episode of the Albigensian crusade was the sack of Béziers. The bishop of that city, who was with the crusaders, desired to spare his parishioners and secured from the leaders in his camp the promise of immunity if a number of heretics listed by name were delivered up. The townsmen unanimously refused. Thereupon, while the crusade's leaders conferred, the rabble of camp followers, "inspired by God," rushed the city and took it. The problem then was to know who were the Catholics to be spared and who the heretics to be killed. The question was referred to Arnold, the abbot of Cîteaux and papal legate. He answered, "Kill them all, for God knows his own." He reported to Pope Innocent III that neither rank, age, nor sex was spared. Twenty thousand fell, and the town was fired, "divine vengeance thus marvelously raging against it." (Cf. Henry C. Lea, *History of the Inquisition in the Middle Ages* [New York, Harper & Brothers, 1887, reprinted 1922] I, pp. 153–54. The illustration is from the French manuscript 25.425, a near-contemporary chronicle, in the Bibliothèque Nationale, Paris.)

70. THE FOURTH LATERAN COUNCIL

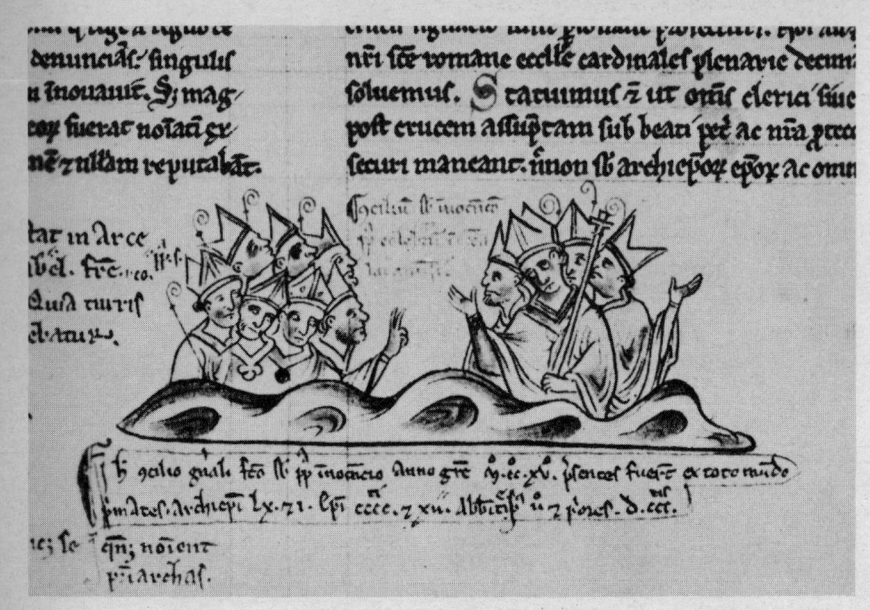

The bishops disputing at the Council which promulgated the doctrine of transubstantiation. The illustration is from the *Chronica Maiora* of Matthew Paris of 1255. The inscription beneath reads: HOC CONCILIO GENERALI FACTO SUB PAPA INNOCENTIO ANNO GRATIAE MCCXV PRESENTES FUERUNT EX TOTO MUNDO/PRIMATES ARCHIEPISCOPI LX ET I EPISCOPI CCCC ET XII ABB[ATES . . . ?] ET PRIORES DCCC. "In this general council convened under Pope Innocent in the year of grace 1215 there were present from all the world primates [of the Church] archbishops 61, bishops 412, abb[ots . . . ?] and priors 800." (I am indebted to my colleague, Professor Edmund T. Silk, for help in deciphering the abbreviations.)

71. FRANCIS AND DOMINIC

St. Dominic, 1170–1221 (Fig. 71a), founded the Dominican order, not simply to preach "penance," like the Franciscans, but to instruct in the great doctrines of the faith. His followers were from many countries and went out to labor in many lands: the first generation alone had French, German, English, Italian, Spanish, Norman, Polish, and Czech members. (From an illustration of the thirteenth century.)

St. Francis, 1182–1226 (Fig. 71b), renowned for his sermon to the birds, is depicted here in a woodcut from the fifteenth century.

71a

71b

72. CHRISTIAN PIETY

72

From the eleventh century on, it was increasingly centered on the sufferings of the crucified Redeemer, who was portrayed as deceased, his head falling on the right shoulder. We have noted how the theme of the passion was invested with greater tenderness by St. Bernard. Franciscan piety led in the thirteenth century to the introduction of a number of new features in the delineation. Christ wears the crown of thorns. The arms droop, the body sags, and the legs are crossed and held by only one nail. The body, consequently, assumes the shape of the letter S, exhibiting at the same time the utter helplessness of death and the agony preceding it. All these features appear in this sketch from the *Album de Villard de Honnecourt*, from the second half of the thirteenth century, now in the Bibliothèque Nationale, No. 212.

73. MEDIEVAL PREACHING

73

The friars were greatly renowned as preachers in the late Middle Ages. Whether the priests had so neglected their duties in this regard as to justify the invasion of their parishes is a point of debate. Excellent preaching manuals were provided for the priests, but did they use them? At any rate, the friars preached, often out of doors and to vast audiences. Because they were instructed to avoid doctrine, they concentrated on morals. The allusions in most medieval sermons were often to fantastic legends of the saints or to bizarre allegories of birds and beasts, but morals had to do with daily life: the vices were reprimanded, the virtues extolled. The active life was to be no less esteemed than the contemplative. (This illustration is from Caoursin, *Rhodiae Obsidio*, 1496.)

74a

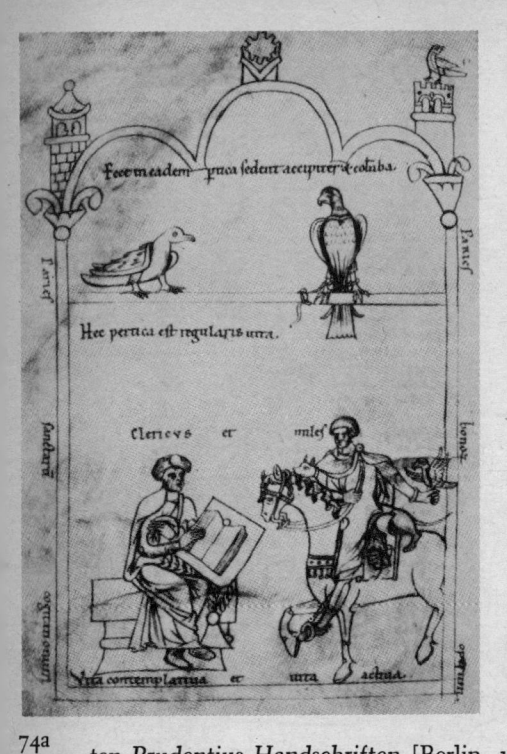

At its best medieval preaching reached high levels with prophetic thunders and mystical rhapsodies. The virtues and the vices were personified and portrayed by word and brush. Fig. 74a depicts the active and the contemplative life. The latter is symbolized by the dove and the monk, the former by the falcon and the hunter. The writing on the left reads: "The wall of holy meditations," and that on the right: "The wall of good deeds." (MS. Cistercian Cloister at Zwettl, No. 253, f. 145, dated 1180.)

Fig. 74b represents the virtue Patience enduring the darts of his assailants without retaliation (from the *Psychomachi* MS. of the ninth century, reproduced in Richard Stettiner, *Die illustrierten Prudentius Handschriften* [Berlin, 1905].)

Luxury (Fig. 74c) was always allegorized as a woman primping, and Pride (Fig. 74d) invariably as a man thrown from his horse. The style of the portrayal was taken from classical representations of an unhorsed cavalryman. (These last two illustrations are from the *Luttrell Psalter* of 1325.)

MEDIEVAL PREACHING

Catholicis in templo diuini fontis ad aram
Consecrat aeterna splendens ubi luxe corusco
PACIENTIA INTER VARIAS ACIES VITIORUM INTREPIDA STAT

Et cum modesta
Per mediasimmota acies...

74b

74c

74d

75. WORKS

75a

75b

OF MERCY

Fig. 75a, from the fourteenth century, shows St. Louis washing the feet of beggars. Almsgiving is depicted in Fig. 75b, a woodcut dated 1507. Fig. 75c depicts St. Louis feeding a leper, as represented on a window in the abbey of St. Denis, dating from the fourteenth century. A leper is at confession in Fig. 75d, a fifteenth-century woodcut. The priest holds a handkerchief over his mouth to ward off infection.

75c

75d

76. MINSTRELS

They sang not only of lords and ladies, but also of the saints. Peter Waldo renounced the world when he heard from a minstrel the legend of St. Alexius. (From *Queen Mary's Psalter*.)

77. ARISTOTLE

Aristotle might be used by Christians, provided theology would ride upon him as upon a donkey. Carving in the stalls of the church at Montbenoît, in Louis Réau, *Iconographie de L'Art* (Paris, 1955), pp. 80–81.

l'Agence Roubier, Paris

78. THE CHURCH AT THE APEX

In the Middle Ages and long after, the Church was regarded as standing at the apex of all religions, all institutions, and all disciplines. She is depicted here as enthroned, the pope and the emperor doing homage on either side. The emperor's features are those of Maximilian, who was reigning when this cut was published. On the sides, in the center, are the false religions with broken staves: Mohammedanism and Judaism on the left, represented in conventional style as blindfolded. On the other side, paganism bears the name "gentilitas," meaning not gentility, but "of the gentiles." To the far right is the religion of the Tartars. At the bottom are the representatives of the learned disciplines. (From Stamler's *Dialogus*, published in 1508.)

79. DANTE'S DIVINE COMEDY

Sandro Botticelli (1447?–1510) did a series of illustrations for the *Divine Comedy*, which were published in Florence in 1491. The drawing reproduced above illustrates the scene in *Paradiso* II, where Dante and Beatrice converse as they enter the Circle of the Moon. Beatrice became Dante's guide in Paradise, since Virgil, as a pagan, could not go beyond Purgatory.

are Paolo and Francesca, slain when discovered in an illicit love, with nothing to live for in all eternity save a romantic infatuation. And here are Ugolino and Archbishop Ruggieri. The former was a Guelph, who, to oust Nino, his nephew and a fellow Guelph, conspired with the Ghibelline Ruggieri. With Nino disposed of, Ruggieri then turned on Ugolino and imprisoned him with four small children, leaving them to die of hunger in a tower. Ugolino, in hell, having related to Dante how the children preceded him in death before his eyes, then fastens his fangs, strong like a dog's, into the skull of Ruggieri, to gnaw forever and forever and forever.

Purgatory and Paradise differ from Hell primarily in that man is there no longer doomed to be forever what once he was. Purgatory introduces the hope of change. Passion is purged, ambition curbed, pride cowed, envy expunged. In Paradise, the eternal law of justice reigns, and the whole cosmos pulses in the harmony of love.

VIII

The Decline of the Papacy

OFTEN the fourteenth and the fifteenth century are treated by historians of the Church as a period of decline. This judgment is shared by Catholic and Protestant scholars alike, though not for precisely the same reasons. They are of course agreed that the prevalence of clerical concubinage and the financial extortion of the papacy were abuses, but whereas the Catholics have been disposed to see a recession in the declining prestige and power of the papacy, the waning quality and influence of the monastic orders, the rise of sectarianism and the popularity of nominalism, Protestant historians have often looked upon these developments with favor as preludes to the Reformation. But, despite differing value judgments, there is agreement as to what took place.

The papacy certainly declined in power and prestige. A number of causes were contributory. The swarming of sectarian movements is certainly one. The rise of nationalism is another, and the accommodation of ecclesiastical finances to the new monied economy gave the national states an advantage in contests with the Church. The shift in theology undercut the theoretical foundations of the hierarchical structure of the Church and society, and certain secularist tendencies weakened the grip of the Church on the culture of the age. These varied shifts are not to be dated as commencing precisely in the year 1300. Some had been in process of development for several centuries.

The Rise of Nations

By 1300, nationalism had not yet assumed its modern form, and the word nation was used for groups that would not be so designated today. The word was first employed to demark student groups at the universities. At Paris there were four such nations: the English, including the Germans and the Scandinavians; the French, including the Spanish and the Italians; and, in addition, the Picards, and the Normans. At Prague also, the university had four nations: the Germans, the Czechs, the Bavarians, and the Silesians. At the same time, in point of fact, three of the modern nations were in process of formation, Spain, England, and France. In each land a populace with a common tradition and a common language was consolidating contiguous territories under an increasingly centralized government and was rounding out borders to naturally defensible frontiers. The achievement of political autonomy within these limits called for a rejection of the overall authority of the two great universal powers of the Middle Ages, the empire and the Church. The kings took over the roles of the emperors, and the slogan was, *Rex est imperator in regno suo* (The king is the emperor in his own domain). Likewise, the sovereigns sought to control the Church in their territories, even in defiance of papal authority, and in the sixteenth century the king of England came very close to saying that he was the pope in his own domain.

The degree to which the three incipient nations exhibited these tendencies varied. Spain was least in a position to be assertive because it was not yet united. The *Reconquista* had gone far enough to include Toledo, but the Moors still held Granada for nearly two centuries longer because the Christian states were not consolidated. Castile was pushing south, while Aragon sought to build a Mediterranean empire on the islands and in Naples. England had moved further on the road to consolidation. What is now England was then under a single monarch but was weakened by continual strife with Scotland and with France, owing to the unwillingness of England to abandon her continental claims and to relinquish Aquitaine. Of the three lands, France had reached the largest degree of consolidation and centralization of authority. Although Aquitaine and Brittany were not included in her domain, nothern and southern France were united following the annexation of the *midi* after the Albigensian crusade.

England and France were both to clash with the papacy and particularly so France, the very kingdom which in the early Middle Ages had done so much to build up the papacy. The clash centered not on land as in the Investiture controversy but on money, and the reason was that the Church had taken advantage of the new monied economy to develop her finances on an international scale. Her international operations required extensive outlays for which her resources in Italy no longer sufficed. Many of the lands held by the papacy in the days of Gregory I had been lost to the Saracens and the proceeds from papal monopolies on salt and alum mines were not an adequate compensation.

If the Church aspired to be an international power, she must build up an international income. A beginning was made at the end of the eleventh century by the imposition of a small monetary levy, called Peter's Pence, on England and the Scandinavian countries. Further steps involved the imposition of tithes on all local churches throughout Europe, with a penalty of excommunication for noncompliance. In the collection of these monies, the Church set aside her aversion to those tainted with filthy lucre and availed herself of the services of Lombard bankers who delivered the money in Rome on credit and reimbursed themselves by pocketing the tithes at the point of collection.

The rulers of Europe objected to the export of gold beyond their borders, particularly because it was frequently spent to their disadvantage. They objected also to the crusading tax, which continued to be exacted even after the last Christian outpost in Palestine had fallen to the Turks in 1291. Even before the crusades were over, it was being spent for wars called crusades, but actually waged by Christian princes at the pope's behest to discipline other

Christian princes who failed to do the pope's bidding. The nobles were not inclined to pay for their own chastisement. When the papacy backed a crusade of the French ruling House of Anjou to expel the great German imperial House of Hohenstaufen from Sicily, neither the Germans nor the English were disposed to contribute. Kings would finance wars only in their own interest; for such ends they had long been willing to lay hands on the wealth of the Church. This had come to mean not the expropriation of land but the sequestering of money.

England's quarrel with the papacy in these centuries involved principally the feudal tribute to which King John had committed the country in perpetuity by making England a fief of the papacy in 1213, and which was no longer being paid. Legacies of land to the Church were forbidden by a statute in 1279, and papal appointments to English sees were made illegal in 1351, to keep foreigners from settling in lucrative English bishoprics. Appeals to the courts of Rome were forbidden by the Statute of Praemunire in 1353.

In France, the clash at the outset was also largely over money. King Philip the Fair levied taxes on the French clergy of one-half their annual income. In 1296, Pope Boniface VIII replied with threats of excommunication against any layman who exacted and any churchman who paid such taxes without the pope's permission (in the bull *Clericis Laicos* of 1296). Philip, in turn, forbade the exportation of gold to Rome and Boniface countered by flinging at Philip the most far-reaching claims ever made by the medieval papacy. They were not invented by Boniface, but were taken over from the statements of Innocent IV, who, when the papacy had already passed the peak of power, compensated for its decline with heightened pretensions; he stated that Christ, being a king as well as a priest, had committed to Peter not one key but two, and not one sword but two—the temporal as well as the spiritual. Peter had renounced for himself the actual use of the temporal sword, but had delegated it to kings to be employed under papal direction. Thus the direct institution of kingship by God was flatly denied. This assertion was now cast at Philip by

Boniface, together with the claim that, to be saved, every human being must be subject to the Roman pontiff. When this claim had been stated earlier by Thomas Aquinas, the word *subject* was ambiguous; but here the context eliminated any ambiguity. Boniface made this assertion in the bull *Unam sanctam* in 1299.

But the previous successes of the papacy in the struggle for power had paradoxically reduced the pope's chances of making good his pretensions. The universal Church had weakened the universal empire by pitting against it the northern Italian cities and the rising national power of France. After 1250, the imperial throne was vacant for two decades, and stability for the empire was not recovered until 1356, when it was reconstituted on an elective basis. The papacy had upset the balance of power, and Boniface could raise no champion to challenge Philip. In 1303, some of Philip's henchmen captured the pope in his summer residence at Anagni, near Rome, and did such violence to his person that he died shortly thereafter.

Avignon

The papacy was then transferred from Rome to Avignon, a little principality in the south of France, at that time not under the French crown. This city was to be the papal residence from 1305 to 1378, a span so close to seventy years that, in memory of the seventy-year captivity of the Jews, this period was called the Babylonian captivity of the papacy. It was, however, not an actual captivity because the popes were free to return to Rome.

Knights Templars

During these years, all popes were French and exercised even the spiritual sword only at the behest of the kings of France. The shift is well evidenced by the way in which King Philip the

Fair turned the Inquisition into an instrument of the state. His object was to disband the Knights of the Temple. This body of knights in France was an obstacle to the consolidation of monarchical power because subject only to the pope. The knights were wealthy and armed and had nothing to do now that the crusades in the Holy Land were at an end. In Spain, the orders of Calatrava, Santiago, and Alcántara were still needed for the *Reconquista*, and in Germany the Teutonic Knights were subduing Prussia. There was no comparable assignment for the Templars in France, and the sensible procedure would have been demobilization. But, this would have been tantamount to admitting that the crusades in the Holy Land were over, and no one was willing to concede as much.

Philip's dilemma was most felicitously solved when a renegade brought charges of heresy, claiming that the Templars worshiped the head of a cat, blasphemed the Mass, practiced unnatural vice, and had betrayed the holy places to the infidels. They certainly did not betray the holy places. No cat-headed idol has ever been found. The Templars may have been guilty of blasphemy. As a matter of fact, blasphemy was not uncommon in the Middle Ages, though nobody was ever burned for it because blasphemy was, after all, an affirmation of faith. Blasphemy is neither shocking nor funny unless one believes in that which is blasphemed. Unnatural vice is probable enough, but that is not heresy, and the charge was heresy. The entire membership of the Order of the Templars in all of France was arrested overnight. The incriminated were confronted with lists of charges varying somewhat from place to place. Torture extracted confessions corresponding exactly to the charges in each locality and nothing more. Even the Grand Master of the order, Jacques de Molay, was alleged to have confessed. The case was then committed to the Inquisition. Thereupon, Pope Clement V intervened. Those who had confessed repudiated now their confessions, but instead of being released they were treated as heretics who had relapsed and were sentenced to death. Fifty-nine Templars were burned in Paris, including Jacques de Molay (1314). The Inquisition was thus being used to serve the state, and such pressures were placed upon the pope that he offered no remonstrance.

Church Revenues

The transfer of the papacy to Avignon raised for the popes other financial problems. The Patrimony of St.Peter had been overrun by the Italian nobles, and the Church could no longer collect the revenues. The popes at Avignon recruited armies of mercenaries to recover the lost domains. To defray the costs of the military operations, levies were imposed upon the local churches in France, England, and Germany. The wizard who reorganized the papal finances was John XXII. He exploited all the old money-raising devices and concocted many more. One method was to impound for the papacy all of the first year's income of a newly appointed bishop. The term *Annates* was used in case the see was small, *Servitia* if large. When a vacancy in a bishopric occurred, the pope might fill it by transferring a bishop from another see, thus creating another vacancy. Or, he might refrain from naming any bishop at all and, pending an appointment, reserve all the revenues for himself. This system was called Reservation. A fee was exacted for a promise of appointment to a see when a vacancy should occur, with a waiting list of descending chances. When the pope visited a bishopric, his expenses were paid by the see. The costs of entertainment ran so high that it was cheaper to pay him not to come, in which case he could accept several invitations. New offices were created with charges for installation, and fees were exacted for all manner of petty services.

One of the great money-raising devices came to be the dispensing of indulgences. The practice went back to the crusades. To one who took up the cross, the bishop granted an indulgence, remitting some penance imposed previously. Later, the right to do so was reserved solely for the popes. Then, similar remissions were given to those who, staying at home, helped to finance the crusades, whether in the Holy Land or in Europe. Indulgences were granted also to support charities, such as the construction of a cathedral, a hospital, or even a bridge. The great Gothic structures were financed in part by indulgences. One factor in the theory of indulgences was the old German practice of commuting a corporal punishment into a monetary fine.

Another factor was the doctrine of the treasury of the merits of the saints. The assumption was that the saints were better than need be for their own salvation. Their excess credits were stored in a celestial deposit called the *Thesaurus meritorum sanctorum*. From this treasury, the pope could draw and make transfers to those whose accounts were deficient. This treasury would never be exhausted because the merits of Christ were included. There was a question whether the pope acted out of the fullness of his own power or whether he simply petitioned God to pardon, having full assurance that God would honor the request. Late in the fifteenth century, the popes claimed authority to remit penalties imposed not only on earth but also in purgatory, and some indulgences forgave not only penalties but also guilt. Strictly speaking, indulgences were not sold, but in return for the gift of this grace the recipient made a contribution. Still, the granting of the pardon was timed to coincide precisely with the contribution.

By these many devices, the popes and the cardinals together reaped a larger income during the period of their residence at Avignon than the kings of France. Almost two-thirds of the Church's revenue were expended to finance wars for the recovery of Peter's Patrimony in Italy. Why the kings of France succeeding Philip should have permitted so much gold to go to Avignon, whereas he did not allow it to pass to Rome, is perplexing. Perhaps the papacy under French control was regarded an asset sufficiently great to warrant the expense. But it became ever less of an asset when other countries were indisposed to take directives from a papacy under French control. England and Germany were restive and, had this Babylonian captivity lasted longer, the Protestant secession might have been anticipated by a century and a half.

This came very near to happening when the emperor, Louis of Bavaria, defied Pope John XXII over a most crucial point, in that he made marriage a purely civil affair, and by his own imperial authority granted a divorce to a woman among his subjects, so that she might be free to marry his son. The pope declared a crusade against Louis, and Louis branded the pope a heretic The pope put him under the ban, invoking upon him the wrath of almighty God and the apostles Peter and Paul, coupled with the wish that Louis should be smitten with blindness and madness, that the earth should swallow him alive, and his memory be forever erased. But the earth did not open, and his memory is preserved in all the textbooks.

Louis summoned to his aid an Italian lawyer, Marsilius of Padua, a layman, who set forth a theory of church-state relations in which the state was exalted even more than in the system of Justinian. Marsilius proposed that the ownership (*dominium*) of all property should reside with the state. The Church should own absolutely nothing but should be allowed the use of property in amounts to be determined by the state. All the clergy would receive their stipends from the government. This would make them essentially civil servants.

Even more radical views were set forth by some of the Franciscans. The whole company of the followers of the Poverello were welded together in common opposition to John XXII, the financial wizard. John resolved to have no more nonsense about *dominium* and *usus*. The Church would no longer take the onus of ownership and let the Franciscans have the benefits. Let them either own or starve. This set a problem for the Conventuals. Then John decided to suppress the few remnants of the Spirituals altogether. Next, he alienated all Franciscans by his pronouncement that Christ himself owned property, contrary to the expressed view of an earlier pope. The Franciscans branded the pope a heretic. He turned some of the Spirituals over to the Inquisition, and they were burned. The Spirituals as a party then disappeared, only to be succeeded by the Fraticelli, who placed the Rule of St.Francis above the authority of the Church, appropriated the eschatology of Joachim of Fiore and identified the pope with Antichrist. Thus one branch of the Franciscans became sectarian.

Some of the order who escaped the papal talons took refuge with Louis in Bavaria. Among them was one of the Conventuals, William of Occam, an Englishman, who wrote a hefty tome on the errors of Pope John XXII. In a treatise on the powers of emperors and popes, he reverted to the old imperial theory, insisting on the direct, divine institution of the civil power and maintained that the clergy should confine themselves to reading, preaching, ordaining, and administering the sacraments. Much more radical was William's theory of the Church. His nominalist philosophy led him to think of the Church in terms of her individual members rather than as a corporate entity. He analyzed the Church by her components, and inquired with regard to each whether it was able to err. He concluded promptly that the pope can err, a general council can err, the laity can err, at least all men can err, and the truth may reside only in godly women. There was no reason, of course, why women might not err also, provided that some other portion of the Church at that moment upheld the truth. On this basis, one cannot see why all of the parts might not have erred at the same time, but he was deterred from this conclusion by the word of Christ, that against the Church the gates of Hell should not prevail. At any given moment, therefore, some part would be right. Historically, there is much to be said for his position. We have noticed that when the papacy was at the nadir, monastic reform and missionary endeavor were initiated elsewhere. William raised another point: if all the parts save one may be wrong, how is anyone to know that this one part is right? What is the ground of authority? His answer was an appeal to the Bible, but he scarcely perceived that if there is no authoritative body to interpret the Bible, each individual must do so for himself.

The Great Schism

The Babylonian captivity ended in 1377. Pope Gregory XI perceived that the papacy must cut loose from France if other countries were not to renounce obedience to the Holy See. Gregory XI went back to Rome, but his cardinals refused to accompany him and elected another pope, who stayed on in Avignon. This pope took the title Clement VII. He and his successors at Avignon are not recognized by the Roman Church today, and that is why at the time of the Reformation another pope bore the title Clement VII. Gregory XI at Rome was succeeded by Urban VI who created a new college of cardinals. There were then two popes and two sets of cardinals. Thus began the Great Schism, which was not fully terminated until 1459. All Europe was, in consequence, divided. France supported the popes at Avignon; Naples, often quarreling with Rome, lined up with France. England, Bohemia, Germany, and Flanders, out of opposition to France, sided with Rome. But Scotland, at war with England, sided with France and therefore against Rome; so did Castile after some wavering. Then, as in the days of St. Bernard, rival bishops arose in each country in the name of rival popes, and monarchs were often not able to enforce an absolute uniformity within their own domains. These alignments had political consequences. Anne of Bohemia would have married the king of France had not the two countries supported opposite popes. She married instead Richard II of England.

What then was to be done? A group of thinkers in Germany, and more particularly in France—the most distinguished among them were Jean Charlier Gerson, the chancellor of the University of Paris and Pierre D'Ailly, a cardinal—came forward with the suggestion that the only way out of the impasse would be to revive Conciliarism. This would be not an innovation but a revival of that system which had obtained during the period of the great ecumenical councils from the fourth through the eighth century. All the great doctrinal decisions had then been made by councils.

To be sure, the decisions of the councils had been ratified by the popes, yet the sixth council had declared an earlier pope a heretic. Now, more was involved, however, than heresy, for never had councils gone so far as to depose and create popes. Over against the immediate past, Conciliarism certainly was a terrific innovation, reversing the trend toward centralization of the previous two centuries. Conciliarism meant constitutionalism. Authority in the Church would be lodged in a representative assembly. The Conciliarism of this period achieved its first objective and ended the schism, but did not arrest papalism. Nor did the councils redress the moral and financial abuses in the Church. Yet Conciliarism was not devoid of long-range consequences, partly in the religious sphere in the Protestant Reformation, but more particularly in the political. The Puritan pamphleteers for Parliamentarianism in the seventeenth century drew from the arsenal of the conciliarists.

The ending of the schism was no light accomplishment and not easily achieved. Whenever a pope died at Avignon or Rome, his cardinals promptly elected a successor on the ground that the dispute should not be settled by default. When the conciliar idea was broached, each pope avowed willingness to join in summoning an assembly but evaded fulfillment by proposing a spot for the council at ever greater distance from the territory of the other. The cardinals of both popes were at last so utterly disgusted that they assembled at Pisa in 1409 without either pope, a full thirty-four years after the outbreak of the schism. The popes at the time were Benedictus and Gregorius. The cardinals dubbed them "Benefictus" and "Errorius" and deposed them both. In their place, the cardinals elected a new pope who died shortly and was then succeeded by John XXIII, who so debased the name of John that it was not taken again by a pope until assumed by the most beloved pontiff of the twentieth century. The earlier John XXIII was a condottiere, who had been defending the estates of the Church against the king of Naples.

The other two popes, however, did not resign. Consequently, instead of two, there were now three. What was wrong? The answer given was that the Council of Pisa had been assembled only by the cardinals. If a council were summoned by a pope and an emperor, surely it would mend the schism. John XXIII had no disposition to call a council until the king of Naples drove him out of Rome. Then only did he consent, assuming that he would be able to manipulate the assembly. The Emperor Sigismund was happy to join in issuing the invitation because he wished to be crowned by the authentic pope. He had his way with regard to the place for the council. It was to be not Rome, but Constance, in what is now Switzerland. In 1414, a great conclave gathered there, including such noble and distinguished men as Gerson, the mystic, and D'Ailly, the theologian, whose views about the rotundity of the earth influenced Columbus. But the bulk of the bishops in attendance were not distinguished for learning or sanctity. John XXIII tried to swamp the council by creating a large number of new Italian bishops. The council thwarted him by organizing itself according to nations. The term was coming to have its modern meaning. The participants were Italians, Germans, French, and English; the Spaniards were listed among the French. All of John's Italian bishops put together had then only one vote. At this juncture John ran away from the council but was captured, returned, deposed, deprived of his fisherman's ring, and incarcerated. His successor made him a cardinal, and he sleeps now in the baptistry at Florence beneath his cardinal's hat. A new pope was elected who took the name Martin V. One of the other two popes resigned, one was deposed. The council, before disbanding, asserted the principle of Conciliarism and provided for future meetings.

John Wycliffe

There might never have been another council had not sectarianism, conjoined with nationalism, presented a new threat to the unity of the Church. The nations involved were England and Bohemia, linked, as we observed, by the marriage of Anne of

Bohemia to Richard II of England. Cultural interchange ensued and the students of both countries went back and forth between Oxford and Prague. The heretic in England was John Wycliffe, a priest of the Church, an advisor to the king, and a staunch upholder of English opposition to exploitation by the French popes at Avignon. He had extended the doctrine of Marsilius of Padua with regard to *dominium* and *usus*. Wycliffe held that all *dominium*, or ownership, is vested in God, and man has only the *usus*. *Abusus* justifies deprivation of *usus*. This meant that the state might confiscate the goods of a recreant Church, a very convenient doctrine to justify the expropriation of Church properties by John of Gaunt, the practical ruler of England at the time.

In 1378, when the papal schism occurred, Wycliffe's views became vastly more radical, because he applied to the Church a philosophy of history resting upon the doctrine of predestination. We have observed that the prediction of the imminent end of the age weakens the power of the institutional Church since it becomes ephemeral. The doctrine of predestination undercuts the institution by starting not with the end but before the very beginning of history, when, prior even to birth, God elects some souls to bliss and consigns others to perdition. This view, as held by St. Augustine, had no bearing on the structure of the Church because he saw no way of distinguishing the elect from the non-elect. But, if a tangible test for identification could be discovered, then the sheep in the Church could be segregated from the goats, the wheat from the tares. Wycliffe found this test in ethical deportment and concluded that popes, whose lives were in glaring contradiction to those of the apostles, were not the successors of the apostles, nor the true Church of the elect, but manifestly the reprobate, "the damned limbs of Lucifer" and the very seat of Antichrist. In the hands of such prelates, the sacraments lose their power. In any case, the priest does not have the ability to change the bread and wine into the body and blood of Christ by transubstantiation, because there is no transubstantiation. Wycliffe was a philosophical realist, who held that substance as one of the universals cannot be annihilated. This was not to say, however, that Christ is not in the sacrament. He is there, in addition to and along with bread and wine, whose substance remains. This was called the doctrine of remanence.

But where, then, does authority reside in the Church? Wycliffe, like Occam, had recourse to the Bible, again without perceiving the problem as to who has authority to interpret the Bible. To his mind, the Bible needed no interpreter, for its meaning was self-evident. To disseminate the Bible and instruct the people, he sponsored a translation into the newly emergent English tongue. This was the age of Chaucer. The task of spreading the word was committed to an order of poor priests who came to be called Lollards in derision. Wycliffe had no confidence in the older monastic orders and especially detested the friars as meddling interlopers in the domain of the parish priest. Nor had he any higher regard for their sincerity than Chaucer, who derided them in his *Canterbury Tales,* where the most amiable character is the village priest. The Lollards were priests whose mission was to minister to their flocks and to the region round about. Whereas the Franciscans began as laymen and ended as priests, the Lollards, who began as priests, were deprived by the Church of their status and ended as laymen. Wycliffe, enjoying the patronage of the government, was not executed for heresy, but in the next reign the act *De heretico comburendo* sent his followers to the stake (1401). Wycliffe's critique of the Church was basically theological, but there was also an element of English national feeling against foreign exploitation.

John Huss

Even more marked was the national feeling in Bohemia where Catholicism had been introduced by way of Germany, with the consequence that anti-clerical sentiments of the Czechs had inevitably a tinge of anti-German resentment. But here, too, the national element was not primary. The great reformer, John Huss, headed a movement for preaching in the vernacular, not to make the people more Czech, but to make them more Christian. His critique of contemporary Catholicism was, at the outset, moral. He upbraided the luxury and license of the prelates and drew a graphic picture of the contrast between Christ, riding on a donkey, and the pope on a stallion with the people crowding to kiss his feet. The contrast of Christ and Antichrist became a popular theme, later to be exploited by the Protestant reformers. Huss was less radical than Wycliffe. He did not hold to the doctrine of remanence. As to the validity of acts performed by unworthy priests, Huss made a distinction between the sacramental and the pastoral. The sacraments at the hands of the unworthy are nevertheless valid and efficacious, but the pastoral usefulness of the priest is utterly vitiated by unseemly behavior. From Wycliffe, Huss did carry over without diminution the doctrine of the Church as the company of the predestined, recognizable in some measure by the quality of their deportment. Such a view, as we noted, is disruptive of the whole hierarchical structure of the Church. A point that came to be distinctive of the Hussite movement was the restoration to the laity of the cup in the Mass. The Church had, not too long previously, restricted the cup to the priest, lest the clumsy laity should spill any of the "blood of God." The Hussites pointed to the words of Christ, "Drink of it, all of you."[1] The Church replied that these words were addressed to the apostles, and that the apostles all were priests. This the Hussites denied. They were resisting the growing tendency to increase the gulf between the clergy and the laity by always requiring of the clergy a distinctive clerical garb, by excluding the laity from the chancel, and by the withdrawal of the cup. The chalice came to be the symbol of the Hussite movement.

The story of Huss' relations with King Wenzel and Archbishop Zbynek is not clear cut. The archbishop approved of vernacular

[1] *Bibite ex hoc omnes*, Matt. 26:27.

preaching but condemned Wycliffe's views, assuming that they were shared by Huss. The king supported Huss against the archbishop until alienated by Huss' denunciation of an indulgence issued to finance the pope's war against Naples. Huss did not controvert the entire doctrine of indulgences, as Luther was later to do, but was outraged that indulgences should be used as a device for raising money and even more that the money should be spent to pay for papal wars. The students at the University of Prague burned the papal bull of indulgence. Wenzel thereupon executed some of the students. Huss protested and was sent into retirement where he wrote his great work *On the Church*.

Then came the Council of Constance. The proposal was made that Huss should be examined by the council. He welcomed the suggestion, for he was certain that all instructed theologians would perceive the cogency of his contentions. The Emperor Sigismund, heir to the domain of his brother Wenzel, wanted the council to see to it that his inheritance should not be tainted by heresy. He therefore gave Huss a safe-conduct to go and to return from the council. On arrival, Huss was profoundly shocked by the blatant immorality of the clerics. Pope John XXIII, not yet deposed, caused him to be imprisoned and induced Sigismund to withdraw his safe-conduct on the ground that the Church is not obligated to keep faith with him who has no faith. But Huss did not clash primarily with the disreputables at Constance but rather with the noblest churchmen, such as Pierre D'Ailly. The saints are often the persecutors of the saints, because only they care enough. Huss' theory of the Church as the company of the predestined, recognizable by their conduct, was just as subversive of a council such as that at Constance, as of the papacy itself. D'Ailly wanted to end the schism and establish the principle of Conciliarism. He was aghast at the prospect of disintegrating the visible Church. Huss was accused of teaching the doctrine of remanence and of holding that even the sacramental acts of priests depend upon their character. He replied that these views he had never held. He was then asked to repudiate them anyway. He replied that to take back what he had never held would be false. At the stake, he recited the litany, "O Christ, thou son of the living God, have mercy upon me. O thou, who wast born of the Virgin Mary. . . ." The very earth was dug up from around the stake and removed, lest his followers have any relics to take back to Bohemia.

Even without relics Bohemia was aflame. The moderates, called Utraquists (from the Latin word *uter*, meaning both, that is, both the bread and the wine), were ready to make peace with Rome if the chalice were conceded to the laity. But they were overrun by a more radical group called the Taborites who would have no truck with Rome, whatever the concessions. Though reviving the eschatology of Joachim of Fiore with the date for the new era set a little in advance of their own time, they did not in consequence sit back in tranquil expectation. Peasant hordes were organized under the leadership of the blind General Zizka and, though armed at times only with flails, repulsed the formidable armies of the Emperor Sigismund and carried their crusade into Saxony.

Council of Basel

The Council of Basel was summoned in 1431 to deal with this situation. It was more democratically organized than that of Constance, because any priest could vote this time. The details of the negotiations with the Hussites are not significant because in the end their armies suffered a reverse, and Catholicism was reintroduced with the important proviso, however, that Hussitism was to be tolerated. This was the first definitive breach in the unity of the medieval Church and a foretaste of religious pluralism. One land now permitted two forms of the Christian religion.

The Council of Basel had then little left to do, but it continued to sit and began to appropriate papal revenues for its own support. Then, there came an appeal which might well have occupied its best endeavors. Constantinople was beset by the Turks. The Eastern Empire asked for help. The West would meet the need only if the East would accept its creed. There would have to be a theological discussion, and since the council was still in session, Basel might well have been the appropriate place, but it was too remote from the East. The pope adroitly invited the Greeks to Ferrara. They accepted. Later, the sessions were transferred to Florence (1438-39). The Council of Basel continued to sit. Thus, instead of a papal schism, there was a conciliar schism. Nothing could have discredited anti-papal Conciliarism more thoroughly. Basel elected an anti-pope. Both, council and anti-pope, flickered out in 1449. In the meantime, the Council at Florence arrived at a compromise formula with the Greeks, which was promptly repudiated when their delegates returned home. The military support at Constantinople was negligible, and the city fell to the Turks in 1453.

Renaissance

By that year, the Renaissance was well under way in Italy. The Renaissance is most commonly regarded as marking a recession, not only of ecclesiastical control over society but also of a prevailingly Christian view of life. In assessing such a claim one must be clear as to what is meant by *Renaissance*. Some historians use the term simply to describe a chronological period: some would go back to 1300 to include Dante, and others would go forward to 1600 to take in Shakespeare. Those who view the question from the standpoint of the Church commonly prefer to start with the pontificate of Nicholas V in 1450 and to end with the sack of Rome in 1527. But, most often the term is used to describe an attitude toward life, which valued earth more than heaven; the immortality of fame more than the immortality of the soul; self-cultivation more than self-effacement; the delights of the flesh more than asceticism; the striving for success more than justice; individual and intellectual freedom more than authority; and classical Humanism more than Christianity. If this be the Renaissance, then the historian must ask to what degree such attitudes and behavior are more clearly discernible in this period than in the preceding, to what extent they were prevalent throughout the entire culture after the fourteenth century, and what bearing they had upon the character and continuance of a Christian society.

Humanism

At the outset, the Renaissance was in a cultural sense Italian, urban, and aristocratic. The Italian city-states, especially during the last half of the fifteenth century, enjoyed comparative peace and sufficient affluence to enable their rulers to patronize arts and letters. There was a gorgeous burgeoning of genius. Later, all Europe from Spain to Poland sought to emulate the Italian example. The movement was everywhere aristocratic, subsidized by the wealthy and cultivated by artists and literary men called Humanists because of their concern for the humanities. They were learned antiquarians, delving into classical literature. Their common medium was Latin, although they created at the same time a splendid literature in the vernaculars modelled on classical forms. They did not utilize the invention of printing to disseminate widely their ideas. The earliest books were sumptuous, expensive, and imitations of manuscripts even to the point of carrying over traditional abbreviations. The cheap popular pamphlet was first introduced by the propagandists of the Reformation. The Humanists did not bespeak the mind of the entire culture.

Skepticism did not exist among them in the sense of a denial of any of the great Christian affirmations. The closest approach to skepticism was fideism, that is to say, blind faith without rational support. But this was an inheritance from the Middle Ages. There were two Christian affirmations which in this epoch lacked a philosophical undergirding. The first was the doctrine of the Trinity. We have already noted the difficulties created for this doctrine by the philosophy of nominalism, which latter, rather than Thomism, was then dominant. The nominalists did not deny the doctrine of the Trinity, but maintained only that it is philosophically indefensible. There are, they said, two kinds of logic, the philosophical and the theological, which lead to irreconcilable conclusions. There are not two kinds of truth, and the philosophical conclusion will have to yield to the theological, which is derived from revelation. Such a position becomes skepticism only if revelation is called into question, and at that time it was not.

The other doctrine was that of immortality. The Arabic philosopher Averroes had interpreted Aristotle to mean that the soul after death is absorbed into the world-soul and loses its personal identity. This view, he well knew, did not comport with the Koran, and for him, too, there had to be a double logic, if not a double truth. The problem passed from the Arabs to the Christians, and in the late fifteenth century Pietro Pomponazzi, a philosopher at Padua, wrote a book *On Immortality*, wherein, with great acumen, he examined the problem of the relation of mind to body and concluded that no evidence demonstrates and no analogy suggests that the soul can survive dissociated from the body, as the Platonists supposed. Yet he, too, accepted immortality as the revealed doctrine of the Church.

We do find skepticism of a sort in the form of historical criticism used to expose the spuriousness of famous forgeries and to examine critically sacred documents. Historical criticism was the task of Humanists whose delving into the classics made them aware of the differences between ancient and medieval Latin and enabled them to date documents by philological criteria. Using such tests, Lorenzo Valla (1407-57) exposed the *Donation of Constantine* as a forgery. The language, he pointed out, was not that of the age of Constantine. There were references to the iconoclastic controversy of the eighth century. Documents of the period of Constantine never once mentioned the *Donation*, and at no time did the popes actually exercise the authority which Constantine was supposed to have bestowed upon them. Valla disproved also the common assumption that the Apostles' Creed was the work of the twelve apostles. More daring was his application of historical criticism to the study of the Bible, even though he came up with no startling conclusions. As far as the Church was concerned, the demonstrations of Valla were not especially disturbing. She could survive the exposure of a forgery.

The Humanists did not attack the Church, and in the only instance in which the Church attacked the Humanists, the victory was theirs. This was the Reuchlin controversy, which took place not in Italy, but in Germany in the early sixteenth century and had to do with the freedom to pursue Hebrew studies. A converted Jew named Pfefferkorn exhibited his zeal for the Christian faith by clamoring for the destruction of all Hebrew books. The Emperor Maximilian asked the advice, among others, of the great Christian Hebrew scholar, Johann Reuchlin, who reported that very little Hebrew literature should be destroyed, and nothing at all without examination by competent persons, for whose training he proposed the establishment of chairs in Hebrew at the universities. The Dominicans rallied to the cause of Pfefferkorn, and the case went to the pope. But, although Reuchlin was saddled with the costs of the trial, he never paid and was not barred from teaching. The Church herself had appropriated the tools and the methods of Humanist scholarship.

If the Renaissance is said to have substituted a secular for a religious view of life, then one must analyze the meaning of the term secular. Sometimes it is used to signify a roisterous, unscrupulous, lecherous, and frivolous deportment. Certainly, there were those in the fifteenth century who so demeaned themselves, but how novel were they? The Sforzas, the Visconti, and the Medici scarcely outdid the Plantagenets in disposing of rivals and gratifying the flesh. As to frivolity, the levity of Boccaccio does not outdo that of Aucassin who preferred Hell with Nicolette to Paradise with stuffy saints. Perhaps the newness of the Renaissance may be held to consist in making pornography a branch of belles-lettres as with Aretino, but what shall one say of Ovid, who was read throughout the Middle Ages?

The term secular is again used to describe the ideal of the

cultivated man whose ambition is to round out his personality by the acquisition of many skills like Leonardo da Vinci, a painter, sculptor, inventor, and among the first natural scientists, or like Michelangelo Buonarroti, a sculptor, painter, architect, and poet. The cultivated man is interested in the development of the body as well as in that of the mind, and in the *Cortegiano* of Baldassare Castiglione he receives counsel on how to run, race, hunt, dance, and swim. All this adds up to a revival of the Greek ideal of *Paideia*. Repeatedly, we have seen that it has disquieted Christians, and yet Christians have held self-cultivation and self-renunciation in an uneasy tension. If a comparison is made with the Middle Ages, are not the sports of Castiglione more genteel than tournaments?

A third meaning of the word secular has to do with the image of man. The Renaissance is said to have made him autonomous, self-sufficient, without any need for God. An example of this view is found in the writings of Pico della Mirandola, founder of the Neoplatonic Academy at Florence. Pico said that man is the sculptor and modeller of his destiny. By this he meant that man, finding himself at the center of the great hierarchy of beings, has the freedom of choice to descend to the level of the brute or to ascend until united with the ineffable One. This is simply Neoplatonic mysticism. It presents a danger to Christianity if no need is felt for Christ's aid in the ascent. Yet this view had been accommodated to Christianity by the early Christian Fathers who had declared that God became man in Christ in order to assist man to become God. Similarly, Pico, though suspect in the eyes of the Church, thought of himself as a good Christian.

Perhaps the most subversive aspect of Humanist thought was a tendency to discount the absolute uniqueness of Christianity. One way of so doing was to introduce into Christianity a body of occult Oriental lore, the Jewish Cabala, the Zoroastrian Oracles, and the Hermetic literature of Gnostic origin with some Christian interpolations, in the hope of supporting, but with the danger of perverting, Christian teaching. More direct was the effort to find common elements in Judaism, Islam, and Christianity. The great German cardinal, Nicholas of Cusa, imagined a world parliament of religions in which Christianity obtained universal acceptance because the differences were minimized. Giovanni Boccaccio gave a new turn to the ancient story of the father who called in each of his three sons separately and to each gave a ring which should make him the heir. After the father's demise the rings were discovered to be identical. These three rings, said Boccaccio, signified Judaism, Islam, and Christianity.

The Renaissance Popes and Princes

But, if now we ask how far Christianity affected life in this period, we have a varied picture with advances in some areas over the Middle Ages. If we take the political scene, we find among the princes of the Italian cities the type of behavior described and apparently approved by Niccolò Machiavelli in his work *The Prince*. Machiavelli himself is an anomaly because in his history of Florence he shows his attachment to republican government, although in *The Prince* he exalts the despot. Perhaps Machiavelli had become disillusioned with republicanism. Perhaps he was merely saying that a state to be strong must have a despot, and a despot to remain in power must be unscrupulous. Yet, with no apparent reservation Machiavelli indicates that the despot must be sufficiently moral not to goad his subjects to rebellion and sufficiently immoral to let no one take advantage of him or of the state. Machiavelli definitely recognized that he was combatting Christianity, for he attributed the ills of his country to the "weakness (*debolezza*) of our religion." *The Prince* became the classic exposition for the starkest *Realpolitik*. But, in his generation, how representative was Machiavelli? The prevailing opinion was voiced rather in the *Institute of the Christian Prince* of Erasmus and in the *Utopia* of Thomas More, both in the tradition of Christian political morality.

Yet no one can deny that Machiavelli had living models for the *Prince* and in particular Cesare Borgia, the son of a pope. In general, the popes of the period were scarcely to be distinguished from the secular princes with their splendid vices and dazzling endowments. Spirituality was not among their distinguishing marks. A few thumbnail sketches of Renaissance popes will illustrate this judgment. Sixtus IV engaged in the machinations of the Renaissance despots. He desired to dislodge the Medici at Florence. His nephews promised to dispose of Lorenzo and Giuliano. The pope insisted there should be no killing. The nephews told him to leave the matter to them and be content. He answered, "*Io sono contento*" (I am content). The rivals of the Medici at Florence, the Pazzi, and the Archbishop Salviati were enlisted. Giuliano de'Medici was assassinated at Mass in the Duomo. Lorenzo, escaping, rallied his men and overcame the conspirators. Several members of the house of Pazzi, as well as the Archbishop Salviati, were hanged. The pope protested against such treatment for an ecclesiastic but was advised that he would do well not to say too much.

The career of Alexander VI reveals that the prevalent practice of clerical concubinage had reached the papacy itself. This pope had four illegitimate children. The most notorious were Lucrezia Borgia and Cesare Borgia. The best that can be said for Alexander is that he acknowledged his concubine and assumed responsibility for his children. In his political dealings, he was quite ready to make treaties with the Turks against Christian princes. No longer Spain, but rather the papacy had now become the link between Christendom and Islam.

Pope Julius II was a disciplined person, a reformer of a kind, a Titan in energy, a noble patron of the arts, the discoverer of Bramante, Raphael, and Michelangelo, but a pope who led his own troops to regain the estates of the Church, and himself scaled the walls of Bologna. Erasmus was more shocked by the travesty of a pope in armor than by the carnality of the Borgia.

Leo X, a Medici, was an elegant dilettante, whose chief distinction was his ability to make impromptu speeches in Latin. He spent more on gambling than on artists, loved the chase, and disliked leaving his hunting lodge to come into Rome and have his toe kissed. He is said to have said, "The papacy is ours. Let us enjoy it." He was pope when Martin Luther posted his theses.

Such were the popes of the Renaissance, but happily the papacy was not the whole Church and, in these same Italian cities, for a good forty years, from the Peace of Lodi in 1454 to the French invasion of Italy in 1494, reality was again given to the ideal of the just war. The reason was not so much a more acute ethical feeling as that five city states had achieved a balance of power: Venice, Milan, Florence, Rome, that is the papacy, and Naples. These five had a community of culture; they did not refrain from conflict, but their struggles were conducted by bands of armed mercenaries who, in seasonable weather, engaged in skirmishes designed to win the greatest advantage for their employers with the least damage to themselves and their fellow mercenaries in the opposing camp. The object of battles, as in the old tournaments, was to take prisoners, count the score, pay the chips, release the captives, and settle down for the winter. The old code of the just war was revived, rules were observed, ambassadors respected, private reprisals suppressed, and cannons despised.

If we look at Europe as a whole, we discover during the fourteenth and the fifteenth century an amazing number of disputes settled by arbitration, disputes sometimes between the great powers, though more commonly between the lesser: dukes, counts, cities, bishops, and monastic military orders like that of the Teutonic Knights. Since the arbiters were seldom churchmen, one may infer that the ecclesiastical direction of society was diminishing. The judge might be a king, a nobleman, or a board set up by the contestants, yet seldom, save in Italy, a cleric. But that laymen should undertake to obviate warfare by voluntary submission to impartial judgment is better evidence of the Christianizing of culture than the acceptance of ecclesiastical control.

In the domestic sphere, the period of the Renaissance was the one when romantic love was increasingly domesticated through the romanticizing of marriage. In the economic area, the Church was ever more drawn into the processes and mentality of incipient capitalism. We have already noted the way in which the Church came to rely on the bankers for credit. She was also driven to turn to them for loans when her own revenues, wherever located, proved insufficient. Although the Church exacted no interest when making loans, she was compelled to give it when borrowing. Then, even the theoretical condemnation of usury started to break down. Aquinas had approved a contract of mutual risk with no fixed return. He had no objection to profits, but only to the demand for definite payment by a specific date, even though the enterprise for which the loan had been made had failed. But, later theologians pointed out that whether or not the enterprise failed, the lender forfeited the gain that might have accrued had he invested the funds, and therefore he was entitled to compensation for the cessation of gain. The doctrine of the just price, which Aquinas had determined in terms of material cost and labor, now began to include also the market value.

Renaissance Art

The realm of art is one of the most elusive. The Gothic church was cruciform, the Renaissance church circular. The Gothic church used the spire, the Renaissance the dome. Whether one style is more religious or more Christian than the other is perhaps a question of taste. Certainly, the architects of the Renaissance, Leo Battista Alberti and Andrea Palladio, sought to inspire religious edification. For them, the circular form exhibited the unity, infinity, uniformity, and the very essence of God. The circle, they pointed out, comprises the harmonies of music and geometry. In their view, a church should be of such proportions that no part could be removed without destroying the whole. This end might be achieved by a simple circle, or by a polygon inserted within a circle, or by a cluster of noduled chapels gathered about the periphery. The sense of elevation, so characteristic of the Gothic, should be achieved by making the cathedral a part of the landscape. It should be set upon an elevated piazza reached by stairs so that the very approach to the sanctuary would induce awe and aspiration. The interior should be of staggering beauty, with windows so high as to exclude the bustle of the world. Buildings dedicated to the Omnipotent should be strong and everlasting, resplendent with jewels. Enveloped by their mysterious amplitude, the believer is transported into ecstasy.

The painting of religious subjects in the Renaissance discloses both a closer approach and a greater withdrawal from the common life. The biblical characters were portrayed as contemporaries with great realism. The Magi were nobles from the Italian cities, the shepherds were peasants of the Apennines, the Virgin Mary was Madonna, a buxom Italian maid, and the Christ Child, a bambino, a cuddly infant. But, the Renaissance with its sense of history felt that the landscape should be set back in time and displayed therefore the biblical scenes amidst classical ruins. The religious art of the Renaissance did not depart from the Christian tradition but shifted the emphasis to another aspect of Christian teaching. The art of the early Church stressed the Resurrection, that of the high Middle Ages the Passion, that of the Renaissance the Incarnation of God in the infant Jesus.

We are reminded, of course, that pagan allusions and artifices appear in the art and literature of the period. This is indisputable, but of itself indicates no departure from the Christian world view, for by this time pagan mythology had come to be innocuous, since no one believed it any longer.

In assessing Humanism, we must remember that it was not an integral entity. There were Humanists and Humanists. Some of them were obsessed by that pessimism, which had plagued late Roman antiquity, owing to the belief that man is not autonomous but subject to Fortuna, personified either as capricious chance or as predetermined destiny. Astrology played a major role. The

Church condemned what was called judicial astrology, that is predictive astrology, rather than what today is known as astronomy. Nevertheless, kings had court astrologers and so did popes. Though Pico, the Neoplatonist, would have no truck with astrology, he was rather an exception among the Humanists.

Then, among the populace at large, there was the cult of the macabre. Particularly after the Black Death of 1348, when nearly one-third of the population of Europe died, survivors were preoccupied with the theme of death. Tombs bore sculptures of corpses with entrails protruding, infested with worms. One of the most popular literary forms, well after the introduction of printing, was the *Ars Moriendi*, the "Art of Dying," with lurid presentations of death scenes, showing angels and devils contending for a soul and even more lurid portrayals of the fate of those unreconciled to the Church. In the course of centuries, these ghastly exhibits lost some of their emotional impact, and when corpses were left unburied, the people would at times have picnics beside the cadavers. Some of the Humanists began to maintain that he who is of clean hands and a pure heart need not worry. Nevertheless, the theme of purgatorial and infernal anguish must have been very vivid to induce the people to contribute so lavishly to indulgences and, except for such beliefs, the spiritual upheavals of Luther and Loyola are inexplicable.

Finally, we are to remember that some of the outstanding men of the Renaissance were themselves divided spirits. Petrarch suffered from despondency and was tempted to destroy his work because conceived in pride. Michelangelo wrote sonnets worthy of St. Francis prostrate before the Crucifix, and renounced his art in the end because the Ineffable defied all representation. Even Florence of the Medici experienced a medieval revival when summoned by the Dominican friar Girolamo Savonarola to repent and burn the vanities of lewdness and luxury. The sequel, too, was medieval. Because Savonarola, in the wake of a French invasion and the expulsion of the Medici, took over the government of the city, he incurred the wrath of the Spanish pope, Alexander VI, who inhibited him from preaching. The recalcitrant friar, some of whose predictions had not come true, was condemned as a false prophet and sent to the stake in the Piazza Pubblica, quite after the manner of the high Middle Ages.

The Mystics

Then, next to such secularist tendencies as have been manifest in the age, we meet in the north with a great revival of mystical religion among the Friends of God and the Brethren of the Common Life. The Friends of God originated early in the fourteenth century in the lands of the Emperor Louis of Bavaria, which lay under an interdict for roughly a quarter of a century. Devout souls, deprived of the sacraments, came to believe that they were not thereby excluded from the presence of God. The Friends of God were a loose association of those with mystical inclinations. They were greatly influenced by Meister Eckhart (1260–1327), whose mysticism went even beyond Neoplatonism in considering the goal of man to be not only detachment from all the things of sense but absorption into the Godhead. Less extreme was the most outstanding member of the group, John Tauler (1300–1361), for whom the chief end of man is to be wholly enraptured by the love of God and the love of man.

Toward the end of the fourteenth century, the Brethren of the Common Life arose in the Netherlands and had their center at Deventer. They represented a much freer type of monasticism and at first took no life-long vows. In placing their members as teachers in schools and universities throughout Europe, their practice resembled that of the Dominicans. Their piety more nearly resembled that of the Franciscans. The supreme example is *The Imitation of Christ,* commonly associated with the name of Thomas à Kempis (1380–1471). The emphasis is placed here upon walking in the steps of the Saviour, sharing with him in the cup of his Passion, rather than upon theological formulations, inasmuch as the Blessed Trinity is better pleased by adoration than by speculation. As with St. Francis, there is a lyricism of love here with deeply mystical notes, for the lover is embraced by the very Godhead. A representative of the Brethren in the period of the high Renaissance was Wessel Gansfort (1420–1489). When he visited Rome, Pope Sixtus IV asked what he might do for him, expecting confidently that he would ask for a benefice. Wessel amazed the pope by his unwillingness to accept anything other than a Greek manuscript. Wessel disparaged indulgences by pointing out that nothing of the sort was necessary in order that the prodigal son should receive his father's kiss. The sacrament of the altar is of no avail, said Wessel, apart from a burning heart, and if this be present, the external rite is not essential. The penitent thief could have been the patron saint of Wessel and his school, because the thief was saved by so little theology; he knew and believed only this: that Christ would take him into Paradise. Wessel was a precursor of Desiderius Erasmus and of Martin Luther.

80. PAPAL PRETENSIONS

Alinari–Art Reference Bureau

As papal power waned, papal pretensions increased. The art of the mid-fourteenth century stresses the hierarchical claims of the Church. The Orcagna altarpiece (1354–57) in S.M.Novella at Florence affords a striking contrast to the mosaic in the Lateran of St. Peter (Fig. 49), conferring authority upon Pope Leo III and Charlemagne, with the emperor on St. Peter's right. In this painting Christ confers authority on St. Peter and St. Thomas Aquinas; the emperor has disappeared altogether. One wonders whether there is any significance in the placing of St. Peter on the left and of St. Thomas on the right. When the Church was not too successful on the administrative level, was there a disposition to emphasize her teaching role?

81. EDWARD I RESISTS POPE BONIFACE VIII

81

Edward I of England, much like Philip the Fair of France, defied Pope Boniface VIII by refusing to pay tribute to Rome. The conflict was less dramatic, but the outcome no less a victory for the king. Edward outlawed the clergy until they paid the taxes he imposed, and they submitted. The claim of the papacy to secular supremacy in England had thus been refuted. (From the Cotton MSS. in the British Museum.)

82. ST. CATHERINE PERSUADES THE POPE TO RETURN TO ROME

The daughter of a poor dyer of Siena, St. Catherine (1347-80) was so emboldened by her visions as to clang the bells of doom alike at Rome and at Avignon. Summoned to give an account of her behavior before the General Chapter of the Dominicans, to which she belonged, she was cleared of the suspicion of heresy, and her appeal to Pope Gregory XI to return the seat of the papacy from Avignon to Rome was heeded. St. Catherine was frequently opposed by the doctors of the Church, whom she would confute by persuading them of the verity of her divine mission. On her life, see Johannes Jorgensen, *Saint Catherine of Siena* (New York, Longmans Green, 1938).

83. THE COUNCIL OF CONSTANCE

83a

83b

John XXIII, wishing to ingratiate himself with the Emperor Sigismund, conferred on him the coveted honor of the Golden Rose (Fig. 83a), but did not thereby save himself from deposition. This illustration is from the contemporary chronicle of the Council of Constance by Ulrich Richental. Fig. 83b shows Cardinal Pierre D'Ailly at the Council of Constance (From *Concilium Constantiense*, Société archéologique Russe).

84. PREACHING AND MARTYRDOM OF JOHN HUSS

84a

84b

84c

These illustrations are from a German tract (*Geistlicher Bluthandel Johannis Hussz, zu Constentz verbrannt anno Domini MCCCCxv* . . .), which appeared around 1520, after Luther had discovered the similarity of many of his teachings to those of Huss, in whose preaching a common theme (borrowed from Wycliffe) was the contrast between the lowly Christ riding on a donkey (Fig. 84a) and the lordly pope on a stallion (Fig. 84b). Fig. 84c shows the martyrdom of Huss. His head has been shaved prior to his execution at the stake, to remove the anointing of his ordination. The little figure emerging from his head is his soul being received by a wingless angel.

85a

A page from a manuscript of Wycliffe's New Testament, written prior to 1400, is reproduced here (Fig. 85a) with the permission of

hem, These ben the
wordis that Y spak to ȝou, whanne Y was ȝit with ȝou;
for it is nede that alle thingis ben fulfillid, that ben writun
in the lawe of Moises, and in prophetis, and in salmes,
45 of me. Thanne he openyde to hem wit, that thei schulden
46 vnderstonde scripturis. And he seide to hem, For thus
it is writun, and thus it bihofte Crist to suffre, and ryse
47 aȝen fro deeth in the thridde dai; and penaunce and re-
myssioun of synnes to be prechid in his name in to alle
48 folkis, bigynnynge at Jerusalem. And ȝe ben witnessis
49 of these thingis. And Y schal sende the biheest of my
fadir in to ȝou; but sitte ȝe in the citee, til that ȝe be clothid
50 with vertu from an hiȝ. And he ledde hem forth in to
Betanye, and whanne his hondis weren lift vp, he blesside
51 hem. And it was don, the while he blesside hem, he
52 departide fro hem, and was borun in to heuene. And thei
worschipiden, and wenten aȝen in to Jerusalem with greet
53 ioye, and weren euermore in the temple, heriynge and
blessynge God. Here eendiȝ ye gospel by ye seiynge of Luke.
and next folewynge bigynneȝ Joon in ye gospel

Capitulum Primum

1 IN the bigynnyng was the word, and the word was at God,
2 and God was the word. This was in the bigynnyng at God.
3 Alle thingis weren maad bi hym, and withouten hym was
4 maad no thing, that thing that was maad. In hym was lijf,
5 and the lijf was the liȝt of men; and the liȝt schyneth in derk-
6 nessis, and derknessis comprehendiden not it. A man was
7 sent fro God, to whom the name was Joon. This man cam
in to witnessying, that he schulde bere witnessing of the liȝt,
8 that alle men schulden bileue bi hym. He was not the liȝt,
9 but that he schulde bere witnessing of the liȝt. There was a
very liȝt, which liȝtneth ech man that cometh in to this world.
10 He was in the world, and the world was maad bi hym, and
11 the world knew hym not. He cam in to his owne thingis,
12 and hise resseyueden hym not. But hou many euer resseyueden hym, he ȝaf to hem power to be maad the sones of
God, to hem that bileueden in his name; the whiche not
13 of bloodis, nether of the wille of fleische, nether of the
14 wille of man, but ben borun of God. And the word was
maad man, and dwellyde among vs, and we han seyn the
glorie of hym, as the glorie of the oon bigetun sone of
15 the fadir, ful of grace and of treuthe. Joon berith witnessyng
of hym, and crieth, and seith, This is, whom Y seide, He that
schal come aftir me, is maad bifore me, for he was tofor me;
16 and of the plente of hym we alle han takun, and grace for
17 grace. For the lawe was ȝouun bi Moises; but grace and
18 treuthe is maad bi Jhesu Crist. No man sai euer God, no
but the oon bigetun sone, that is in the bosum of the fadir,
19 he hath teld out. And this is the witnessyng of Joon, whanne
Jewis senten fro Jerusalem prestis and dekenes to hym, that
20 thei schulden axe hym, Who art thou? He knoulechide,
and denyede not, and he knoulechide, For Y am not Crist.

the Yale University Library. The passage begins in the last chapter of Luke (24:44, in the middle of the verse) and continues into John, through 1:20. The transliteration (Fig. 85b) is taken from *The New Testament of Wycliffe and Purvey* (Oxford, 1879). The sign ȝ stands for y in *yit* = yet, you, ye; for g in *agen* = again, *gaf* = gave, *gouun* = given; for gh in light. Other signs in the original are spelled out in the transliteration. Note that, in the original, þ = th.

86. THE RENAISSANCE

86a

The portrayal of the Nativity during the Renaissance diverges from that in the Middle Ages in several respects. A greater humaneness is evident in that the scene is usually set in the artist's locale. In Italy, the mother is the *Madonna* and the child the *bambino*. The Wise Men become the nobles of Florence or Siena, the shepherds are the peasants of the Apennines. There is a feeling for historical periods in that classical ruins make up the background. The miraculous is enhanced. In the Middle Ages, Mary was shown lying in bed after the pangs of childbirth, but in the Renaissance, due to the visions of St. Brigit (Fig. 86a) she would be shown kneeling before the child right after delivery, apparently having experienced no pain. Then again, not one star appeared to guide the Wise Men but three, in honor of the Holy Trinity (Fig. 86a). Increased geographical knowledge had led to the discovery that Africa was a continent, as much as Europe or Asia, and thus a continent was assigned to each of the Three Kings; one of them —Gaspard—therefore became black (Fig. 86b).

(Fig. 86a is from an undated manuscript at Bern, and appears in Henrik Cornell, "The Iconography of the Nativity of Christ," *Uppsala Universitets Arsskrift*, Heft 3, 1924. Fig. 86b is from Bertholdus, *Horologium devotionis circa vitam Christi* [Basel, *ca.* 1489].)

87. CLASSICAL MYTHOLOGY AND CHRISTIAN FAITH

The blending of the classical and the Christian in the art of the Church did not originate in the Renaissance. This pulpit in the baptistry at Pisa was executed by Niccolò Pisano in 1260. In the central panel above is a depiction of the crucifixion. One of the pillars is Hercules with his club. The pillar to the far left is of the Church suckling two infants. In 1926 the pulpit was "purified" and plain pillars were substituted. This drawing is taken from Charles Yriarte, *Florence* (London, 1882), p. 239.

88. THE DANCE OF DEATH

88

A mural painting from the first half of the fifteenth century in L'Église de la Chaise-Dieu, built by Pope Clement VI at Auvergne in the middle of the fourteenth century. This theme became very popular in the Middle Ages, particularly after the Black Death of 1348.

89. CHRIST THE JUDGE

89

Coincident with the cult of death in the late Middle Ages was the enhancement of the terror of death by the depiction of the judgment to come: Christ as Judge, seated upon a rainbow, usually with a sword (wrath) pointed at one ear, and a lily (mercy) directed toward the other. In this example, we have the very height of terror since there are two swords. Interceding with Christ are Mary on our left and John the Baptist on the right. Below, a devil herds souls toward hell. A figure with a halo, presumably St. Peter, has a soul under his arm, but a devil has lassoed the soul's foot and is tugging hellward. In the corners below, the prophet Jonah on the left tears his hair over the sins of Nineveh, on the right the Apostle Philip points to Christ. The German text is not clear. (This illustration is reproduced in Johannes Geffcken, *Der Bildercatechismus des fünfzehnten Jahrhunderts* [Leipzig, 1855].)

90. RELIGIOUS SENTIMENT ON THE EVE OF THE REFORMATION

Nowhere does it receive nobler expression than in the sculptures (chiefly in wood) of Tilman Riemenschneider (1455/60–1531). From 1483 he labored in Würzburg in central Germany. Though he lived through the earlier years of the Reformation, he was not affected by the new currents. His sculptures exhibit that foreboding of doom that beset the late medieval spirit and without which Luther's upheaval is inexplicable. Riemenschneider's St. Dorothea (left), for all its tranquility, suggests a wistful sadness. Her figure is regal, the hands posed in an unusual manner and with exceeding grace. The headdress resembles that of the Empress Kunigunde. During the Peasants' War, Riemenschneider was tortured on a charge of spreading a false rumor about the bishop's conduct during the struggle. His hands were not crippled, as legend declares, but his spirit was broken. The sculpture of St. Dorothea was destroyed in World War II. (The illustration and this brief description are from Kurt Gerstenberg, *Tilman Riemenschneider* [München, 1941 and 1950], No. 124, opp. p. 194.)

Atlantis Verlag, Zürich

91. BIBLES OF

Jm frid ist gemacht oder worden sein stat.

David Salomon

Jch schlaff vnd mein hertz wachet

91a

One cause of the reform movements in the sixteenth century was the groundwork laid in the instruction of the people in the knowledge of the Bible. Before the invention of movable type, the technique of the block book was used to present biblical themes: a picture was stamped from a wood block and the text written in by hand. The Bible of the Poor (*Die Biblia Pauperum,* Deutsche Ausgabe, 1471) done in this way showed, in the center, a scene from the New Testa-

THE POOR

91b

ment, flanked by two from the Old Testament suggestive of the same theme. In Fig. 91a we have Jesus in the center going down into the tomb and, on the sides, Joseph going down the well and Jonah into the whale. Fig. 91b shows the temptation of Jesus in the center and, on the sides, Adam and Eve being tempted by the serpent and Esau by the "mess of potage."

92. THE EXECUTION OF SAVONAROLA

This occurred on May 23, 1498, in the Piazza Pubblica at Florence. The building at the rear of the square toward our right is the Bargello. On the left are the Duomo and the Campanile.

Selected Bibliographies

CHAPTER I

For the entire Bible consult *The Interpreter's Dictionary of the Bible* (New York, Abingdon, 1962), 4 vols.

Old Testament History: Noth, Martin, *The History of Israel* (New York, 1958); Bright, John, *A History of Israel* (New York, 1959).

Old Testament Theology: Rad, G. von, *Old Testament Theology* (New York, Harper & Row, 1962).

Special Phases: Childs Brevard, *Memory and Tradition in Israel* (Naperville, Ill., 1962); Napier, B. D., *Song of the Vineyard* (New York, Harper & Row, 1962).

Intertestamental Period: Perowne Steward, *The Life and Times of Herod the Great* (New York, 1959); ———, *The Later Herods* (New York, 1958).

Dead Sea Scrolls: Gaster, Theodor H., *The Dead Sea Scriptures in English Translation* (Garden City, N. Y., Anchor, 1956); Burrows, Millar, *The Dead Sea Scrolls* (New York, 1955); Schubert, Kurt, *The Dead Sea Community* (New York, Harper & Bros., 1959); Howlett, Duncan, *The Essenes and Christianity* (New York, Harper & Bros., 1957).

Classical Background: Jaeger, Werner, *Early Christianity and Greek Paideia* (Cambridge, Mass., 1961); Cochrane, C. N., *Christianity and Classical Culture* (Philadelphia, 1959); Pohlenz, Max, *Der hellenische Mensch* (Göttingen, 1947).

CHAPTER II

NEW TESTAMENT

Introduction: Grant, Robert N., *Historical Introduction to the New Testament* (New York, Harper & Row, 1963).

Interpretation: Bultmann, Rudolf, *Primitive Christianity in its Historical Setting* (Cleveland, Meridian, 1956); Bultmann, R., et al., *Kerygma and Myth*, ed. H. W. Bartsch (New York, Harper Torchbook, 1961); Bornkamm, Günther, *Jesus of Nazareth* (New York, Harper & Bros., 1956); Robinson, James M., *A New Quest of the Historical Jesus* (London, 1959).

CHAPTER III

General Histories of the Christian Church: Fliche, Auguste et Martin, Victor, *Histoire de l'Église* (Paris, 1946–52), 21 vols.; Walker, Williston, *A History of the Christian Church* (Rev. ed., New York, 1959); Latourette, Kenneth Scott, *A History of Christianity* (New York, Harper & Bros., 1953).

The Early Church: Kidd, B. J., *A History of the Christian Church to A.D. 461* (Oxford, 1922), 3 vols.; Lietzmann, Hans, *The Beginnings of the Christian Church* (New York, 1937–38), 4 vols.; Daniélou, Jean and Marrou, Henri, *The Christian Centuries* (New York, 1964), Vol. I; Bainton, Roland H., *Early Christianity* (Princeton, N.J., Van Nostrand, 1960), documents and commentary.

Christian Thought: Harnack, Adolf, *History of Dogma* (New York, Dover, 1961), 4 vols.; Seeberg, Reinhold, *Textbook of the History of Doctrines* (Grand Rapids, Mich., 1964), 2 vols.

SOURCES

Translation of Creeds: Schaff, Ph., *Creeds of Christendom* (New York, Harper & Bros., 1877), 3 vols.; *Creeds of the Churches*, ed. John H. Leith (New York, Anchor, 1963). The bulk of the early Christian literature is available in translation in the *Ante-Nicene Fathers* and the *Post-Nicene Fathers*, Series I & II. New translations are in progress: *The Fathers of the Church* (by Catholic scholars); *The Library of Christian Classics* (by Protestant scholars). For this period, especially, *Early Christian Fathers*, ed. C. C. Richardson, Vol. I.

Excerpts from sources in single volumes: Ayer, J. C., *A Source Book for Ancient Church History* (New York, 1920); Kidd, B. J., *Documents Illustrative of the Early Church* (Oxford, 1920), 3 vols.; Gwatkin, Henry M., *Selections from Early Writers* (London, 1893); Stevenson, J., *A New Eusebius* (London, 1957); Grant, Frederick C., *Hellenistic Religions* (New York, 1953); Grant, Robert M., *Second-Century Christianity* (London, 1946); Owen, E. C. E., *Some Authentic Acts of the Early Martyrs* (Oxford, 1927); Shotwell, J. T., and Loomis, Louise R., *The See of Peter* (New York, 1927); Latin Fathers only: Wright, F. A., *Fathers of the Church* (London, 1929).

Persecutions: Hardy, E. G., *Christianity and the Roman Government* (London, 1925); Guterman, Simeon L., *Religious Toleration and Persecution in Ancient Rome* (London, 1961); Stauffer, Ethelbert, *Christ and the Caesars* (Philadelphia, 1955).

Rival Religious Systems: Cumont, Franz, *The Oriental Religions in Roman Paganism* (Chicago, 1911); ———, *The Mysteries of Mithra* (Chicago, 1910); Vermaseren, Maarten Jozef, *Mithras, the Secret God* (New York, 1963); *Pagan and Christian Mysteries*, ed. Joseph Campbell (New York, Harper & Row, Torchbook, 1963); Jonas, Hans, *The Gnostic Religion* (Boston, 1958); Carrington, Philip, *Christian Apologetics of the Second Century* (New York, 1921).

Internal Development of the Church: Harnack, Adolf, *Mission and Expansion* (New York, Harper & Bros., 1953), 3 vols.; Latourette, Kenneth Scott, *History of the Expansion of Christianity* (New York, Harper & Bros., 1937), Vol. I; Hatch, Edwin, *The Organization of the Early Christian Churches* (London, 1881); Duchesne, Louis, *Christian Worship* (New York, 1931); Watkin, O. D., *History of Penance* (Reprint, New York, 1961), 2 vols.; Souter, Alexander, *The Text and Canon of the New Testament* (Oxford, 1924); James, M. R., *The Apocryphal New Testament* (Oxford, 1924); Bethune-Baker, J. F., *An Introduction to the Early History of Christian Doctrine* (London, 1903, reprint 1958); Kelly, J. N .D., *Early Christian Doctrines* (London, 1958); ———, *Early Christian Creeds* (London, 1960); Cadoux, Cecil J., *The Early Church and the World* (Edinburgh, 1925); Giordani, Igino, *The Social Message of the Early Church Fathers* (Paterson, N.J., 1944); Bainton, Roland H., *Christian Attitudes toward War and Peace* (New York, 1960); Rice, D. Talbot, *The Beginnings of Christian Art* (New York, 1957); Morey, C. R., *Early Christian Art* (2nd ed.; Princeton, 1953).

CHAPTER IV

The Christian Roman Empire: Baynes, Norman H. & Moss, H. St. L. B., eds., *Byzantium* (Oxford, 1961); Baynes, Norman H., *Constantine the Great and the Christian Church* (London, 1931); Alföldi, András, *The Conversion of Constantine and Pagan Rome* (Oxford, 1948); Doerries, Hermann, *Constantine and Religious Liberty* (New Haven, 1960); Frend, William H. C., *The Donatist Church* (Oxford, 1952); Gwatkin, H. M., *The Arian Controversy* (New York, 1898); Simpson, William D., *Julian the Apostate* (Aberdeen, 1930); Waddell, Helen, *The Desert Fathers* (Ann Arbor, Univ. of Michigan, 1957); Workman, H. B., *The Evolution of the Monastic Ideal* (London, 1927); Kidd, B. J., *The Churches of Eastern Christendom* (London, 1927); Zernov, Nicholas, *Eastern Christendom* (New York, 1961); Bevan, Edwin, *Holy Images* (London, 1940).

Biographies (recent): Campenhausen, Hans von, *The Fathers of the Greek Church* (New York, 1959); Daniélou, Jean, *Origen* (New York, 1955); Prestige, G. L., *St.Basil the Great* (London, 1956).

CHAPTER V

THE MIDDLE AGES

General: Stephenson, Carl, *Medieval History*, rev. B. Lyon (New York, Harper & Row, 1961), excellent bibliographies; Cantor, Norman F., *Medieval History* (New York, 1964).

EARLY MIDDLE AGES

Duckett, Eleanor, *Gateway to the Middle Ages*, I, Monasticism; II, Italy; III, France and Britain (Ann Arbor Paperback, 1961).

Lopez, Robert S., *Naissance de L'Europe* (Paris, 1962).

Lot, Ferdinand, *The End of the Ancient World and the Beginning of the Middle Ages* (New York, Harper & Row, Torchbook, 1961).

Southern, R. W., *The Making of the Middle Ages* (New Haven, Yale Paperback, 1961).

ECONOMIC HISTORY

Thompson, James Westphal, *Economic and Social History of the Middle Ages 300–1300* (New York, 1928).

Dopsch, A., *The Economic and Social Foundations of European Civilization* (London, 1937).

THE MEDIEVAL CHURCH
Sources:
Library of Christian Classics (Westminster Press, Philadelphia):
- IX *Early Medieval Theology*, ed. George E. McCracken.
- X *Scholastic Miscellany*, ed. Eugene Fairweather.
- XI *Nature and Grace: Selections from the Summa Theologica of Thomas Aquinas*, ed. A. M. Fairweather.
- XII *Western Asceticism*, ed. Owen Chadwick.
- XIII *Late Medieval Mysticism*, ed. Ray C. Petry.
- XIV *Advocates of Reform, from Wyclif to Erasmus*, ed. Matthew Spinka.

Gregory of Tours, *History of the Franks* (New York, 1927), 2 vols.

The Portable Medieval Reader, eds. J. B. Ross and M. M. McLaughlin (New York, Viking Press, 1955).

Basic Documents in Medieval History, ed. Norton Downs (New York, Van Nostrand, 1959).

Kidd, B. J., *Documents Illustrative of the History of the Church* (New York, 1949), Vol. III.

Bettenson, Henry, *Documents of the Christian Church* (London, 1944).
Coulton, G. G., *Life in the Middle Ages* (Cambridge, Eng., 1928-30), 4 vols.
Petry, Ray C., *History of Christianity*, Vol. I, *Readings in the History of the Early and Medieval Church* (Englewood Cliffs, N.J., 1962).

HISTORIES OF THE MEDIEVAL CHURCH
Hauck, Albert, *Kirchengeschichte Deutschlands* (Leipzig, 1887-1920), 6 vols.
Bainton, Roland H., *The Medieval Church* (Princeton, Anvil Paperback, 1962).
Baldwin, M. W., *The Medieval Church* (Ithaca, N.Y., 1960).
Deanesley, M., *A History of the Medieval Church* (London, 1934).
Dawson, Christopher, *The Making of Europe* (New York, 1932); *Medieval Religion* (New York, 1934); *Religion and the Rise of Western Culture* (New York, 1950); *Medieval Essays* (New York, 1954).
Coulton, G. G., *Five Centuries of Religion* (Cambridge, Eng., 1923-36), 3 vols.
Schubert, Hans von, *Geschichte der christlichen Kirche im Frühmittelalter* (Tübingen, 1921).
Taylor, Henry Osborn, *The Emergence of Christian Culture in the West* (New York, Harper & Bros., Torchbook, 1958).

CONVERSION OF THE BARBARIANS
Latourette, Kenneth Scott, *Expansion of Christianity* (New York, Harper & Row, 1938), Vol. II.
Addison, James T., *The Medieval Missionary* (London, 1936).
Robinson, Charles H., *The Conversion of Europe* (New York, 1917).
Rückert, Hanns, *Die Christianisierung der Germanen* (Tübingen, 1934).
Spinka, Matthew, *History of Christianity in the Balkans* (Chicago, 1933).
Stutz, Ulrich, "The Proprietary Church," *Studies in Medieval History*, ed. Geoffrey Barraclough (Oxford, 1938).

BIOGRAPHIES
Augustine: Battenhouse, Roy, *A Companion to the Study of St. Augustine*, a symposium (Oxford, 1938); Bourke, Vernon J., *Augustine's Quest of Wisdom* (Milwaukee, 1945); D'Arcy, M. C., *A Monument to St.Augustine*, a symposium (London, 1930).

Ambrose: Dudden, Frederick H., *The Life and Times of St.Ambrose* (Oxford, 1935), 2 vols.
Benedict: Washburn, Henry B., *Men of Conviction* (New York, 1931).
Gregory I: Dudden, F. H., *Gregory the Great* (London, 1905), 2 vols. Howorth, Henry II., *St.Gregory the Great* (London, 1912).
Patrick: Bury, H. B., *Life of St.Patrick* (London, 1905).

CHAPTER VI

ADDITIONAL SOURCES

The Letters of St.Boniface, tr. Ephraim Emerton (New York, 1940).
The Correspondence of Pope Gregory VII, tr. Ephraim Emerton (New York, 1932).

CHARLEMAGNE

Easton, S. C. and Wieruszowski, H., *The Era of Charlemagne* (New York, Van Nostrand, 1961).
Fichtenau, Heinrich, *The Carolingian Empire* (New York, Harper & Row, Torchbook, 1964).
Sullivan, Richard E., *The Coronation of Charlemagne* (Boston, 1959).
Beumann, Helmut, "Nomen Imperatoris," *Historische Zeitschrift* CLXXXV (1958), 515–49.
Havinghurst, Alfred E., *The Pirenne Thesis* (Boston, 1958).

TENTH CENTURY

Lopez, Robert S., *The Tenth Century* (New York, 1959).
Focillon, Henry, *L'An Mille* (Paris, 1952).

CHURCH PROPERTY

Lesne, Emile, *Histoire de la Propriété ecclésiastique en France* (Lille, 1910–43), 8 vols. in 7.
Herlihy, David, "Church Property on the European Continent 701–1200," *Speculum* XXXVI (1961), 81–105.

CLUNY MOVEMENT

Smith, Lucy M., *Cluny in the Eleventh and Twelfth Centuries* (London, 1930).

INVESTITURE CONTROVERSY

Brooke, Zachary N., *Lay Investiture* (London, 1939).
Cantor, Norman F., *Church Kingship and Lay Investiture in England 1059–1135* (Princeton, 1955).
Schieffer, Th., "Cluny et la Querelle des Investitures," *Revue Historique*, CCXXV (Jan.–Mars, 1961), 47–72.

Tellenbach, Gerd, *Church, State and Christian Society at the Time of the Investiture Controversy* (Oxford, 1940).
Ullmann, Walther, *The Growth of Papal Government* (London, 1955).

CRUSADES

A History of the Crusades, ed. Kenneth Setton (Philadelphia, 1955 ff.), projected in a number of volumes.
Runciman, Steven, *A History of the Crusades* (Cambridge, Eng., 1951–54), 3 vols.
Duckett, Eleanor S., *Anglo-Saxon Saints and Scholars* (New York, 1947); *Alcuin, Friend of Charlemagne* (New York, 1951); *St. Dunstan of Canterbury* (New York, 1955); *Alfred the Great* (Chicago, 1956); *The Wandering Saints of the Early Middle Ages* (New York, 1959).

CHAPTER VII

ADDITIONAL SOURCES

The Letters of St. Bernard of Clairvaux, tr. Bruno S. James (Chicago, 1953).
Francis of Assisi, *The Little Flowers* (London, Dent & Sons, Everyman's Library, 1912).
Selected Letters of Pope Innocent III, eds. C. R. Cheney and W. H. Semple (New York, 1953).
Dante Alighieri, *The Divine Comedy*, tr. and comment by John D. Sinclair (New York, Oxford Univ. Press, 1961), 3 vols.
Aquinas, Thomas, *The Truth of the Catholic Faith* (Garden City, Doubleday, 1960), 2 vols.
Fremantle, Anne, *The Age of Belief* (New York, New American Library, 1960).
Waddell, Helen, *Wandering Scholars* (Ann Arbor, Mich., Univ. of Michigan, 1955).

UNIVERSITIES

Rashdall, Hastings, *The Universities of Europe in the Middle Ages*, eds. F. M. Powicke and A. B. Emden (Oxford, 1936), 3 vols.
Haskins, Charles H., *The Rise of Universities* (Ithaca, Cornell Univ. Press, 1963).

SCHOLASTICISM

Coppleston, F. C., *Medieval Philosophy* (New York, Harper & Row, Torchbook, 1961).
De Wulf, M., *History of Medieval Philosophy* (New York, 1952), 2 vols.
Gilson, Etienne, *Reason and Revelation in the Middle Ages* (New

York, Scribner, 1938); *The Spirit of Medieval Philosophy* (New York, 1940); *Christian Philosophy* (New York, 1940); *The Christian Philosophy of St.Thomas Aquinas* (New York, 1956).

Hawkins, D. J. B., *A Sketch of Medieval Philosophy* (New York, 1947).

Leff, Gordon, *Medieval Thought from St.Augustine to Ockham* (Baltimore, Penguin Books, 1958).

McGiffert, Arthur C., *A History of Christian Thought* (New York, 1953–54), 2 vols.

Vignaux, Paul, *Philosophy in the Middle Ages* (London, 1959).

COURTLY LOVE

André le Chapelain (Andreas Capellanus), *The Art of Courtly Love*, introduction J. J. Parry (New York, 1941).

Bainton, Roland H., *What Christianity Says about Sex, Love and Marriage* (New York, Association Press, 1957).

Denomy, Alexander J., *The Heresy of Courtly Love* (New York, 1947).

THE GOTHIC STYLE

Adams, Henry, *Mont-Saint-Michel and Chartres* (Garden City, Doubleday, 1959).

Coulton, G. G., *Art and the Reformation* (New York, Harper & Bros., Torchbook, 1958), 2 vols.

Gimple, Jean, *The Cathedral Builders* (New York, Grove Press, 1961).

Harvey, John, *Gothic England* (London, 1948).

———, *The Gothic World* (London, 1950).

Mâle, Émile, *The Gothic Image* (New York, Harper & Bros., Torchbook, 1958).

Morey, Charles R., *Medieval Art* (New York, 1942).

Panofsky, Erwin, *Abbot Suger* (Princeton, 1946).

Pevsner, Nikolaus, *An Outline of European Architecture* (Baltimore, Penguin, 1958).

Prentice, Sartell, *The Heritage of the Cathedral* (New York, 1936).

———, *The Voices of the Cathedral* (New York, 1938).

Simson, Otto von, *The Gothic Cathedral* (New York, Harper & Row, Torchbook, 1964).

Worringer, W., *Form in Gothic* (New York, Schocken, 1964).

BIOGRAPHIES

Abelard: Gilson, Etienne, *Heloise and Abelard* (Ann Arbor, Mich., Univ. of Michigan, 1960); Waddell, Helen, *Peter Abelard* (London, 1933), a historical novel.

Bernard: Williams, Watkin W., *St.Bernard of Clairvaux* (Manchester, Eng., 1952).

Innocent III: Packard, Sidney R., *Europe and the Church under Innocent III* (New York, 1927); Tillmann, Helene, *Papst Innocenz III* (Bonn, 1954); Clayton, Joseph E., *Pope Innocent III* (Milwaukee, 1940).

Langton: Powicke, Frederick M., *Stephen Langton* (Oxford, 1928).

Francis: Cuthbert, Father, *The Romanticism of St.Francis* (London, 1915); ———, *Life of St.Francis* (London, 1927).

Dominic: Jarrett, Bede, *The Life of St.Dominic* (Westminster, Md., 1947).

SECTS AND INQUISITION

Waldenses: Comba, Emilio, *A History of the Waldenses of Italy* (London, 1889); Watt, George B., *The Waldenses in the New World* (Durham, N.C., 1941); Davison, Ellen S., *Forerunners of St.Francis* (Boston, 1927).

Albigenses: Warner, H. J., *The Albigensian Heresy* (New York, 1922). Runciman, Steven, *The Medieval Manichee* (New York, Viking, 1961).

Inquisition: Lea, Henry C., *History of the Inquisition of the Middle Ages* (New York, 1922), 3 vols.; Tuberville, Arthur S., *Medieval Heresy and the Inquisition* (London, Archon, 1964).

LITURGY

Dix, Gregory, *The Shape of the Liturgy* (London, 1952).

CHAPTER VIII

CAPTIVITY AND COUNCILS

Mollat, G., *The Popes at Avignon* (New York, Harper & Row, Torchbook, 1965).

Jacob, Ernest F., *Essays in the Conciliar Period* (Manchester, Eng., 1943).

Tierney, Brian, *Foundations of Conciliar Theory* (Cambridge, Eng., 1955).

———, *The Crisis of Church and State 1050–1300* (Englewood Cliffs, N. J., 1964).

SECTS

Wyclif: Workman, Herbert B., *John Wyclif* (Oxford, 1926), 2 vols.; Winn, Herbert E. ed., *Select English Writings: Wyclif* (Oxford, 1929).

Huss: Spinka, Matthew, *John Huss and the Czech Reform* (Chicago, 1941).

LATE MEDIEVAL MOOD

Huizinga, John, *The Waning of the Middle Ages* (Garden City, Doubleday, 1956).
Manning, Bernard L., *The People's Faith in the Time of Wyclif* (Cambridge, Eng., 1919).
Pantin, William A., *The English Church in the Fourteenth Century* (Cambridge, Eng., 1955).
Meiss, Millard, *Painting in Florence and Siena after the Black Death* (New York, Harper & Row, Torchbook, 1964).

PREACHING

Hefele, Karl, *Die franziskanische Wanderpredigt in Italien* (Freiburg i. Br., 1912).
Owst, Gerald R., *Preaching in Medieval England* (Cambridge, Eng., 1926).
———, *Literature and Pulpit in Medieval England* (Oxford, 1961).
Petry, Ray C., *No Uncertain Sound* (Philadelphia, 1948).
Robertson, D. W. Jr., "Frequency of Preaching in Thirteenth Century England," *Speculum* XXIV (1949), 376–88.

SOCIAL QUESTION

Jarrett, Bede, *Social Theories of the Middle Ages* (Westminster, Md., 1942).
Noonan, John T., Jr., *The Scholastic Analysis of Usury* (Cambridge, Mass., 1957).
Baldwin, John W., *Medieval Theories of the Just Price* (Philadelphia, 1959).

POLITICAL THOUGHT

Ullmann, Walther, *Medieval Papalism* (London, 1949).
———, *Principles of Government and Politics in the Middle Ages* (New York, 1961).

RENAISSANCE

The Renaissance Philosophy of Man, eds. Ernst Cassirer, Paul O. Kristeller and John H. Randall, Jr. (Chicago, 1948).
Chabod, Frederic, *Machiavelli and the Renaissance* (London, 1958), with a valuable bibliography on religion in the Renaissance.
Pastor, Ludwig von, *The History of the Popes* (London, 1891–1953), 40 vols.
Ferguson, Wallace, "The Church in a Changing World," *American Historical Review*, LIX (Oct. 1953).

Kristeller, Paul O., *The Classics and Renaissance Thought* (Cambridge, Mass., 1955).
———, *Renaissance Thought* (New York, Harper & Row, Torchbook, 1961 and 1965), 2 vols.
Spitz, Lewis, *The Religious Renaissance of the German Humanists* (Cambridge, Mass., 1963).

ART

Benesch, Otto, *The Art of the Renaissance in Northern Europe* (Cambridge, Mass., 1947).
Panofsky, Erwin, *Studies in Iconology* (New York, Harper & Row, Torchbook, 1962).

LATE MEDIEVAL PIETY

Seesholtz, Anna, *Friends of God* (New York, 1934).
Meister Eckhart, tr. Raymond B. Blakney (New York, Harper & Row, Torchbook, 1957).
Treatises and Sermons of Meister Eckhart, tr. J. M. Clark and J. V. Skinner (New York, Harper & Bros., 1958).
Hyma, Albert, *The Christian Renaissance* (New York, 1924).

Index
Volume I

Abbasids 154
Abelard, Peter 189f, 197f; *Sic et Non* 190
Abgar of Edessa 87
Abraham 3, 4ff, 9
Acts of the Apostles 24, 42, 55, 67, 165, 212
Adeodatus 123, 125
Adhemar, bishop of Puy 179
Aesculapius 60
agape 42
Agilulf, king of the Franks 150
Ahasuerus 4
Ahaz, king of Judah 12
Aidan 152
Aimable, St. 149
Alaric, king of the Visigoths 107, 132, 140
Alberti, Leo Battista 250
Albigenses 210, 213, 215f, 218
Albigensian crusade 216, 226
Alcuin 161f
Alexander, bishop of Rome 72
Alexander III, pope 203, 214
Alexander VI, pope 248, 252f
Alexander Jannaeus 22
Alexander Severus 73
Alexander the Great 16ff, 21, 46, 102
Alexius, St. 214
Ambrose, St., bishop of Milan 121, 124f
Anacletus 72
Anacletus II, pope 193
Anjou, House of 227
Anne of Bohemia 234, 237
anointing 10f
Anselm, St. 186, 197, 220; *Cur Deus Homo* 197
Ansgar 143, 167
Antiochus Epiphanes 4, 21f
Anthony, St. 104, 149
Antonines 87
Apocrypha 12, 69f
Apollo 91, 93
Apollonia, St. 149

apostasy 81f
apostles 31, 56
Apostles' Creed 66, 108, 162, 244
apostolic succession 71ff
Aquinas, St. Thomas 219ff, 228, 250
Aramaic language 9
architecture 112f, 195f, 198f, 250f,
Aretino, Pietro 245
Arianism 97f, 100, 103, 121, 133, 135, 150
Aristotle 17, 18, 19, 211, 219, 220, 244
Ark of the Covenant 8, 11, 13, 24
Armenian Church 87, 110
Ars Moriendi 252
art 79, 112, 132f, 183, 250
Artemis, cult of 49
asceticism 105
Assyrians 12f
Astarte 75
astrology 251f
Athanasius, bishop of Alexandria 69, 86, 97, 101
Athanasians 100
Attis 75, 76
Augustine, St., bishop of Hippo 60, 97, 114, 121, 131, 164, 178f, 196, 218, 222, 227; *City of God* 127, 161; *Confessions* 122
Augustine, St., bishop of Canterbury 143, 152
Augustinians/Augustinianism 187, 220
Augustus, Roman emperor 1, 2, 24, 37, 53, 73, 90
Aurelian, Roman emperor 74
authority, papal 165, 238
Averroes 154, 244
Avignon 228, 230, 234f

Baal, cult of 9, 75
Babel, Tower of 4
Babylonian captivity 13, 14ff, 228
Baldwin of Bouillon 179f
baptism 42, 66, 83, 103
Barnabas 48

INDEX

Bartholomew, St. 31
Basel, Council of 241f
Basil, St. 105
Bathsheba 18
Benedict, St. 105, 136f, 138, 169
Benedictine rule 136f, 161, 168, 191
Berengaria of Castile 205
Bernard of Clairvaux, St. 192f, 202, 234
Bertha, queen of England 152
Bible, translations of 106, 116f, 156, 238
bishops 56, 71, 230
Blaise, St. 149, 212
Blanche, queen of France 201
blasphemy 229
Boccaccio, Giovanni 245, 247
Bohemund 179f
Boniface, St. 143, 155ff
Boniface VIII, pope 227f; *Clericis Laicos* 227; *Unam sanctam* 228
Boniface, Roman general 128
Bogomiles 215
Borgia, Cesare 248
Borgia, Lucrezia 248
Bramante 248
Brethren of the Common Life 253f
Byzantine empire 94, 101, 107f, 116f

Cabala 246
Caesar 21, 25, 37f, 46, 90
Caesaropapism 111f, 117, 119
Caiaphas 39
Cain 65
Calatrava, order of 229
Caligula, Roman emperor 53
Callistus, bishop of Rome 80f
cannibalism 63
Canon 3
Canute, king of the Danes 167f
capitalism 250
Caracalla, Roman emperor 82
cardinals, college of 165
Cassiodorus 138
Castiglione, Baldassare: *Il Cortegiano* 246
Carthusians 173
Cathari: *see* Albigenses
cathedrals 200f
Catholicism 130f

Celestine, pope 222
celibacy 56, 80, 94, 104f, 170, 174, 188f, 213
Celsus 61, 85, 103; *True Discourse* 85
Celtic Church 153
Chalcedon, Council of 109, 111
Charlemagne 159-162, 172, 182
Charles the Bald 163
Charles Martel 149, 157
Chaucer: *Canterbury Tales* 238
Chilperic 148
chivalry 182
Christ, birth of 1f, 26ff
Christmas 76f
Chronos 19
Chrysostom, St. John 105, 121, 132
Church and state 87, 111f, 129f, 221, 232
Church Fathers 67, 70, 77ff
Cicero 122f, 128, 131, 139
circumcision 15, 45, 52
Cistercians 173, 191f, 213
Claudius, Roman emperor 49
Clement of Alexandria 78ff
Clement of Rome, St. 71f
Clement V, pope 229
Clement VII, pope 234
Clermont, Council of 178, 179
Clothilda, queen of Gaul 145ff
Clovis, king of Gaul 143, 145ff, 157, 197
Cluny reform 168-173, 191
Columba 152f
Columbanus 151
Columbus 236
Commodianus 88
conceptualism 189
Conciliarism 234ff, 240
confraternities 211
congregationalism 56
Constance, Council of 236, 240f
Constantine, Roman emperor 60, 88, 91ff, 97f, 100ff, 113, 127, 132, 134, 197, 216, 244
Constantine, Donation of: *see* Donation of Constantine
Constantius the Arian 101
Constantius Chlorus 90
consubstantiality 78, 99

contemplation, religions of 3f, 64
Copts 109
covenant, divine 4f, 7
creation 4f, 64
Crespin, St. 212
crucifixion 40, 65, 68f
crusades 179ff, 194, 213, 226f, 229ff
Cynics 19, 30, 61
Cyprian, bishop of Carthage 82f
Cyril, St. 116, 143, 168
Cyrus, king of the Persians 16

D'Ailly, Pierre 234, 236, 240
Damasus, bishop 106
Daniel, Book of 22, 25, 35f, 55
Dante Alighieri 182, 221ff, 242; *On Monarchy* 221; *Divine Comedy* 222f
David 1, 2, 8, 11, 12, 18
David, House of 13, 24, 27
De heretico comburendo 238
deacons 56
Dead Sea scrolls 25
Decius, Roman emperor 74, 82, 84, 89f, 96
Demosthenes 122
Denis, St. 147, 165, 199
Deuteronomy 13
Diaspora 20
Diocletian, Roman emperor 89f, 91f, 96, 160
Dionysian cult 75f
Dionysius the Areopagite 165, 174
Dionysius Exiguus 161
disciples 30f, 41f
Dominic, St. 210
Dominicans 210, 245, 253
Domitian, Roman emperor 54f, 58
Donation of Constantine 158, 244
Donation of Pepin 157f
Donatists 103, 130, 174, 214
Dunstan, St., abbot of Glastonbury 202

Easter 76f
Ecclesiastes 12
Eckhart, Meister 253
ecumenical councils 99, 110, 114, 116, 234
Einhard 159f

Elagabalus 73
Eleanor of Aquitaine 188
Eleutherus 72
Eloi, St. 212
Epicureans/Epicureanism 19, 49
Epistles 68f
Erasmus, Desiderius 248, 254; *Institute of the Christian Prince* 247
Essenes 24f, 59
Esther 4
Ethelbert, king of England 152
Eucharist, the 42, 77, 80, 115f, 215
Eudoxia, empress 132
Eugenius III, pope 194
Eusebius, bishop of Caesarea 92, 95, 127
Eutyches 109
Evaristus 72
excommunication 166f, 176f, 204, 205
Exodus 6f
Ezekiel 69
Ezra 16

faith 220f
Felicitas 73f
Fergus 212
Festus 50
feudalism 164
Fiacre, St. 212
Florence, Council of 242
Francis, St. 118, 207ff, 254
Franciscans 232f, 238, 253
Frederick Barbarossa 203f
Frederick II, emperor 204, 219
Friends of God 253

Gaiseric, king of the Vandals 133
Galerius 89f, 91, 92
Gall, St. 149, 151
Gallienus, emperor 84
Gansfort, Wessel 254
Gelasius, pope 158
Genesis 15
Genevieve, St. 149
George, St. 147
Gerson, Jean Charlier 234, 236
Ghibellines 204
Gideon 10, 22
Gnostics/Gnosticism 64ff, 67, 70, 75, 78, 100, 123, 215, 246

God 5, 7, 33f, 220
God, kingdom of 29f, 34
Godfrey of Bouillon 179
gods, Roman 52f
Golden Age, myth of the 17, 19
good life, the 17f
Gospels 43, 67
Gothic art 182, 195f, 199f
grace 33f, 131
Gratian 183
Gregorians 172f, 179, 201, 213
Gregory the Illuminator 87
Gregory of Tours 145, 148
Gregory I, pope 139ff, 152, 226
Gregory VII, pope 172, 173–177, 196
Gregory IX, pope 218, 234
Guelphs 204
guilds 211f

Hadrian's tomb 140
Hagia Sophia 112
Hammurabi, Code of 4f
Hannibal 53
Hanukkah 4, 22
Harold, king of the Danes 167
Hasmoneans 21f
Hellenism 17–21, 79
Heloise 190, 197
Henry III, emperor 172, 175
Henry IV, emperor 172–177
Henry II, king of England 188, 202f
Hercules 90, 91
heretics 100, 109ff, 130, 214–219, 229
Hermetic literature 246
hermits 104f
Herod Antipas 25, 32
Herod the Great 12, 23ff, 27
Herodians 37
Hezekiah, king of Judah 13
hierarchy 166
Hilary of Poitiers 101
Hilduin, abbot of St. Denis 165
Hincmar, archbishop of Reims 166
history, religion of 3f, 121
Hohenstaufen, House of 204, 227
Homer 19, 20, 59
honor 187
Honorius, bishop of Rome 113, 114
Honorius II, pope 192

Hosius, bishop of Cordova 98, 101
hospitals 59f
Hubert, St. 149
Hugh, abbot of Cluny 176
humanism 242ff, 251f
Huss, John 239ff; *On the Church* 240
Hussites 239ff
Hyginus, St. 72

iconoclasts 115, 157
icons 115, 118f
Ignatius, bishop of Antioch 62f, 71f, 80, 83
immortality 19, 49, 244
incarnation, doctrine of 65, 97, 99
individualism 186, 213
indulgences 133, 230f, 240
infallibility, papal 114f
Innocent II, pope 193
Innocent III, pope 203–206, 209, 213, 216; *De Contemptu Mundi* 204
Innocent IV, pope 227
Inquisition 130, 218f, 229f
investiture controversy 173–177
Irenaeus of Lyons 69ff, 80, 97
Isaac 5
Isaiah 14, 36
Isaiah, the Second 14
Isaurians 115
Ishtar 75
Isidore, bishop of Seville 165
Isis 75, 76
Islam 114, 116, 151, 181, 247f
Isocrates 122
Israel 5
Ivan I, czar 118
Ivan III, czar 118
Ivan IV, czar 119

Jacob 5
Jacobite Church 109
Jacques de Molay 229f
James, St. 31, 41, 45, 147
Jehovah: *see* Yahweh
Jeroboam 12
Jerome, St. 101, 106f, 121
Jesus, birth of: *see* Christ, birth of
Jesus 24ff, 29ff, 69

Joachim of Fiore 217, 233, 241
Job 14
John the Apostle 31, 42f
John the Baptist 29
John XII, pope 172
John XXII, pope 230, 232f
John XXIII, pope 235f, 240
John, king of England 205, 227
John of Damascus 115f
John of Gaunt 237
John, Gospel of 27f, 68f, 77
Joseph 6, 27f
Joshua 7f, 22
Josiah, king of Judah 13, 14
Judah Maccabeus 22
Judaism 2–16, 18–21, 45, 52f, 73, 79, 88, 114, 247
Judas Iscariot 31, 39, 86
Julian the Apostate 88, 102f
Julien, St. 212
Julius II, pope 248
just war, the 19f, 164, 178f, 249
justice 201f
Justina, empress 124
Justinian, Roman emperor 110f, 113, 120, 133, 232
Justinian Code 111, 184
Juvenal 48

Kenotic 117
kingship 10f
knighthood 187
Knights Templars 194, 229f

Lanfranc, archbishop of Canterbury 177
Langton, Stephen 205
Last Supper 38, 42
Lateran Council 206
law 183f, 202
Law, Mosaic 3, 7, 15, 32f, 42, 45
law, Roman 184
Leo III, pope 159
Leo X, pope 248f
Leo III, emperor 115
Leonardo da Vinci 246
Liberius, bishop of Rome 101
Licinius 91ff
light, imagery of 199
Linus 72

liturgy 142, 161f
Logos 28
Lollards 238
Lord's Day 94
Lothair 163, 172, 176
Lothair II, 166
Louis of Bavaria, emperor 232, 253
Louis II, emperor 166
Louis VII, king of France 188, 201
Louis the German 163
Louis the Pious 163, 165
love, romantic view of 187f, 194f, 222, 250, 252
Loyola, St. Ignatius of 252
Luke, St., the Evangelist 1, 35, 54, 69
Luke, Gospel of 27, 68
Luther, Martin 240, 249, 252, 254

Maccabees 21f
Machiavelli, Nicolo: *The Prince* 247
Magna Carta 205f
Magna Mater 53, 75f
Manichaeanism 123, 130f, 215
Mar Thoma Church 109
Marcion 60, 66ff
Marcus Aurelius 63; *Meditations* 122
Mark, St., the Evangelist 31, 43, 69
Mark, Gospel of 27, 40
marriage 30, 130, 188f
Marsilius of Padua 232, 237
Martin of Poitiers 136
Martin of Tours, St. 1, 47, 197
Martin, pope 159
Martin V, pope 236
martyrs 43, 54, 62f, 64, 73f, 83, 90
Mary, Mother of God 27, 76, 102, 108, 112
Mary Magdalene 31, 40, 85
mass conversions 147
Matilda, Countess 175f
Matthew, St. 31, 69
Matthew, Gospel of 27
Maxentius 91, 93
Maximian 89f
Maximilian, emperor 245
Maximinus Daza 90, 92
Medardus, St. 149
Medici, Lorenzo 248
medicine 183

Mercury 134
Messiah 25f, 35, 42
Methodius, St. 116, 143, 168
metropolitans 118
Michael, Archangel 140, 147
Michelangelo 246, 248, 252
Milan, Edict of 102
Milton, John: *Paradise Lost* 222
miracles 149f
Mirror of Perfection 208
missionary work 43, 45, 138ff, 142
Mithraism 75f
Mohammed 113f
Moira 48
Moloch 53
monasticism 104f, 136ff, 191f, 206f, 213
monasticism, Eastern 117
Monica, St. 122, 124f
Monophysites 109ff, 113f
Monothelites 113, 114
More, St. Thomas: *Utopia* 247
Mosaic Law: *see* Law, Mosaic
Moses 6f, 20, 54
Moslems 114f
Mozarabs 153f
music 79
mystery cults 74ff, 78, 88
mystery plays 212

Nathan 18
Nathanael 31
nationalism 224ff
nature, religions of 3
Nebuchadnezzar 13, 22
Necho, pharaoh 13
Nehemiah 16
Neoplatonism 84f, 102, 123, 125, 131, 165, 199, 246, 253
Nero, Roman emperor 50, 51, 54, 72
Nestorius, bishop of Constantinople 108ff
Nestorians 100, 109ff
New Testament 44, 67–70
Nicaea, Council of 99f, 109
Nicaean Creed 103
Nicholas I, pope 166
Nicholas V, pope 242
Nicholas of Cusa 247

nominalists 184f
Novatianists 104

Occam, William of 233, 238
Occamism 187
Octavian 46
Oedipus 48
Olaf, St. 143, 167f
Old Testament 3, 8, 66, 215
Omayyad dynasty 153f
Origen 60, 78f, 85, 98, 103
Orphic cult 75f
Orthodox Churches 99, 109f, 150, 179
orthodoxy 135
Osiris 75, 76
Oswy, king of England 152f
Othlo 186
Otto I, emperor 172
Ovid 139, 245

pacifism 128f, 131
Pachomius, St. 105
paganism 48, 59, 75
Palladio, Andrea 250
papacy 139ff
Parliamentarianism 235
parochial schools 59
Passion, the 28, 38ff, 200, 208f
Passover 4, 6, 36
patriarchs 118
Patrick, St. 143f, 151
Paul, St. 20, 27, 38, 40, 43ff, 55f, 59, 67ff, 71f, 126, 131, 174, 217
Paul the Deacon 161
Paulinus 152f
Pax Romana 46f
Peace of God 178, 207
penance 83, 133
Pentateuch 15
Pentecost 41
Pepin, king of the Franks 155
Pepin the Short 157f
Perpetua 73f
persecution 62ff, 74
Peter, St. 31, 35, 38ff, 42f, 45, 49, 55, 60, 69–72, 81f, 86, 147, 153, 216
Peter Bartholomew 180
Peter Castelnau 216

Peter Damian 196
Peter Lombard 188
Peter's Patrimony 229, 231
Petrarch 252
Petronius, governor of Syria 53f
Pfefferkorn 245
Pharisees 19, 22ff, 32, 37
philanthropy 141, 211f
Philemon 68
Philip, St., the Evangelist 43
Philip the Fair, king of France 227ff
Philip Augustus, king of France 204, 205
Philistines 8, 9f, 15
Philo 20, 53, 67
philosophers/philosophy 17, 19, 65, 78, 183f
Phoenicians 9, 53
Pico della Mirandola, Giovanni 246, 252
Pierre de Dreux 200f
Pisa, Council of 235f
Pius 72
Plato 20, 88; *Republic* 19
Platonists 18, 19, 49, 244
pleroma 64f
Pliny, governor of Bithynia 57f
Plotinus 84, 88, 123
pluralism, religious 94, 241
Polycarp, St., bishop of Smyrna 62f, 71
polygamy 67, 114
Pompey, Roman general 20, 23, 46
Pomponazzi, Pietro: *On Immortality* 244
Pontius Pilate 25, 37, 39f, 51, 67
Pornocracy 167
Porphyry 84f
poverty 30, 80, 207f, 210
Praemunire, Statute of 227
predestination, doctrine of 45, 126, 131, 217, 237, 239
Premonstratensians 173
presbyterianism 56f
Priscilla 49
Procopius 113
prophets 56
Proverbs 12
Pseudo-Dionysian treatises 165f
Pseudo-Isidorian Decretals 165

purgatory, doctrine of 142, 222f
Purim 4

Quartodeciman Controversy 151
Quirinus, governor of Syria 1, 2, 27
Qumran community 24f, 33

Ramesses II, pharaoh 6
Raphael 248
Raymond of Toulouse 179f, 216
reason 17, 220f
realists 184f
Rebecca 3
Reccared, king of the Visigoths 150
Rechabites 114
Reformation, the 224, 235, 243
Rehoboam 12
reincarnation 215f
relics 149
remanence, doctrine of 238, 239f
Remigius, bishop of Rheims 145f
Resurrection 35, 40f, 44, 68f, 85f
Reuchlin, Johann 245
revelation 221
Revelation, Book of 45f, 54f, 68f, 88, 217
Richard II, king of England 234, 237
Robert of Flanders 179
Robert of Normandy 179
Robert the Pious 178
Roderick, king of the Visigoths 153
Roger of Sicily 193
Roma aeterna 135f
Roman Church 69, 71ff, 80f, 99
Roman empire 40–57, 93ff, 127
Roman empire, fall of 106ff, 120f, 126f
Rublev 119
Rufus, William 177
Russian Church 116f

Sabbath 15, 32, 45f
sacraments 77
Sadducees 19, 22, 24, 32
saints 54, 102, 134, 149f
Salvian 133
Salviati, archbishop 248
Samaritans 12
Samson, abbot at Bury St. Edmunds 149

Samuel 10
Sanhedrin 25, 37, 46
Santiago, order of 229
Saracens 154f
Sargon, king of Assyria 12
Satan 69, 196f, 222
Saturninus, St. 149
Saul 10f
Savonarola, Girolamo 252f
schisms 212f, 234f, 242
scholarship 138f
Scholasticism 182, 186f, 189f, 219f
science 18, 185
Scotus Erigena 166
sects/sectarianism 173, 213, 216f, 219, 224
secular clergy 156
Seleucids 21ff
Seneca 47, 139
Sennacherib, king of Assyria 13
Septimius Severus 73f
Septuagint 20
Serapion, bishop of Antioch 70
Sergius, St. 119
Severus, House of 73, 77, 91
Shepherd of Hermas, The 83
Sigismund, emperor 236, 240f
Simon Magus 70, 170
simony 170, 174
sin 80ff, 122, 126, 196f, 222
Sixtus IV, pope 248, 254
skepticism 243f
slavery 87
Socrates 86
Solomon 2, 11f, 113
Son of Man, the 25, 34, 35f, 42
Song of Songs 12, 194f
Soter 72
Spirit, descent of the 41f
Stabat Mater 204
stations of the cross 200
Stephen, St. 43
Stephen II, pope 157
Stilicho, Roman general 132
Stoics/Stoicism 17ff, 28, 49, 131
Strabo, Walafrid, abbot of St. Gall 171; *Glossa Ordinaria* 171
Suger, abbot of St. Denis 195, 199
Sunday 94, 199

Sylvester, bishop of Rome 158
Sylvester II, pope 172
synagogue 16
Syrian Church 109

Taborites 241
Tacitus 51, 54
Talmud 15
Tamerlane 109
Tammuz 75
Tancred 179
Tauler, John 253
Telesphorus 72
Templars: *see* Knights Templars
Temple, the 12, 13, 15, 22ff, 36
Ten Commandments 4f, 7, 115
Ten Tribes of Israel 5, 12
Tertullian 60f, 64, 77ff, 81, 98, 103
Teutonic Knights 229, 249
Theobald, count of Champagne 202
theocracy 10, 160, 166
Theodolinda, queen of the Franks 150
Theodora, empress 133, 167
Theodore, archbishop of Canterbury 161
Theodoric 133
Theodosian Code 103, 111
Theodosius I, emperor 103, 124
Theodosius II, 103
theology 183ff
Thomas, St., apostle 31, 43, 109
Thomas à Becket 202f, 216
Thomas à Kempis: *The Imitation of Christ* 253
Thomism 182, 187, 243
Tiberius, Roman emperor 27, 37, 51, 54
Tiridates of Armenia 87
tithes 226
Titus, Roman emperor 46
Torah 15f
Tiglath-Pileser III, king of Assyria 12
tradition, oral 70f
Trajan, Roman emperor 57f, 62
transubstantiation, doctrine of 206
treasury of merits of the saints 231
Trinity, doctrine of 78, 99f, 111, 131, 185, 220f, 243f

troubadours 188
Truce of God 178
Tyre, synod of 100

Ugolino, cardinal 209, 223
Ulfilas 135, 143, 156
Urban II, pope 178f
Urban VI, pope 234
usury 211, 250
Utraquists 241

Valerian, Roman emperor 84
Valla, Lorenzo 244f
Vespasian, Roman emperor 54
Victor, bishop of Rome 69
Victorinus 123, 125
Vigilius, pope, 111, 159
Vikings 162f, 167
Vincent, St. 212
Virgil 59, 139; *Aeneid* 107
Vladimir, prince of Russia 117, 143
Vulgate, the 106

Waldenses 210, 213ff, 218
Waldo, Peter 214
war-guilt theory 129
Wenzel, king of Bohemia 239f
Whitby, synod of 153
William the Conqueror 177
William, duke of Aquitaine 168, 193
William of Utrecht 176
Winfrith 155
Wisdom 64ff
Wisdom, Book of 12
Worms, Concordat of 177
Wycliffe, John 237–240

Yahweh 7, 11, 65, 67

Zachariah 36
Zbynek, archbishop 239f
Zealots 24, 32, 35, 37
Zedekiah, king of Judah 13
Zizka, general 241
Zoe Paleologus 118
Zoroaster 246